THE
QABALAH

Frontispiece. The Great Qabalistic Tree, after Kircher (OEdipus AEgyptiacus)

THE
QABALAH

SECRET TRADITION OF THE WEST

PAPUS

SAMUEL WEISER, INC.

York Beach, Maine

First published in 2000 by
Samuel Weiser, Inc.
P. O. Box 612
York Beach, ME 03910-0612
www.weiserbooks.com

Library of Congress Cataloging-in-Publication Data
Papus, 1865-1916.
    [Cabbale. English]
    The Qabalah : secret tradition of the West / by Papus (Gerard
       Encausse).—1st paperback ed.
       p. cm.
    "Preceded by a letter from Adolphe Franck . . . and a study by Saint-
       Yves d'Alveydre, and containing new texts by Lenain, Eliphas Levi,
       Stanislas de Guaita, Dr. Mark Haven, Sedir, J. Jacob, and a complete
       translation of the Sepher Yetzirah; followed by a partial reprinting of a
       Qabalistic treaty by the Chevalier Drach."
    Originally published: 1977.
    Includes bibliographical references.
    ISBN 0-87728-936-0 (pbk. : alk. paper)
    1. Cabala—History. 2. Cabala—Bibliography. I. Sefer Yezirah.
      English. II. Title.
  BM526 .P3613 2000
  296.1'6—dc21
00-043536

BJ

Translated by W. N. Schors

Printed in the United States of America

07 06 05 04 03 02 01 00
8 7 6 5 4 3 2 1

CONTENTS

LIST OF ILLUSTRATIONS

FOREWORD

In 1865, Gérard Encausse, better known as *Papus*, was born in La Corogna, a little town in Spain. His French father was a doctor in chemistry of more than local fame, while his mother was a highly intelligent Spanish lady. Papus's relationship with is parents was excellent and there is no doubt that his father's medical interests were instrumental in shaping the young boy's later career. It must, indeed, have been very stimulating to have had a father who not only invented a new method of treating illnesses – feeding and renewing the organism with the essence of plants and minerals via the skin, and not via the stomach, by means of steam-baths – but whose unorthodox methods proved to be effective as well.

This same unorthodox approach characterized Papus's start to his medical studies in Paris. Instead of spending his spare time in the usual easy way, he became a regular visitor of the Bibliothèque Nationale and the Bibliothèque de l'Arsenal to study alchemical texts, the Hebrew language and Rosicrucian writings. During this period he adopted as nom de plume the name PAPUS, i.e. 'physician'.

The word Papus was used for the first time by Apollonius of Tyana (first century A.D. in his *Nuctameron*, in order to indicate the first genius of the first hour, i.e. medicine. The *Nuctameron*, known largely through Eliphas Lévi's translation, is actually a magical ritual, having as its central and emanative force, the twelve symbolic hours which correspond with the twelve signs of the Zodiac and the allegorical labours of Hercules, representing the various steps of initiation.

Under this pseudonym, the young Gérard Encausse wrote his extensive works. His zeal can be judged by the simple fact that even while fulfilling his military service he could not stop working. On the contrary, during these years, his *Magie pratique* and his *Traité méthodique de science occulte* were born, a miraculous achievement for a man being only in his mid-twenties, and proof of an exceptionally talented mind. Most artists and scientists of great fame have reached their finest efforts at an early age and Papus certainly confirms this rule. The greater part of his work was produced between 1884 and 1897, between the ages of nineteen and thirty-two, and most of what he wrote after this was either an elaboration of earlier thoughts or of a more historical character, such as the books he wrote on Martinism.

One exception should be mentioned; the booklet *Faust de Goethe* (written in 1914 and published in 1921), in which esoteric treatise Papus explains the motivation behind the use of pentacles, their mechanism and their influence on the astral plane. This brochure is still a must for all who want to grasp the esoteric background of Goethe's thinking. It also goes without saying that Papus contributed to all the important occult periodicals of his day, such as *Le Lotus, L'Initiation* and *Voile d'Isis*, and many treasures from his pen can be found in these reviews.

Papus, then, could look back upon considerable achievement in the occult sphere at an age when most ordinary people are only first starting to think. Few human beings, indeed, can say when obtaining their degree – Papus got his Doctorate of Medicine in 1894 – that the bulk of their mental activity has already been printed and that their efforts have already been acknowledged by the Esoteric world. In this respect one only has to remember that in 1888, being only 23 years old, Papus was elected a member of the General Council of the Theosophical Society, on the instigation of Colonel Olcott, co-founder of the Theosophical Society and right-hand man of Mme H.P. Blavatsky.

The question now arises: was this reputation justified? Even though Papus was awarded many high distinctions by the governments of France, Portugal, Russia, Turkey, etc., and held many important masonic and rosicrucian functions, it did not necessarily mean that his fame would be a lasting one. Nevertheless, we are on safe ground when saying that his reputation as a great and honest occult philosopher was justified. Not only have many of his books and brochures been translated into several foreign languages; English, German, Italian, Russian, Czechoslovakian and Spanish (about sixty titles!), but they have been reprinted many times as well. There have been no less than seven reprints of his *Traité élémentaire de science*, and *Le Tarot des Bohémiens*, which took up the idea of a connection between the Qabalah and the Tarot, and is still a standard work on the subject, is in its sixth impression, while *La Cabbale* is now in its eighth edition.

Quite naturally a man of such outstanding talent came into close contact with the contemporary celebrities. In his early youth Papus met the Marquis Joseph Saint-Yves d'Alveydre (1842-1910), in many ways the successor of Fabre d'Olivet (1767-1825), and author of the visionary *Mission des Juifs* (1884), one of the most revealing works on the interchange between destination, occultism and politics. Saint-Yves, who has created with his *Archéomètre* a unique Qabalistic canon in which the Watan-alphabet is reconstituted for the first time, and was initiated both in western and oriental traditions, became Papus's first master. It was Saint-Yves who convinced Papus that he had to leave spiritualism and to start off on the road of mysticism. A development which already had begun in 1882, when Papus wrote: 'We know how much materialism has benefited from the doctrine of evolution. Nevertheless it has been the profound study of this doctrine of evolution which has shown to me the very weakness of materialism ... Oh, yes, the mineral does evolve ... but on one condition, which is that the physico-chemical forces and the sun itself assist this phenomenon, which means, on condition that the superior forces, by their evolution, sacrifice themselves to the evolution of the lower forces ... Summing up: each phase in development, each evolution has asked the sacrifice of one, and more often, of two, superior forces. The doctrine of evolution is incomplete. It represents only one side of the facts and neglects the other. It reveals the law of the struggle for life, but it forgets the law of sacrifice, which rules all phenomena. ...'

His medical knowledge, moreover, enabled him to rediscover the deep truth of the old hermetic laws like the doctrine of 'the three principles of man' and 'the principle of the astral body'. He writes: 'A serious investigation allows me to confirm the truth of the hermetic theory on the constitution of man; a theory which has not changed since the eighteenth Egyptian dynasty, that is to say, for thirty-six centuries ... The same theory enables us to solve the problem of death and of life thereafter. ... ' In 1897 Papus came forward with practical evidence to support such postulations by publishing *La magie et l'hypnose*, which contains only factual material and proof of most things connected with astral qualities and phenomena.

But his development continued and gradually he went through the phases of all esoteric thinkers, finally stating: 'First man believes what is told. Then he wants to find out for himself: the phase of rationalism. Then man discovers that everything is alive, that all things are alive in a central force, in God: man becomes pantheistic ... Finally man wants to penetrate this central force, to live in and become one with it, with God: man has become mystic ... '

Before he had reached this mystic level, however, Papus first launched his *Traité méthodique de science occulte*, a true encyclopedia on occult sciences, containing rare texts from Kircher, Fabre d'Olivet, Wronski, and others; and a second work, characteristic of the rational-magic phase he then passed through: *Traité élémentaire de science occulte*, and based according to the typical disposition of the magical student, on the triangle: theory, adaptation, realization.

Less magical, but in the end far more epoch-making, was his *Tarot des Bohémiens* (1889) which – inspired by Court de Gébelin's (predecessor of Fabre d'Olivet) *Monde Primitif* (1775), the first book representing Egyptian Tarot illustrations, and by Eliphas Lévi's ideas – tries to establish the connection between the Qabalah and the Tarot, by linking the four suits with the four letters of the Tetragrammaton. It was, in fact, the *Tarot des Bohémiens* that sparked off the interest in and the abundance of literature on this mysterious conception; to some a simple method of divination, to most, however, a system of initiation showing man in his successive phases of development. *Le Tarot des Bohémiens* is basically an essay on numbers and Hebrew letters, and as such it is a logical consequence of the translation Papus made (in 1887) of the *Sepher Yetzirah*, one of the main Qabalistic texts, and in a way a forerunner of his main work on Jewish occult tradition entitled *La Cabbale, tradition secrète de l'Occident*, first published in 1892.

The sources of inspiration for Papus's Qabalistic thinking are found in *Fabre d'Olivet*, from whom he obtained his notion of esoteric mysteries as concealed in the *Hebrew language*; in

Prof. Ad. Franck, a French scholar on Qabalistic literature and its history; in *Eliphas Lévi*, who discovered a connection between the Qabalah and the Tarot; and in his spiritual master *Saint Yves d'Alveydre*, from whom Papus derived a systematic view of Jewish history.

Papus's opinion was that the Qabalah was attributable to Moses, and Biblical history was sufficient to prove to Papus that the Qabalah was the most perfect summary of the Egyptian mysteries and as such, via Gnostic, Rosicrucian, Masonic and Martinistic ideas and fraternities, the key-stone of all western tradition. Though this point of view has sometimes been denied (e.g. by A.E. Waite, in spite of his recognition and admiration of both Lévi and Papus) it is to most occult authorities an established fact, as can be seen in the writings of the white-Russian doctor and initiate *Skariatine*, who under the pseudonym *Enel*, wrote his *Langue sacrée*, which most convincingly confirms Papus's theories by tracing basic Qabalistic problems back to the sacred Egyptian writings.

Papus's opinions on the Tarot, which he calls 'the oldest book of the world', can best be understood in relation to his belief in the Egyptian origin of the Qabalah. As the twenty-two Trump Cards correspond with the letters of the Hebrew alphabet, the origin of which can be traced back to the Egyptian hieroglyphics, the Tarot must also be of Egyptian origin. In this context it becomes clear when Papus states: 'We can now understand why Pythagoras, initiated in Egypt into the secrets of the holy word "iod-hé-vau-hé", replaced this word in his esoteric teachings by the sequel of the four first numbers of "Tetractys".' (*Tarot of the Bohemians*, chapter IV). It might be said here, that most occult authors consider Egypt to be the birthplace of the Tarot and that this reasoning is also consistent with their views on the origin of the Qabalah.

Papus's *La Cabbale* is the more valuable since it contains, apart from the theoretical part, his translation of the *Sepher Yetzirah*, Eliphas Lévi's famous *Ten lessons on the Qabalah*, an extensive Qabalistic bibliography, and parts of Rabbi Drach's important and rare treatise *La Cabbale des Hébreux* and a profound analysis of the rabbi's theories. (In 1884 Drach published his *De l'Harmonie entre l'Eglise et al Synagogue ou perpétuité et catholicité de la religion universelle*, in which most solid, but highly unorthodox opinions are brought forward on the Qabalah, Messianism and rabbinical traditions).

Though *La Cabbale* constitutes a peak amongst all the works of Papus, we would nevertheless like to mention here, though it might be considered out of context, as one of his finest achievements: *L'âme humaine avant la naissance et après la mort*, since it represents the true, mystical Papus at his finest, and since we believe the mystical phase to be the most decisive one in man's life. Written as a key to the gnostic Valentine's *Pistis Sophia*, it actually provides us with a final description of the road of man's spiritual evolution. In total concordance with the teachings of Jacob Boehme and Louis Claude de Saint Martin (1743-1803), whose theories consisting of Qabalistic, gnostic and Bohemian elements, exercised a great influence in England, Germany and Italy, Papus states in *L'âme humaine*: ' ... The Illuminate becomes a mystic and when at last science is enlightened by faith and faith consolidated by science, one has to devote his spiritualized faculties to the evolution of the poorer ... One never reaches the Path of the Masters by means of the Astral Body: only the Spiritual Body is capable of doing so.'

No difference can be found between this and Eliphas Lévi's 'Credo', which is to be expected as no fundamental differences should exist between the teachings of those men who discover and reach the road to enlightenment. However, both Eliphas Lévi and Papus suffered from the usual shortcomings of those who did not quite reach the ultimate goal, but in spite of and even because of their shortcomings, their works can lead man to the discovery and acknowledgment of the mysterious forces in life and to the possibility of understanding and mastering them.

From that awareness till spiritual life 'il n'y a qu'un pas'. As such and as a concise and valuable introduction to the sacred science of the Hebrews, and therefore to the esoteric teachings of Christianity, this English translation of *La Cabbale* is offered. To quote Papus from one of his last lectures given shortly before his death in 1916: 'Cabbale ... richesses infinies. Il suffit simplement de savoir de quelle richesse il s'agit.'

W.N. Schors

PREFACE TO THE SECOND EDITION

The first edition of our book *The Qabalah* enjoyed considerable success, and in this second edition we have been at pains to include all relevant research made since the first writing.

We have endeavoured to establish as clear a classification as possible of the books and traditions of which the Qabalah is a part, and we have done our best to draw up as extensive a bibliography as possible. We have retained in full the two principal parts of our first work, and have added the following.

In the Introduction, a work of great interest by Marquis de Saint-Yves d'Alveydre on the Qabalistic tradition reconstituted in the light of the archeometer.

In Part 2 we have called upon the pen of the master Qabalist Eliphas Lévi by publishing his course of ten lessons on the Qabalah. This course is followed by an equally enlightening work by Sedir, thus giving the reader an idea of Qabalistic teaching.

It is then easy to understand the following chapters, particularly Stanislas de Guaita's Study of the Sephiroth preceding our sephirotic table.

In Part 3, The Texts, there is a new translation which seems to us to finally complete the Sepher Yetzirah, or Qabalistic book of creation, including the most important commentaries. It seemed equally useful to review in this section the most important elements of some texts relating either to the Zohar or to the other sections of the written tradition.

Finally, we have completed our bibliography by including the important works of Dr Marc Haven, well-known and much revered by his readers.

Also we give in this edition the elements of the practical Qabalah derived from the divine names of the spirits and an almost complete new impression of Chevalier Drach's brochure so highly priced in the catalogues.

The figures were equally specially chosen, and we hope to help our readers to understand clearly the teaching of the western tradition which is summed up in Christianity. The Qabalah alone has the right to this title of 'Tradition'.

This essay is, to our eyes, the means by which to direct ourselves towards the sanctuary of enlightenment where the four letters of the mystical name of the Saviour of the Three Plans shine forth.

INRI: Christ; God come in the flesh whose bright light is all spirit shunning the pride of the Mental Plan.

PAPUS

To M. ADOLPHE FRANCK,

Member of the Institute,
Honorary professor of the college of France,
President of the National League Against Atheism.

My distinguished sir,

Will you permit me to dedicate to you this modest essay which I am now publishing on the subject of the Qabalah, a subject the elucidation of which is so important for the philosopher?

You were the first, not only in France but also in Europe, to bring forth a considerable work on the 'religious philosophy of the Hebrews', as you yourself call it. This work, which you alone could bring to a satisfactory conclusion thanks, on the one hand, to your perfect knowledge of the Hebrew language and, on the other, to your acquaintance with the history of philosophical doctrines, achieved a position of authority immediately upon publication and certainly has merited the traditions and imitations which have since followed. The few German critics who wished to find fault with you regarding the Qabalah have succeeded only in giving proof of their inadequacy and their prejudice. The 1889 edition will definitely match the success of that of 1843.

But since all of us who nowadays concern ourselves with such study owe such a debt of gratitude to our senior and teacher in this field, how can I personally hope to thank you for the unaccustomed honour you have bestowed on me by encouraging my efforts through the authority of your name, declaring that if you are not a mystic, at least you prefer to see those who come after you taking part in such research, rather than have them partake of the hopeless, anti-philosophical and, let us dare to say the word, anti-scientific doctrines of materialistic positivism.

At the very moment when we raised the shield of intellectual struggle against materialism, at the moment when all adepts of this doctrine, scattered through the Faculties of medicine, through the Press, through the highest and lowest levels of society, considered us as 'dilettanti', clerics or fools, the president of the National League Against Atheism came forward, braving all sarcasm, to protect us with the inarguable authority of a profound philosopher and ardent defender of spiritualism.

You showed that these savants, for the most part eminent men in the domain of analytical discovery, have been by their very specialization itself restricted, bound to a too hasty study of philosophy. This is the source of their scorn for a branch of human knowledge which, alone, could furnish them that synthesis of sciences which they so aspire to achieve; this is the source of their materialistic conclusions, of the *unknowable* and all other formulas indicative of the laziness of the human mind, unadapted to serious study and in a hurry to finish, without sounding the true value or social consequences of its affirmations.

Alongside the official line of religious or secular Universities, of scientific Academies and the Laboratories of Higher Learning, there has always existed an independent line, generally little known and therefore looked down upon, made up of researchers sometimes too steeped in philosophy, sometimes too taken with mysticism, but how interesting to study:

These adepts of Gnosis, these Alchemists, these disciples of Jacob Boehme, of Martinez Pasqualis or of Louis-Claude de Saint-Martin, are the only ones, however, never to have neglected the study of the Qabalah up to the moment when your work appeared to show they had at last found approbation, a leader in the person of one of the most eminent representatives of the University.

It is as an admirer and disciple of Saint-Martin and his doctrines that I myself take the liberty of thanking you, in the name of these 'independents', for the precious ·support that they have found in your person. And if, in conclusion, I dared to ask a request of you, it would be for your intercession on their behalf with the heads of your University.

In the works of Saint-Martin, in those of Fabre d'Olivet, Wronski, Lacuria and Louis Lucas, there is a series of studies which I find quite profound and not at all well-known, on psychology, morals and logic.

Certainly it would be useful, at the very least, to see on the schedule of our Higher Normal School the *Traité des signes et des Idées* by Saint-Martin, *Les Missions* by Saint Yves d'Alveydre or the *Vero dorés de Pythagore* by Fabre d'Olivet, as well as the system of psychology which forms the introduction to his *Histoire philosophique du gene humain*, or yet again the philosophical section of the *médecine nouvelle* or the *Roman alchimigre* by Louis Lucas, not to mention the *Création de la Realité absolve* by Wronski, albeit this latter is perhaps too technical and too abstractly presented.

You may say to me that these authors are 'mystics', writers whose erudition is not always what one might wish; but it is also a 'mystic' who requests that they be read more fully and with greater critical care, if only to better understand the various evolutions of the human mind.

However my request may be greeted, I shall always be thankful to you, distinguished sir, for all you have done for our cause.

What progress we have made has not been without effort or struggle, and we will continue in this way, as we have begun, our labour and our published works answering the attacks with which our books and our very persons are so consistently harassed. In truth, any sincere work lasts a goodly time; but what remains, after only a few years, of perfidious and unjust calumny? A little bitterness and much pity in the hearts of the victims, even more remorse in the souls of the attackers, and nothing more.

But if, with the passage of time, these existing works lose some of their dynamic power, there is still one sentiment which those who come later must feel as strongly as we, and that is a profound gratitude for the one who did not hesitate in the most difficult moments to encourage our efforts by supporting them with all the respect and authority which attaches itself to a great name.

In fullest sincerity,

PAPUS

Paris, 23 October 1891.

LETTER

FROM M. ADOLPHE FRANCK TO THE AUTHOR

Sir,

I accept with the greatest pleasure the dedication which you have been so kind as to offer me in your work on the Qabalah, a work which is not, as you choose to call it, an *essay*, but a book of the highest importance.

As yet I have been able only to leaf through it rapidly; but I am well enough acquainted with it to tell you that in my opinion it is the most intriguing, the most instructive, the most knowledgeable publication to have so far made its appearance on this obscure subject.

I can find fault with nothing save the far too flattering terms contained in the letter addressed to me which precedes it.

With rare modesty, you ask my opinion only on the bibliographical material which closes your study.

I dare not say that nothing is missing; for the bounds of Qabalistic Science may extend to the infinite; but I have never anywhere encountered a bibliography as complete as yours.

I offer you my felicitations and my thanks.

Sincerely,

AD. FRANCK

To the Marquis SAINT-YVES d'Alveydre

My Dear Sir,

I am about to publish a new edition of my study on the 'Qabalah', quite an elementary one in the light of your considerable work in the reconstruction of this ancient patriarchal synthesis, of which antiquity possessed only the barest odds and ends.

But when I think of the way of pain and suffering which our Lord has given you to tread in the pursuit of your labours, when I think of the superhuman soul-rending which must have preceded the certainty of eternal Union with your beloved Angel, I find it a costly business to come forth and illuminate with divine light a century in which almost nothing remains but the way of Salvation.

But to return to the technical question of the 'Qabalah', I wish to appeal to the exactitude of the Archeometer so as to resolve a question which has been discussed for centuries and which, like so many others of all kinds, thanks to your admirable accomplishment, can be definitively settled.

I am speaking of the spelling of the word which exactly translates the meaning and origin of the secret tradition of which the Sepher Yetzirah and the Zohar are the radiant columns.

Allow me then to be entirely indiscreet and in addition to the exact definition of the word Cabala, Kabbala or Qabalah, may I also ask the Archeometer for some opinions on the ten numbers concerning which the Pythagoreans spread so much error. Thank you for your response, to the greatest glory of Jesus Christ, our Lord.

PAPUS

NOTES
ON THE QABALISTIC TRADITION

My Dear Friend,

It is a pleasure for me to answer your kind letter. I have nothing to add to your remarkable book on the Jewish Qabalah. It has taken a position of eminence from the well deserved appreciation shown it by the late M. Franck of the Institute, the foremost authority in this field.

Your work completes his, not only due to its erudition, but also to its bibliography and the exegesis of this quite particular tradition; I find this fine book definitive.

But, aware of my respect for tradition and, concurrently, my need for universality and verification using all known procedures, acquainted furthermore with my works, you do not seem to fear that I might enlarge on the subject; on the contrary, this is precisely what you ask of me.

In reality I have accepted only conditionally the books of the Jewish Qabalah, no matter their interest. But having once taken note of them, my personal research has been borne on the universality from which these archaeological documents evolved, and on the principle as well as the laws which might have motivated these actions of the human mind.

For the Jews, the Qabalah came from the Chaldeans through Daniel and Esdras.

For the Israelites who preceded the dispersion of the ten non-Jewish tribes, the Qabalah came from the Egyptians through Moses.

For the Chaldeans as for the Egyptians, the Qabalah was a part of what all the metropolitan Universities called Wisdom, that is, the synthesis of sciences and arts reduced to their common Principle. This Principle was the Word.

An invaluable witness from pre-Mosaic patriarchal antiquity affirms that this wisdom was lost or cast away about

3,000 years before our Lord. This witness is Job and the antiquity of the book is fixed by the position of the constellations he mentions. 'What has happened to Wisdom, where is it then?' asks this holy patriarch.

According to Moses, the loss of previous unity, the breaking-up of patriarchal Wisdom are indicated by the division of Languages and the Era of Nimrod. This Chaldean epoch corresponds to that of Job.

Another witness from patriarchal Antiquity is Brahmanism. It has preserved all the traditions of the past, superimposed like the geological layers of the earth. All those who have studied it from a modern point of view have been struck both by its documentary richness and by the impossibility of a satisfactory classification, from a chronological as well as scientific angle. The division into brahmanic, vishnavist and sivaist sects, to mention only a few, adds to this confusion.

It is nonetheless true that the Brahmins of Nepal date the rupture of ancient universality and the primordial unity of teachings from the beginning of the Kali-Yuga.

This primitive synthesis carried, well before the name of Brahma, that of Ishva-Ra, Jesus-King: *Jesus Rex Patriarcharum*, say our litanies.

Allusion is made to this primordial synthesis by Saint John at the beginning of his Gospel; but the Brahmins are far from suspecting that their Ishva-Ra is our Jesus, King of the Universe, the Creative Word and the Principle of the human word. Otherwise, they would all be Christians.

The oblivion into which fell the Patriarchal Wisdom of Ishva-Ra dates from the time of Krishna, the founder of Brahmanism and its Trimurti. On this point again there is agreement among the Brahmins, Job and Moses, as to the fact as well as the historical epoch.

Since the time of Babel, no people, no race, no University has possessed more than fragmentary remains of the ancient Universality of divine, human and natural knowledge, reduced to their Principle: the Word-Jesus. Saint Augustine designates this primordial Synthesis of the Word under the name *Religio vera*.

The rabbinical Qabalah, of relatively recent composition, was known thoroughly as to its written or oral sources by the Jewish adepts of the first century. Certainly it contained no secrets for a man of such worth and knowledge as Gamaliel. Nor did it hold any for its first and most eminent disciple, Saint Paul, who became the apostle of the resurrected Christ.

Here are the words of Saint Paul in his first epistle to the Corinthians, chapter II, verses 6, 7, 8:

> Yet among the mature we do impart wisdom, although it is not a wisdom of this age or of the rulers of this age, who are doomed to pass away.
>
> But we impart a secret and hidden wisdom of God, which God decreed before the ages for our glorification.
>
> None of the rulers of this age understood this; for if they had, they would not have crucified the Lord of glory.

All these words are carefully weighed, like gold and diamonds, and there is not one which is not infinitely precious and precise. They proclaim the insufficiency of the Jewish Qabalah.

Having thus cast some light on the Universality of the question which interests you, let us concentrate this light on the nevertheless precious fragment of ancient wisdom which is or may be the Jewish Qabalah.

First and foremost, let us examine the exact meaning of the word Qabalah.

This word has two significations, according to whether it is written, as with the Jews, with a Q, that is, the twentieth letter of the Assyrian alphabet, bearing the number 100, or with a C, the eleventh letter of this same alphabet, bearing the number 20.

In the first case, the word signifies Transmission, Tradition, and the question remains indecisive; for the worth of the thing transmitted is proportionate to the value of the transmitter.

We believe that the Jews were quite faithful in their transmission of what they had received from the savant Chaldeans, with their writing and the recasting of the former books by Ezra, himself following the guidance of the great Master of the University of Magi of Chaldea, Daniel. But, from a scientific point of view, this does not advance the question, which is in fact drawn backward to an inventory of Assyrian documents and beyond to the primordial source. In the second case, Ca-Ba-La signifies Power, La, XXII, CaBa, since $C = 20$, $B = 2$.

But now the question finds an exact resolution, for it concerns the scientific character which patriarchal antiquity assigned to alphabets of twenty-two numerical letters.

Must we make of these alphabets a racial monopoly by referring to them as Semitic? Perhaps, if such a monopoly is real; not, however, if the opposite is true.

Now, according to my investigation of ancient alphabets of Ca-Ba-La, of XXII letters, the most hidden, the most secret which certainly served as a prototype, not only for all others of the same kind, but also for the Vedic and Sanskrit symbols and letters, was an Aryan alphabet. This is the one I was so happy to communicate to you; I was given it by eminent Brahmins who never once thought to ask me its secret.

It differs from the others, called Semitic, in that its letters are morphological, that is, each form holds its particular meaning, which makes of it an absolutely unique variety. In addition, an attentive study has shown me that these same letters are the prototypes of the zodiacal and planetary signs, a fact which is also of great importance.

The Brahmins call this alphabet Vatan; and it seems to go back to the first human race, for, through its five rigorously geometric mother forms, it provides its own signature, Adam, Eve and Adamah.

Moses seems to speak of it in the nineteenth verse of the second chapter of his Sepher Barashith. Moreover, this alphabet is written from bottom to top, and its letters are grouped so as to form morphological images. Pandits erase these characters from their slates as soon as the lesson of the guru is finished. They also write it from left to right, like Sanskrit, thus, in the European fashion. For all these reasons, this prototypical alphabet of all the Kaba-Lim belongs to the Aryan race.

Therefore this type of alphabet can no longer be called Semitic, since it is not a monopoly held by the races which, rightly or wrongly, we designate as such.

But we can and ought to call alphabets of this kind schematic. Schema signifies not only a sign of the Word, but also Glory. This double meaning must be kept in mind while reading the above passage of Saint Paul.

The same sort of thing exists in other languages like Slavonian. For example, the etymology of the word slavic is slovo and slava, signifying word and glory.

These meanings carry a weight of conviction, which Sanskrit will serve to deepen. Sama, which can also be found in languages of Celtic origin, signifies similarity, identity, proportionality, equivalence, etc.

Further on we will see the application of these ancient meanings.

For the moment, let us summarize what we have previously said.

The word Cabala, as we understand it, signifies the Alphabet of XXII Powers, or the power of the XXII Letters of this Alphabet. This type of alphabet has an Aryan or Japhethetic prototype, and can be quite justifiably designated under the name of alphabet of the Word or of Glory.

Word and Glory! Why are these two words brought together in two ancient languages as far removed from each other as Slavonian and Chaldean? This is due to a primordial constitution of the human Mind in a common Principle, at once scientific and religious: the cosmological Word and its Equivalents.

Jesus, in his last mysterious prayer, throws light, here as everywhere, on the historic mystery which confronts us here:

'Oh, Father! Crown me with the Glory which was mine before the creation of this World!'

The Incarnate Word makes allusion here to His Work, to His Creation, acting as the Creative Word, a Creation designated by the name of divine and eternal World of Glory, prototype of the astral and temporal World created by the Alahim on this incorruptible model.

The creative Principle is the Word; on this point the voice of Antiquity is unanimous. To speak and to create are synonymous in all languages.

With the Brahmins, documents anterior to the cult of Brahma give ISOu-Ra, Jesus-Rex, as the creative Word.

For the Egyptians, the books of Hermes Trismegistus say the same; and OShI-Ri is Jesus-Rex read from right to left.

For the Thracians, Orpheus, initiated to the Mysteries of Egypt toward the same epoch as Moses, wrote a book entitled *The Divine Word*.

As for Moses himself, the Principle, the Beginning, is the first word and the subject of the first sentence of his Sepher. It is not yet a question of God in Essence, IHOH, who is not named before the seventh day, but of His Word, creator of the

divine Hexad: BaRa-Shith. BaRa means speak and create;
Shith means Hexad. In Sanskrit, we find the same meanings:
BaRa-Shath.

This word BaRa-Shith has occasioned innumerable
discussions. Saint John, like Moses, sets it before us at the very
outset of his Gospel, and says, in Syrian, a Qabalistic language
of XXII letters: The Beginning is the Word. Jesus said: I am
the Beginning.

The exact meaning is thus clarified by Jesus and accords
with all anterior pre-Mosaic Universality.

The foregoing explains why truly ancient Universities
considered the creative Word as the Influence of which the
human Word is the exact Reflection, while the alphabetical
process exactly follows the Planisphere of the Cosmos.

The alphabetical process, together with all its equivalents,
represents then the eternal world of Glory; and the cosmic
process represents the world of astral heavens.

This is why the Prophet-King, echo of all patriarchal
Antiquity, says: *Cœli enarrant Dei Gloriam.* Or in English: The
astral world tells of the world of divine Glory. The invisible
Universe speaks through the visible.

Two things remain to be determined: 1. the cosmic process
of the ancient schools; 2. that of the corresponding alphabets.

Firstly, III parent forms: the centre, the radius or diameter
and the circle; XII involutionary signs; VII evolutionary signs.

Secondly, to which the ancients gave first place: III
constructive letters; XII involutionary; VII evolutionary.

In both cases:

$$III + XII + VII = XXII = CaBa,$$

the pronunciation of:

$$C = 20, B = 2, \text{a total of } 22, \text{C.Q.F.D.}$$

Thus the alphabets of twenty-two letters corresponded to a
solar or solar-lunar Zodiac embodying an evolutionary
septenary.

These were the schematic alphabets.

The others, following the same method, came to
correspond, with 24 letters, to the hourly periods; with 28
letters, the lunar periods; with 30, the solar-lunar monthly
periods; with 36, the decans, etc.

In alphabets of twenty-two letters, the central one, the
Emissive of going forth and the Remissive of return, was I or Y
or J; and this letter, posed on a triangle, formed with two

others the name of the Word and of Jesus: IShVa-(Ra), OShI-(Ri).

Contrary to this, all those who have embraced the naturalist and lunar schism have taken the Central letter to be M, which rules the second elementary trigon.

The entire Vedic, then Brahmanic, system was thus arranged after the fact by Krishna at the beginning of the Kali-Yuga. This is the key to the *Book of the Wars of IEVA*, wars between the Central I or Y and the usurper M.

You, my dear friend, have seen the contemporary proofs, that is, proofs of simple observation and scientific experimentation, with which I have re-established and verified the most ancient tradition. Thus I will restrict myself here only to what is necessary in the elucidation of the historical fact of the Qabalah.

In accordance with the patriarchs who preceded them, the Brahmins divided human languages into two groups: 1. Devanagaries, languages of the celestial city or of civilization reduced to the divine cosmological Principle; 2. Pracrites, languages of wild or anarchic civilizations. Sanskrit is a Devanager language of forty-nine letters; Vedic also, with its eighty letters or symbols derived from the OM, that is, the letter M.

These two languages are Qabalistic in their particular systematization, with the letter M forming the point of departure and of return. But they have been, from their inception till the present day, articulated in a temple language of twenty-two letters, whose primitive Centre was I.

All corrections thus become possible, even easy, thanks to this key, to the great triumph and glory of Jesus, Word of IEVE, in other words, the primordial Synthesis of the earliest Patriarchs.

Present day Brahmins ascribe to their alphabet of twenty-two letters a magical virtue; but for us this word signifies only superstition and ignorance.

Superstition, decadence and paralysis of archaeological elements or more or less altered forms, but which careful study can sometimes, as in this case, link to an earlier system of teaching, conscious and scientific, not metaphysical or mystical.

Ignorance of the facts, laws and principle which motivated this primordial teaching.

Moreover, the lunar Vedo-brahmanic school is not the only one where science and its solar synthesis, the religion of the Word, have degenerated into magic. It is enough to investigate terrestrial trends of a general nature from the time of Babel onwards in order to become aware of a growing decadence which attributed more and more of a superstitious and magical character to ancient alphabets.

From Chaldea to Thessaly, from Scythia to Scandinavia, from the Koua of Fu-Hi and the Musnads of ancient Arabia to the Runes of the Varangians, this same degeneration can be observed.

In this as in everything, truth is far stranger than fiction, and you, my dear friend, are acquainted with this admirable truth.

And so, since no part of terrestrial Humanity is lost, just as nothing in the entire Cosmos can be lost, what was still is, testifying to the ancient universality about which Saint Augustine speaks in his *Retractions*.

The Brahmins participate in their personal Qabalah with the eighty Vedic signs, with the forty-nine letters of Devanager Sanskrit, with the nineteen vowels, semi-vowels and dipthongs, that is, the whole massorah which Krishna added to the Vatan or Adamic alphabet. The Arabs, Persians and Subahs do likewise with their lunar alphabets of twenty-eight letters, and the Moroccans with theirs, the Koreisch.

Also the Manchu Tartars with their mouth-oriented alphabet of thirty letters. The same observations can be made with the Tibetans, the Chinese, etc., with the same reservations pertaining as to the alterations of ancient Science concerning the cosmological equivalents of the Word.

It remains to be known in what order these XXII equivalents should be functionally arranged on the planisphere of the Cosmos.

You have before you, dear friend, a model which conforms exactly to that which has been legally registered under the name and title of archeometer.

You know that the keys to this precision instrument, destined for the higher studies, were given me by the Gospels, by certain precise words of Jesus linked to those of Saint Paul and Saint John.

Now allow me to recapitulate as briefly as possible.

All Asiatic and African religious Universities, equipped

with cosmological alphabets, solar, solar-lunar, horary, lunar, monthly, etc., use their letters in a Qabalistic fashion.

Whether it is a question of pure Science, or Poetry interpreting Science or of divine Inspiration, all ancient books written in the devanagaries, and not pracrites, languages, cannot be understood without an understanding of the Qabalah of these languages.

But even these must be reduced to the XXII schematic equivalents, which in turn must be referred to their exact cosmological positions.

The Jewish Qabalah is thus motivated by the entire constitution of the human Mind; but it must be archeometered, that is, measured by its regulating Principle, verified on the precision instrument of the Word and primordial Synthesis.

I know not, dear friend, if these pages answer your expectations. I have necessarily summarized whole chapters in a few lines.

Be good enough then to excuse the imperfections and to find in all that precedes a simple testimony to my good will and my long-lasting feelings of friendship.

                                        SAINT-YVES

10 January 1901

THE
QABALAH

Part One

The Divisions of the Qabalah

THE HEBREW TRADITION AND THE CLASSIFICATION OF RELATED WORKS

He who wishes, for the first time, to undertake a study of the *Qabalah*, must be informed of the exact place to be occupied by purely Qabalistic works, such as the *Sepher Yetzirah* and the *Zohar*, as distinct from other treatises related to the Hebrew tradition.

It is generally known that in the Qabalah are to be found the theoretical and practical rules of Occult Science; but it is difficult to distinguish between the sacred text *per se* and the esoteric tradition.

This difficulty arises from the confusion natural to any mind wishing to *classify* the immense Hebrew compilations which have come down to us.

In the following exposé, we shall attempt to establish as clear as possible a classification of the diverse works the object of which is to stabilize the oral tradition.

To our knowledge there exists no work of satisfactory thoroughness summarizing in one or several tables the given techniques complete with a serious bibliography.

At the end of our study will be found a list of the contemporary works consulted for our enterprise, and referring to this list one can easily see the difficulty which this task has given us. It is for this reason that we cannot be certain of having definitively exhausted the question, and we are entirely ready to recognize our possible errors, should one more knowledgeable than we point them out to us.

*
* *

All those who are even slightly aware of subjects pertaining to Israel know that alongside the Bible there has existed, if not always, at least for a long, long time, a *tradition* aimed at instructing a certain class of initiates in the explanation and comprehension of the Law (the Torah).

This tradition, transmitted for many years by almost solely oral means, bore upon several different points:

1. First there was all which concerned the *material body* of the Bible. Just as in the Middle Ages we will see certain groups in possession of strict, hidden rules for the construction of the cathedrals, so the *physical construction* of each copy of the Hebrew Bible was subject to fixed rules, constituting a portion of the tradition.

2. In addition there was all which concerned the *spirit* of the sacred text. Commentaries and interpretations can be divided into two major sections: on the one hand, the LAW, the collection of rules governing the social relations of members of Israel among themselves, with their neighbours and with the Divinity; on the other, the SECRET DOCTRINE, the body of theoretical and practical knowledge by which one might become acquainted with the relationships between God, man and the Universe.

The physical construction of the sacred text, along with the legislative and the doctrinal sections, form the three great divisions which make of the esoteric tradition a complete whole, formed of body, life and spirit.

*

* *

When, given the commentary which heads the *Sepher Yetzirah*, 'in view of the ill-conditioned affairs of Israel', it was decided to set down the diverse points of the oral tradition, several great works came into being, each of them intended to transmit a part of this tradition.

An understanding of the above classifications permits an easily established and clear classification of these works.

All of which had a bearing on the *constitution* of the text, the rules concerning the ways to read and write the Torah (Law), the special considerations having to do with the mystic meanings of the sacred letters, all this was put down in the MASSORAH.

The *traditional* commentaries on the legislative part of the Torah make up the MISHNAN, and *later* additions (corresponding to our current-day jurisprudence) make up the

Various TRADITIONS connected with the TORAH

Traditions touching the MATERIAL part of the text. (*Fixation of the text*).

- Word. — Writing. — How to read and write the text. Some mysterious meanings of the sacred characters. → **MASSORAH**
- **BODY** — Legislative part. THE LAW. Diverse rules. Customs. Ceremonies. Civil life. **LIFE**
  - Primitive tradition of Moses and the great prophets. → **MISHNAH** ⎫
  - Commentaries on this tradition. (*Jurisprudence*) → **GHEMARAH** ⎬ **TALMUD** (General code of THE LAW)

Traditions touching the SPIRITUAL part of the sacred text. (*Explanation of the text*).

- Religious and philosophical part. **THE SECRET DOCTRINE**. Esoterism of the Bible. **SOUL**

  THEORY
  - *Bereschith.* Generation, mystical constitution and relationship of the 3 worlds. → **SEPHER YETZIRAH** (Theoretical Qabalah);
  - *Mercavah.* Mystical study of the divine world and its relationships. → **ZOHAR**

  PRACTICE
  - *Synthetic hieroglyphism.* — Evolution. — Division. Mystic transposition of letters and numbers. → **TAROT** (Virtually nothing published).
  - *Magic manuscripts* attributed to Solomon. (*Practical magic*). → **CLAVICULA** (Schemamphoras)

  THE QABALAH (Practical Qabalah)

GEMARAH. The union of these two parts of the legislative section into a whole constitutes the TALMUD.

The secret Doctrine was equally divided in two, theory and practice, disposed in three degrees: a historic degree, a social degree and a mystic degree.

The totality of knowledge contained in these two divisions constitutes the Qabalah as such.

Only the theoretical part of the Qabalah has been fixed in writing, especially with the invention of printing. This theoretical part contains two studies: 1. that of the *creation* and its mysterious laws (BERESCHITH), summed up in the *Sepher Jetzirah*; 2. a more metaphysical discussion of the *divine essence* and its modes of manifestation, and which qabalists refer to as the *Heavenly Chariot* (MERCAVAH), summed up in the *Zohar*.

The practical part of the Qabalah is only rarely referred to and/or exposed in a few manuscripts scattered here and there among large collections. The Bibliothèque Nationale in Paris possesses one of the most beautiful, the origin of which is attributed to Solomon. These manuscripts, generally known under the name of *clavicula*, little keys, formed the bases of all the old grimoires which are to be found more or less in abundance (*Large* and *Small Albert, The Red Dragon* and *Enchiridion*) and even of those which have driven priests to the insanity of witchcraft (*The Grimoire of Honorius*).

We shall now give some details concerning each of the works we have mentioned; but first, let us summarize the preceding in a table which will allow a clear-cut overall view.

THE MASSORAH

We may now turn our attention to each of these collections in detail in order to determine their separate characters.

MASSORAH. – The Massorah forms the *body* of tradition, treating everything which concerns the material part of the Torah.

The Massorah centres around two principal points:

'1. It teaches how to read doubtful passages by means of periods and vowels, how to group and pronounce words and sentences by means of accents.

'2. It expounds on the consonants, as well as on the exterior and material form of the Bible, and gives an account of the hieroglyphs indicated by the tangible form of the Torah, such as the divisions of books, of chapters, or verses, the shapes of the letters, etc., without, however, explaining the meaning of these hieroglyphs[1].'

Occultists who have specialized in the Qabalah, such as Saint-Yves d'Alveydre[2], Fabre d'Olivet[3], Claude de Saint-Martin[4], claim that the *Massorah*, a collection of entirely exoteric formulas, is aimed at removing from the Hebraic tongue anything which might give a clue as to the secret meaning of the Torah.

The Massorah is often divided into Major and Minor. The *Rabbinical Bible* was printed for the first time by Daniel Bemberg, printer in Venice (1525), then in Amsterdam (1724-1727).

MISHNAH[5]. – The Mishnah contains six sections (*sedarim*)

[1] *Monitor*, p.249.

[2] The primary pedagogical reform of Ezra was this: He exchanged the primitive characters of Moses for those of the Chaldean priests, using Assyrian notation, thus constituting the earliest Massorah. (*Mission des Juifs* p.646).

[3] *La Langue Hebraique Reghfule.*

[4] *Le Crocodile* (various works).

[5] In addition to the Bible, orthodox Jews recognize certain translations which call for the same respect as the precepts of the *Pentateuch*.

First disseminated mouth to mouth in all directions, then reassembled and drafted by Judas the Saint under the name of Mischno, and finally copiously augmented and developed by the authors of the Talmud, today these writings leave not the least room for reason or freedom. Ad. FRANCK, op.cit.

which are divided into sixty paragraphs or treatises
(*M'sachoth*); each of these in turn being subdivided into
chapters (*Perakim*).

We will give an outline of the Mishnah so that the reader
may have an idea of its content[1].

THE MISHNAH

Section 1

Agriculture, comprising eleven chapters

1. Prayer and daily benediction; 2. the corner of the field
belonging to the poor; 3. fruits unsuitable for tithe, how they
should be used; 4. animals which should not be bred; crops
which must not grow together on the same earth; threads
which must not be woven together; 5. produce from the
Sabbatical year; 6. gifts destined for the priest; 7. the tithe of
the Levites; 8. the second tithe which a property holder must
pay to Jerusalem; 9. kitchens of the priests; 10. prohibition
concerning the eating of fruit from trees during their first three
years; 11. the first fruits, which must be brought to the temple.

Section 2

Feast days, comprising twelve chapters

1. Produce from the Sabbath; 2. social possessions, that is, the
entire city envisaged as a single household; 3. Easter; 4. the
shekel which everyone is obliged annually to give to the
Church; 5. duties pertaining to propitiatory feast days; 6. the
feast of tabernacles; 7. various dishes prohibited on feast days;
8. new year's day; 9. the various days of abstinence; 10. the
reading of the book of *Esher*; 11. feast half-days; 12. annual
sacrifice; the three visits to Jerusalem.

[1] *Molit.*, op. cit., p.17.

Section 3

Marriage and divorce contracts, comprising seven chapters

1. Permission and prohibition of marrying one's brother's wife; 2. the marriage contract; 3. the engagement period; 4. divorce; 5. vows; 6. persons consecrated to God; 7. women suspected of adultery.

Section 4

Damages, comprising ten parts

1. Rights concerning damages suffered; 2. rights over objects which are found, loaned, left in storage; 3. buying, selling, inheritance, deposits and other social exchanges; 4. jurisdiction in general and punishments; 5. the forty blows less one; 6. pledges; 7. general conclusions, law and testimony; 8. what a judge must do who has erroneously passed false sentence; 9. idolatry and commerce with the pagans; 10. moral proverbs.

Section 5

Sacred offerings, comprising eleven parts

1. Offerings; 2. the offering of flour; 3. the first born; 4. the sacrifice of healthy and sick animals; 5. tax on those things consecrated to God and its payment; 6. exchanging the offering; 7. violation of sacred things; 8. the 36 sins punishable by death; 9. the daily offering; 10. the construction of the temple; 11. doves and turtle-doves.

Section 6

Purifications, comprising twelve parts

1. Furnishings and their purification; 2. the tent where death has come; 3. leprosy; 4. the ashes of cattle used for

purification; 5. various purifications; 6. purificatory ablutions; 7. menstruation; 8. concerning the caution against eating anything impure unless a liquid has been poured over it; 9. the seminal flow; 10. he who has bathed is still impure until sundown; 11. the washing of hands; 12. how a fruit's stem makes it impure.

GEMARAH. – The Gemarah is a veritable anthology of *jurisprudence* based on the Mishnah. Together the Mishnah and the Gemarah form the *Talmud*.

With regard to these two collections, it is my great pleasure to bring attention to a very personal and most valuable piece of work by the author of the *Mission des Juifs*; it is a history of various traditional elements concerning the *Talmud* (p. 650 and following). Here is an extract from this history:

The bulky agglomeration of casuistic and scholastic literature, which since the return from exile replaced the powerful intellectuality of the prophets and continued to grow after the destruction of the third temple, for ten centuries, is generally grouped under the name of *Midrash*, commentary.

The two principal sections of this forest of paper are called *Hallachah*, rhythm or order of the march; *Haggada*, hearsay or legend.

It is in this last section that the influence of the esoteric communities can be discerned: Qabalah, Shemata.

The first volumes of the *Hallachah*, or *Halakha*, are an inextricable tangle of civil and canonical law, of national politics and individual methodology, of divine and human laws, jumbled together and branching out into infinite details.

Still, from many points of view, it is an interesting work to consult and evokes the famous names of Hillel, Akiba and Simon B. Gamaliel.

But the final draft is the work of Judah Hamassi in A.D. 220.

This, then, is the *Mishnah*, from *shana*, to learn; and its supplements are known under the name of *Tosephftoth*, the Boraitha.

Writers of the Mishnaic period, after the Soferim of Ezra, are the Tannim, succeeded by the Amoraim.

Controversies over and developments of the *Mishnah* by these last mentioned form the *Gemarah* or the complement.

It had two compilations: that of Palestine or Jerusalem in the middle of the fourth century, and that of Babylon in the fifth century A.D.

The Mishnah and Gemarah combined are known under the name of TALMUD, a continuation and conclusion of the first reform of Ezra.

THE TALMUD. – From the preceding, one can see that the Talmud is composed of the two principal collections which pertain to the legislative section of the Torah.

The Talmud thus constitutes the very *Life* of tradition, condensed in several treatises. In addition to the two collections we have mentioned (Mishnah and Gemarah) the Talmud contains (providing we consult authors other than Molitor) a whole new series of commentaries (*Midrashim*) and other additions (*Tosephftoth*).

In short, these are the names of the collections of writings which go together to make up the Talmud:

Mishnah	
Gemarah	TALMUD
Medrashim	
Tosephftoth	

The reader whose curiosity has been aroused is well advised to consult the *Philosophie de la tradition* by Molitor, and especially the *Mission des Juifs* by Saint-Yves (p. 653 and following). This last work contains a very fine history of the vicissitudes to which the Talmud has been subject throughout the ages.

THE QABALAH

And now we come to the higher part of tradition, to the Secret Doctrine or *Qabalah*, the veritable soul of this tradition.

It can be seen from the table given above that the theoretical part of the Qabalah is the only section known to us, the practical or magic parts still being kept secret, or being scarcely touched on in a few rare manuscripts.

1 THEORETICAL QABALAH

Authors who have concerned themselves with the question

have considered this theoretical part of the Qabalah from quite different points of view as to internal classification. Let us examine briefly the most important of them.

The largest group of researchers follows the divisions given by the Qabalists themselves. This is the plan followed by M. *Ad. Franck* in his fine work (1843), by *Eliphas Lévi* (1853) and by M. *Isidore Loeb* (Entry Cabala in the *Grande Encyclopédie*).

The principal subjects of mystic speculation of the time are the *work of the chariot* (*maasse mercavah*), by allusion to Ezekiel's Chariot, and *work of creation* (*maasse bereschith*).

The work of the chariot, which is also the great work (*dabar gadol*), discusses the beings of the supernatural world, God, the powers, the fundamental ideas, the 'heavenly family' as it is sometimes called; the work of creation discusses generation and the nature of the terrestrial world[1].

Here is this division:

QABALAH { Maasse Mercavah. – ZOHAR (work of the chariot). Maasse Bereschith. – SEPHER YETZIRAH (work of creation).

*

* *

Other writers, such as M. *S. Munk*[2] divide the Qabalah in the following fashion:

QABALAH {

1. Symbolic. { Mystic calculations. – Themurah. – Gematria. – Notarikon.

2. Positive, dogmatic. { Angels and demons. Divisions. Transmigration of souls.

3. Speculative and metaphysical. { Sephiroth, etc.

As can be seen, M. *S. Munk* tends toward the old division adopted by certain qabalists, notably *Kircher*.

*

* *

[1] Isid. LOEB.
[2] S. MUNK, entry *Kabbale* (*Dict. de la conversation*).

But in our opinion, the most complete division of the Qabalah is that of *Molitor*[1]: this is the one which we ourselves have adopted in the general table given previously, for it has the virtue of conforming in an over-all way to the generally adopted divisions while going beyond them, completing them as it were by the inclusion of a practical part.

	BERESCHITH	First degree
THEORETICAL	Sepher Yetzirah.	Historical legends.
		Haggadah.
	MERCAVAH	Second degree
	Zohar	Practical morals.
	Virtually nothing	Third degree
PRACTICAL	written.	Mystical doctrine.
	MAGICAL	*(Practical magic)*
	MANUSCRIPTS.	
	(Clavicula)	

QABALAH

Traditional teaching, tri-part like human nature and human needs, was at the same time *historical, moral* and *mystical*; thus holy writing had a triple sense: 1. the literal, historical sense (*pashut*), which corresponded to the court of the temple;

2. Moral teachings (*drusch*), which corresponded to the soul or the holy;

3. A mystical sense (*sod*), representing the spirit and the holy of holies.

The first, composed of certain stories taken from the lives of the ancient patriarchs, was transmitted from generation to generation, like so many popular legends. It is found scattered here and there in the form of glosses and explanatory notes in Biblical manuscripts and Chaldean paraphrases.

The moral sense looked at everything from a practical point of view, while the mystical, rising above the visible transitory world, hovered unceasingly in the sphere of the eternal.

[1] J.-F. Molitor, *Philosophie de la tradition*, trans. from the German by Xavier QURIS.

The mystical sense thus required a secret discipline, an uncommon piety of soul.

These two conditions called for the initiation of disciples, regardless of age or status; it sometimes happened that a father would instruct his children along these lines while they were still very young.

This high tradition is called *Qabalah* (in Hebrew, **KIBBEL**, to join together). Within its exterior form the word conceals the essential aptitude of the soul for conceiving supernatural ideas.

The Qabalah was divided into two parts: the theoretical and the practical.

1. Patriarchal traditions on the holy mystery of God and the divine persons;

2. On spiritual creation and the fall of the angels;

3. On the origin of chaos, matter and the renovation of the world during the six days of creation;

4. On the creation of visible man, his fall and the divine ways leading to his reinstatement.

Otherwise stated, it treated:

The work of creation (*Maasse Bereschith*).

The heavenly chariot (*Mercavah*).

*
*   *

The work of creation is contained in the *Sepher Yetzirah*.

We were responsible for the first French translation of this book to appear (1887).

Since then, a new translation has appeared, enhanced by more complete originals, the work of M. *Mayer-Lambert*[1].

We recommend this very studious work with great enthusiasm. Only one regret: the absence of a bibliography which would have been most useful for all concerned.

So that the reader may, in so far as possible, supplement our translation, which is to be found further on, we give here a table summarizing the supplementary developments of the *Sepher Yetzirah*. We have modified the relation of the planets and the days of the week, since the earlier relations seem to us

[1] MAYER LAMBERT, *Commentaire sur le Sepher Jesirah* or *Livre de la création*, by the Gaon Saadya of Fayoum, published and translated by Mayer Lambert, graduate of the Practical School of Higher Studies, professor at the Israelite seminary (Paris, Bouillaud, 1891).

to have been erroneously established due to a poor understanding of the connection between the order of the planets and the order of the days. The Egyptian clock given by Alliette (Etteila) clearly shows the source of this error.

The work of the heavenly chariot is contained in the *Zohar*. Since we do not have space here to give a translation of this book, let us make do with the excellent summary of M. *Isidore Loeb* in the *Grande Encyclopédie* (entry *Cabbale*).

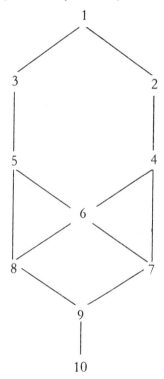

The Zohar is a cabbalistic commentary on the Pentateuch; it is not certain that we possess it in its original form, and the form we do possess may be the work of several persons. It is a vast compilation including, along with the ideas of the writer or writers, other more or less ancient works, such as the *Book of the Secret, The Great Assembly, The Lesser Assembly, The Book of Heavenly Tents, The Faithful Shepherd, The Discourse of a Young Man,* and others.

The basic theories are already contained, in large part, in the book of Azriel. An analysis follows, sufficient for a general understanding of all the Qabalah.

Table of Relations according to the Sepher Yetzirah

LETTERS		UNIVERSE	YEAR	MAN	MORAL WORLD
א	Aleph AIR	Atmosphere	Temperate (spring or autumn)	Chest	Rule of Equilibrium
מ	Mem WATER	Earth	Winter	Stomach	Plane of Fault
ש	Shin EARTH	Heaven	Summer	Head	Plane of Worth
ב	Beth	Saturn	Saturday SATURDAY	Mouth	Life and Death
ג	Gimel	Jupiter	Sunday THURSDAY	Right eye	Peace and Misfortune
ד	Daleth	Mars	Monday TUESDAY	Left eye	Wisdom and Foolishness
כ	Kaph	Sun	Tuesday SUNDAY	Right nostril	Richness and Poverty
פ	Pe	Venus	Wednesday FRIDAY	Left nostril	Culture and Barrenness
ר	Resh	Mercury	Thursday WEDNESDAY	Right ear	Grace and Unsightliness
ת	Tau	Moon	Friday MONDAY	Left ear	Domination and Servitude
ה	He	Aries	March	Liver	Sight and Blindness
ו	Vau	Taurus	April	Bladder	Hearing and Deafness
ז	Zayin	Gemini	May	Spleen	Smell and Absence of Smell
ח	Cheth	Cancer	June	Loins	Speech and Muteness
ט	Teth	Leo	July	Right Kidney	Fulness and Hunger
י	Yod	Virgo	August	Left kidney	Coitus and Castration
ל	Lamed	Libra	September	Large intestine	Activity and Powerlessness
נ	Nun	Scorpio	October	Small intestine	Soundness of Step and Lameness
ס	Samekh	Sagittarius	November	Right hand	Anger and the Removal of the Liver
ע	Ayin	Capricorn	December	Left hand	Laughter and the Removal of the Spleen
צ	Tzaddi	Aquarius	January	Right foot	Thought and the Removal of the Heart
ק	Qoph	Pisces	February	Left foot	Sleep and Languor

ANALYSIS OF THE ZOHAR
by M. Isidore Loeb[1]

God is the source of life and the creator of the universe, but he is
infinite (*en sof*), inaccessible, incomprehensible, he is unknown
(*ain*, nothing, nothingness for our intelligence, he is the great
problem (*mi*, who?), he would be profaned if he were in direct
relation with the world; between him and the world are the ten
sephiroth, through which he created the world, they are his
instruments (*kelim*), the channel (*cinnorot*) which his doings are
transmitted to the world of Faces (see below). The whole the the
ten *sephiroth* forms the prototypal man. Higher or eternal Adam
(or Pre-Adam), which is the macrocosm, the intellectual type of
the material world. The *sephiroth* are generally represented by the
cabbalists with a diagram called the *tree* of the *sephiroth*.

Their names, following the numerical order of the diagram
are:1. crown (*keter*); 2. wisdom (*hokhma*); 3. intelligence (*bina*); 4.
grace (*hesed*); 5. justice (*din*); 6. beauty (*tiferet*); 7. triumph
(*nessah*); 8. glory (*hod*); 9. foundation (*yesod*); 10. royalty or
kingdom (*malkhut*). The first nine *sephiroth* are divided into groups
of three, each containing two opposing principles and a principle
of conciliation. This is the Balance of the Book of Creation. The
first triad (Nos. 1,2,3) represents the metaphysical attributes of
God, or in other words, the intelligible world; the second (Nos.
4,5,6), the moral world; the third (Nos. 7,8,9), the physical
world; the last (No. 10) is nothing more than a resumé and
embodiment of all the others, the *harmony* of the world. The most
important role in this world of the *sephiroth* is played by the first
(No. 1), the Crown, which created the other *sephiroth* and then the
entire world. This is the Metatron of the ancient Qabalah, a kind
of demiurge. As it is almost as intangible and immaterial as God
himself, it is also sometimes called *infinite* or *nothingness* (*en sof*,
ayin); in any case, it is the *first point* (without dimension or any
material qualities), primary substance, the holy Face, the great
Face, and all the other *sephiroth* together are only the small Face.
It is also the Will of God, unless Will is within God and identical
with him. The triad with this first *sephirah* at its head is the plan of
the Universe, the triad of the world; the seven *sephiroth* which
follow are inferior to these three, they are only the *sephiroth* of
execution (of *construction*, as the Qabalists say). Considered from
another viewpoint, the *sephiroth* can be divided into *sephiroth* of the
right (Nos. 2,4,7), of the left (Nos. 3,5,8) and of the middle (Nos.
1,6,9).

[1] *Grande Encyclopédie*, entry *Cabbale*.

Those of the right represent the masculine element, which is considered superior to the other, better; this is the active principle, possessing the attributes of goodness and mercy; those of the left represent the feminine element, the passive principle, having the attributes of concentrated reflection and strict justice; the middle group is the group which reconciles the opposite principles. The three units making up the whole represent respectively, beginning at the top, the intelligible world, the moral world and the sensible or material world. In other qabalistic writings, it is the three triads, Nos. 1 to 9, which respectively represent these three worlds, worlds corresponding, let us note, to the three parts of the human soul as they are found in the Neo-Platonists: intelligence (*self*), heart (*psyche*), vegetative soul (*physis*). The introduction of the union of sexes in God is one of the most remarkable traits of the Qabalah. In the division of the *sephiroth* into parallel triads going from top to bottom, colours also come into play: the right-hand group is white, the left-hand group is red, the middle group is of an intermediate colour (blue, yellow or green). Finally, the *sephirah* No. 6 is linked one way or another to the lateral *sephiroth*, giving occasion to various combinations.

The ten *sephiroth* are like the *logoi* or mother ideas of the world. Together they compose a world which comes directly from God and which, unlike the inferior worlds proceeding from it, is called the world of emanation (*acilut*). By successive evolutions, three other worlds were formed, each provided also with ten *sephiroth*: 1. the world of creation (*beria*), which is likewise the world of the celestial spheres; 2. the world of formation (*yezira*), which is also the world of angels or spirits animating the spheres; 3. the world of termination (*atzigya*), which is the material world, the visible universe, the outer shell of the other worlds. God tried out many worlds before the present one, the Talmud speaks of worlds created and destroyed before this one; this myth represents either the perpetual activity of the creative force, which produces ceaselessly and never tires, or the theory of optimism by which this world is the best of all possible worlds.

This world, however, contains evil, inseparable from matter. Evil comes from the successive diminishing of divine light which, by its irradiation or emanation, created the world; it is an absence or lack of light, or else the remains, the residue of the attempted worlds which were found to be bad. This residue is an external, an appearance, evil is always represented as an external, there is even a world of evil, populated by fallen angels who are likewise external shells or appearances (*kelippot*).

Terrestrial man is the most elevated being of creation, the image of prototypal Adam, the microcosm. As we have seen, the cosmic triad is to be found in the three souls of which he is composed and whose seats, respectively, are the brain, the heart and the liver. The human soul is the result of the union between the king (No. 6) and the queen (No. 10), and thanks to one of her most remarkable attributes, the queen can ascend to the level of the king, man can, by his virtues, act upon the higher world and better it. From this comes the importance of prayer, by which man acts upon the superior forces in order to render them favourable to himself, setting them in motion and actually becoming their instigator. The soul is immortal, but does not attain heavenly happiness until it has become perfect, and to accomplish this, it is often obliged to live within several bodies; this is the theory of metempsychosis[1]. It even happens that a soul may descend from heaven to join with another soul in a single body (*sod ha ibbur*), in order to better itself from the contact or to aid the other. All souls were created at the beginning of the world and when all are perfected, the Messiah will come. The *Zohar*, as with many other works of Jewish literature, even calculates the date upon which the Messiah will come.

2 PRACTICAL QABALAH

The practical Qabalah explained:

A. The spiritual sense of the law; and

B. Prescribed the mode of purification which would assimilate the soul to the divinity, making of it an organ of prayer, acting in the sphere of the visible and the invisible.

Thus it was possible for it to piously degenerate into mere meditation of the sacred names, writing being, according to the Qabalists, the visible expression of divine forces, a form in which heaven reveals itself to earth.

It is easy to understand that nothing or virtually nothing has been written or published, pertaining to this part of the Qabalah.

Consequently critics have aimed some of their bitterest attacks at Qabalists who claimed to have magical knowledge.

[1] The word *reincarnation* is a better rendering of this idea than that of *metempsychosis*. – The soul is reincarnated in the body of a man, never in that of an animal (P).

See Reincarnation 'by Papus'. Physical, astral and spiritual evolution. The spirit before birth and after death. 250 pp. Ed Dorbon, 1912. 2nd edn., July 1926, with figures and a portrait of Papus, Ed., Adyar.

It must be recognized, however, that criticism based on hearsay could hardly produce a favourable judgement.

The theory of the practical Qabalah is connected with the general theory of magic; union of idea and symbol in Nature, in Man and in the Universe. To act on symbols was to act on ideas and on spiritual beings (angels); this was the mainspring for all acts of mystical evocation.

Above all, the study of the practical Qabalah contained special knowledge of the Hebrew letters and the various changes which they could be made to undergo by means of three operations, well-known to most Qabalists (*Temura, Gematria, Notarikon*).

The point is an important one, for it constitutes the meatiest, most exoteric part of the practical Qabalah, and yet several critics (especially the Germans) have refused to see in the entire Qabalah anything more than a scinece of wordplay, rebus and anagram; and only because they have not taken the trouble to go further to the heart of the matter.

Since it is important to be acquainted with this special *hieroglyphic language*, let us borrow from *Molitor* (op. cit.) a few typical examples on the subject.

*
* *

We have already stated that it was as difficult to write the Torah as to read it. Quite often in a word one letter more or less might be found, sometimes one substituted for another, the finals taking the place of the mediants, and vice versa.

Apart from this particular hieroglyphic system, the Bible contains another where the words are considered to be so many mysterious ciphers.

This first hieroglyphic system is either *synthetic* or *identical*:

1. Synthetic when a work contains several others which one discovers by *developing, dividing* or *transposing* the letters;

2. Identical when several words express the same thing. This identity is based either on the mysterious connection existing among the letters, or on their numerical value, obvious traces of which can be found in the prophets. The Mishna calls this hieroglyphic system *the perfume of wisdom*.

Here are some examples of synthetic hieroglyphics.

1. The *evolution* of letters.

In his testament to his son Solomon, David cries: *He cursed me with grievous curses* (NIMREZETH NMRZTh).

Now the Hebrew word *Nimrezeth* contains these very reproaches which the prophet made to David.

N   *oeph*, adultery.

M   *oabi*, Moabite, because he was a descendant of Ruth.

R   *ozeak*, murderer.

Z   *ores*, violent.

T   *hoeb*, cruel.

2. *Division.*

Dividing the word *Bereschith* gives *Bara-Schith, he created six,* that is, the six fundamental forces presiding at the mysterious work of the six days of creation. The same liberty was used in the construction of entire clauses and sentences.

3. *Transposition.*

In Exodus God says: *I will send M'lachi before you,* that is, *M'lachi,* my angel; by transposition this word becomes Michael, protector of the Hebrew people.

The most remarkable of these evolutions, called *Gilqul,* consists of the regular transposition of the different letters of a single word, such as in the holy name IEVE (*Jehovah*). The twelve mysterious changes which can be effected using these four letters represent the continual play of the primal power which causes variety to spring from unity.[1]

Use of numbers[2]

Aside from the synthetic hieroglyphics which we have just examined, there exists another system based on the numerical relation of letters each having a certain value.

The numbers are of three classes; each class contains nine corresponding letters. The first includes the simple numbers from 1 to 9. These are called the small numbers.

The second, beginning at 10 and ending with 90, is made up of the middle numbers.

Finally, the third, formed from the product of units and tens, is the great number.

As for 1,000, the last degree of numerical progression, it can easily be reduced to a unity: $1,000 = 1$; this is why these two

---

[1] *Molitor,* p. 31, 32, 35 (See also p. 123 for the transformations of IEVE).

[2] See *Science des Nombres,* Papus – Unpublished – 240 p. – 1028.

numbers have the same letter in Hebrew: *Aleph*[1] (See p. 63).

Letters can be replaced by numbers and vice versa. These latter may be added and combined separately, as one wishes.

Let us take as an example the word ADAM $\frac{m\ d\ a}{4041}$ whose sum equals 45 (40 + 4 + 1 = 45); the numerological 'root' (total) is 9.

As one might expect, there is an affinity among words having the same numerical value; thus, *Achad* and *Ahabha* whose corresponding number is 13, and which signify, respectively, *unity* and *love*, love being precisely that force by which unity can be restored. Moreover, the number 13 is the number of eternal love, symbolized by Jacob and his sons, Jesus Christ and his disciples; and even more remarkable, adding the ciphers gives the 'root' 4 (1+ 3 =4), which corresponds to the four letters of the holy name *IEVE*, principle of life and love.

The general key to these curious evolutions to which word and number are subject can be found in the hieroglyphic and numerical book whose scientific bases are still shrouded in mystery: the TAROT.[2]

The mystic explanation of the Tarot formed the basis of the oral teaching of *practical magic* which led the initiated Qabalist to prophecy. To our knowledge, nothing has been printed on this subject in Qabalistic books. Our public libraries possess a few manuscripts attributed to Solomon and translated from Hebrew into Latin, and from Latin into modern tongues; these manuscripts contain reproductions, under the name of talismans, of symbols of the Tarot or 'keys', as well as the *explanation* and utilization of these keys. They are known as *The Keys of Solomon* or as *Schemamphoras*; and it must be recognized that the information furnished by them is far from complete.

Be that as it may, it is necessary to mention them so as to determine as exactly as possible the principal divisions which can be established in this part of the secret tradition of the Hebrews. In conclusion, then, here is the manner in which we would divide the Qabalah.

---

[1] The Hebrew language lacks nouns for expressing numbers in excess of 1,000. Thus *Ribbo* which signifies ten thousand has the same 'root' as *Robh* (multitude).

[2] See ELIPHAS LEVI, *Rituel de Haute Magie*, chap. XXI, and PAPUS, *The Tarot of the Bohemians*: the Tarot is considered by some to be the breviary of the initiate. 3rd ed., 349 pages. 1926. Henri Durville, editor.

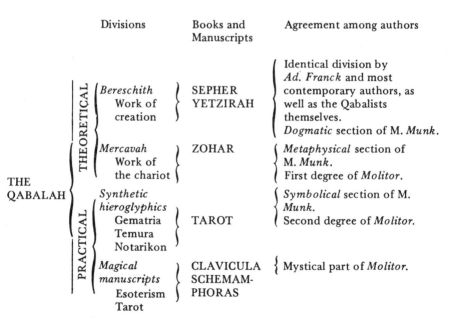

	Divisions	Books and Manuscripts	Agreement among authors
THEORETICAL	*Bereschith* Work of creation	SEPHER YETZIRAH	Identical division by *Ad. Franck* and most contemporary authors, as well as the Qabalists themselves. *Dogmatic* section of M. *Munk.*
	Mercavah Work of the chariot	ZOHAR	*Metaphysical* section of M. *Munk.* First degree of *Molitor.*
PRACTICAL	*Synthetic hieroglyphics* Gematria Temura Notarikon	TAROT	*Symbolical* section of M. *Munk.* Second degree of *Molitor.*
	Magical manuscripts Esoterism Tarot	CLAVICULA SCHEMAM-PHORAS	Mystical part of *Molitor.*

THE QABALAH

Part Two

The Teachings of the Qabalah

THE ELEMENTS OF THE QABALAH IN TEN LESSONS
LETTERS OF ELIPHAS LEVI[1]

FIRST LESSON

GENERAL PROLEGOMENA

Kind Sir and Brother,

I can call you thus because you search for truth in the sincerity of your heart and because, in order to find it, you are prepared to make whatever sacrifices may be necessary.

Truth, being the essence of that which is, is not difficult to find: it is in us and we are in it. It is like light and the blind see it not.

Being is. This is incontestable and absolute. The exact idea of Being is truth; knowledge of it is science; its ideal expression is reason; its activity is creation and justice.

You want to believe, you say. For this, it is enough to know and love the truth. For true faith is the unshakable adherence of the mind to the necessary deductions of science in conjectural infinity.

The occult sciences alone give certainty, for they are based on realities and not on dreams.

They distinguish truth from falsehood in every religious symbol. Truth is the same everywhere, and falsehood varies according to the time, place and persons involved.

These sciences are three in number: the Qabalah, Magic and the Hermetic philosophy.

[1] These letters were kindly given us by a student of Eliphas Lévi, M. Montaut. They appeared in the magazine *Initiation* in 1891.

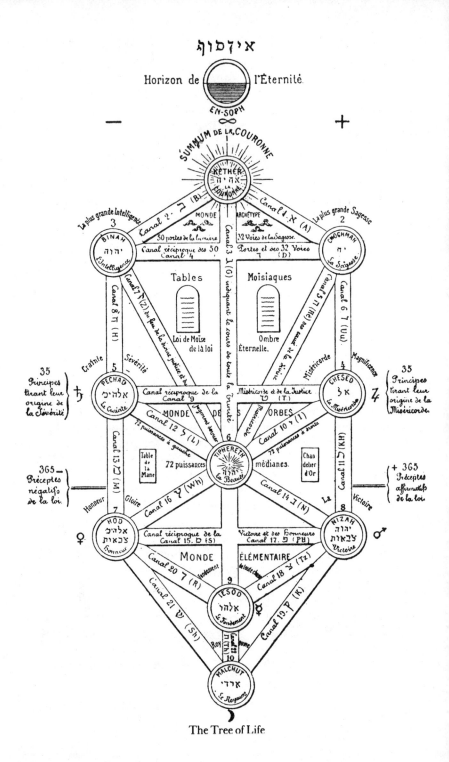

The Tree of Life

The Qabalah or traditional science of the Hebrews could be called the mathematics of human thought. It is the algebra of faith. It solves all the problems of the soul as if they were equations, by isolating the unknowns. It gives to ideas the clarity and rigorous exactitude of numbers; its results are, for the spirit, infallibility (relative, however, to the sphere of human knowledge), and for the heart, profound peace.

Magic or the science of the Magi had as representatives in antiquity the disciples and possibly the masters of Zoroaster. It is the knowledge of the secret and particular laws of nature which produce hidden forces, the magnets, both natural and artificial, which can exist even outside the metallic domain. In short, and to use a modern expression, it is the science of universal magnetism.

The Hermetic philosophy is the science of nature hidden in the hieroglyphs and symbols of the ancient world. It is the search for the principle of life together with the dream (for those who have not yet succeeded) of accomplishing the great work, the reproduction by man of natural and divine fire which creates and regenerates beings.

These, my dear Sir, are the things which you wish to study. The scope is immense, but the principles are so simple that they are represented by and contained within the numbers and letters of the alphabet. 'It is a labour of Hercules which resembles a child's game,' say the masters of the holy science.

The qualifications necessary for success in this study are a great rectitude of judgement and a great independence of mind. One must do away with all prejudice and every preconceived idea, and it is for this reason that Christ said: 'Ye must become as a little child, or ye cannot enter into *Malkuth*,' that is, the kingdom of knowledge.

We shall begin with the Qabalah, whose division is as follows: Bereschith, Mercavah, Gematria and Lemura.

Yours in the holy science.

SECOND LESSON

THE QABALAH – AIM AND METHOD

One's intention in studying the Qabalah must be to arrive at profound peace through tranquillity of mind and repose of the heart.

Tranquillity of mind is an effect of certainty; repose of the heart comes from patience and faith.

Without faith, science leads to doubt; without science, faith leads to superstition. The two together give certainty, but in brining them together they must never be confused. The object of faith is the hypothesis, and this becomes a certainty when the hypothesis is called for by the evidence or demonstrations of science.

Science affirms facts. From the repetition of facts, it ascertains laws. Intelligent laws are necessarily desired and directed by the intelligence. The unity discernible in these laws gives us to suppose a unity of legislative intelligence. This intelligence which we are obliged to posit from so many manifest works, but which we cannot define, is what we call God!

You receive my letter, this is an obvious fact; you recognize my handwriting and my thoughts, and so you conclude that I have in fact written to you. This is a reasonable hypothesis, but the necessary hypothesis is that this letter was written by someone. It might be a forgery of course, though you have no reason to make this supposition. If, however, you do so, you make a very doubtful hypothesis. And if you should think the letter has fallen from the sky fully written, then you would be making an absurd hypothesis.

Here then, following the Qabalistic method, is how certainty is formed:

Evidence	
Scientific demonstration }	certainty
Necessary hypothesis	
Reasonable hypothesis	probability
Doubtful hypothesis	doubt
Absurd hypothesis	error

Following this method, the mind becomes truly infallible, for it affirms what it knows, believes what must be necessarily supposed, admits reasonable suppositions, examines doubtful ones and rejects what is absurd.

The entire Qabalah is contained in what the masters call the thirty-two absolute, real ideas attached to the signs of the basic arithmetical numbers and to the twenty-two letters of the Hebrew alphabet.

Here are these ideas:

NUMBERS

1	Supreme power	6	Beauty
2	Absolute wisdom	7	Victory
3	Infinite intelligence	8	Eternity
4	Goodness	9	Fecundity
5	Justice or severity	10	Reality

LETTERS

Aleph . .	Father	Lamed . .	Sacrifice
Beth . . .	Mother	Mem . . .	Death
Gimel . .	Nature	Nun . . .	Reversibility
Daleth . .	Authority	Samekh . .	Universal being
He . . .	Religion	Ayin . . .	Equilibrium
Vau . . .	Freedom	Pe	Immortality
Zayin . .	Possession	Tzaddi . .	Shadow and reflection
Cheth . .	Distribution	Qoph . .	Light
Teth . . .	Prudence	Resh . . .	Recognition
Yod . . .	Order	Shin . . .	Omnipotence
Kaph . . .	Force	Tau . . .	Synthesis

THIRD LESSON

USE OF THE METHOD

In the preceding lesson I spoke only of the thirty-two ways or paths; later I will specify the fifty gates.

The concepts expressed by the numbers and letters are unquestionable realities. These ideas are connected and agree as do the numbers themselves. One can proceed logically from one to the next. Man is the son of woman, but woman comes out of man, as number comes out of unity. Woman explains nature, nature reveals authority and creates religion which

serves as a basis for freedom, making man master of himself
and of the universe, etc ... Get hold of a Tarot pack (though I
imagine you already have one) and lay out in two ten-card
series the allegorical cards numbered from one to twenty-one.
You will see all the symbols which explain the letters. As for
the numbers from one to ten, you will find their explanation
repeated four times with the symbols of the wand or sceptre of
the father, cup of delights of the mother, épées or swords of
love, and the coins of fecundity. The Tarot is thus included in
the hieroglyphic book of the thirty-two paths and its summary
explanation is found in the book attributed to the patriarch
Abraham, the *Sepher Yetzirah.*

The knowledgeable Court de Gebelin was the first to
discover the importance of the Tarot as a key to the hieratic
hieroglyphics. These same symbols and numbers are to be
found in the prophecies of Ezekiel and St John. The Bible is
an inspired book, but the Tarot is the inspiring work. It has
also been called the wheel, *rota*, from whence *tarot* and *torah*.
The oldest Rosicrucians were familiar with it, and the
Marquis de Suchet speaks of it in his book on the illuminati.

Our packs of playing cards have descended from this book
of symbols. Spanish cards still carry the principal signs of the
primitive Tarot and are sometimes used to play the game of
hombre or man, a reminiscence of a very early usage of the
mysterious book, containing the regulatory oracles of all
human divinities.

The most ancient Tarots were medals which have since
been made into talismans. The keys or lesser keys of Solomon
are composed of thirty-six talismans bearing seventy-two
imprints analogous to the hieroglyphic figures of the Tarot.
These figures, altered by copyists, can still be found in
manuscript copies of ancient keys existing in our libraries.
One of these manuscripts is in the Bibliothèque Nationale,
another, in the Bibliothèque de l'Arsenal. The only authentic
manuscripts of the keys are those giving the series of thirty-six
talismans with their seventy-two mysterious names; the
others, no matter their age, belong to the fantasies of black
magic and contain only unintelligible hocus-pocus.

For a complete explanation of the Tarot, see my *Dogme et
Rituel de la Haute Magie.*

Yours in the name of holy science,

ELIPHAS LEVI

FOURTH LESSON

THE QABALAH

Kind Sir and Brother,

Bereschith means 'genesis', Mercavah means 'chariot', by allusion to the wheels and mysterious animals of Ezekiel.

The Bereschith and the Mercavah are the sum of the science of God and of the world.

I say 'science of God', and yet God is infinitely unknown to us. His nature completely escapes our investigation. The absolute principle of being and beings, he cannot be confused with the effects he produces, and thus it can be said, affirming his existence all the while, that he is neither being, nor a being. This mystifies reason without causing it to stray and keeps us forever from all idolatry.

God is the only absolute postulatum of all science, the absolutely necessary hypothesis fundamental to all certainty, and this is how our ancient masters scientifically formulated this certain hypothesis of faith: Being is. In Being is life. Life manifests itself through movement. Movement is perpetuated by the balance of forces. Harmony is a result of the analogy of opposites. In Nature, there is immutable law and also indefinite progress. A perpetual change of form, the indestructability of matter, these are what one finds on observing the physical world.

Metaphysics presents us with laws and the like of both an intellectual and a moral order, the *true*, immutable on one side, and on the other, fantasy and fiction. On one side, good which is the truth, on the other, evil which is falsity, and from the seeming conflict of the two comes judgement and virtue. Virtue is made up of goodness and justice. Good virtue is indulgent. Just virtue is strict. Good because it is just, and just because it is good, it is ultimately beautiful.

This great harmony of the physical and moral worlds, incapable of having a cause superior to itself, reveals and demonstrates for us the existence of an immutable wisdom, eternal principle and eternal laws, and of an infinitely active creative intelligence. Upon this wisdom and this intelligence, inseparable one from the other, rests that supreme power which the Hebrews call the crown. The crown, and not the king; for the idea of a king would imply that of an idol. For the Qabalists, the supreme power is the crown of the universe, and all of creation is the kingdom, or if you prefer, domain of the crown.

No one can give what he does not have, and this allows us to admit, in a cause, the virtual existence of that which we observe in effects.

Thus God is the power or supreme crown (kether) which rests on immutable wisdom (chokmah) and creative intelligence (binah); in him are goodness (chesed) and justice (geburah) which are the ideals of beauty (tiphereth). In him also are movement, always triumphant (netzach) and the great eternal rest (hod). His will is a continual creating (yesod), and his kingdom (malkuth) is the immensity which fills the universe.

Let us stop here: we know God!

Yours in the name of holy science.

ELIPHAS LEVI

FIFTH LESSON

II

Kind Sir and Brother,

This rational knowledge of the divinity, scaled on the ten figures of which all numbers are composed, furnishes you with the entire Qabalistic method. The method is composed of thirty-two means or instruments of knowledge referred to as the thirty-two ways, and of fifty subjects to which science can be applied, called the fifty gates.

Universal synthetic science is thus seen to be a temple to which lead the thirty-two paths and whose entrances are the fifty portals.

This numerical system, a decimal one, since it is based on the number ten, establishes an exact classification, by analogies, of all fields of human knowledge. Nothing is more ingenious; but also nothing could be more logical, more precise.

This number ten, applied to absolute notions of being of the divine, metaphysical and natural orders, is thus repeated thrice, giving thirty for means of analysis; add syllepsis and synthesis, that unity which awakens in an individual mind and that other which is the universal summary of all, and you have the thirty-two paths.

The fifty gates are a classification of all beings in five series of ten each, embracing all possible knowledge and shedding light on the entire body of human understanding.

But it is not sufficient to have discovered an exact mathematical method; to be perfect, this method must be progressively revelatory, that is, it must furnish the means of drawing all possible conclusions, thereby allowing for the attainment of new knowledge and the development of the mind, leaving nothing to the caprice of the imagination.

Such is obtained through the application of Gematria and Lemura, the mathematics of ideas. The Qabalah has its ideal geometry, its philosophical algebra and its analogical trigonometry. And therefore, so to speak, it forces nature to reveal her secrets.

Once these higher areas of knowledge are mastered, one proceeds to the final revelations of transcendental Qabalism, studying in the shemahphorash the source and reason of all dogmas.

This, dear Sir and friend, is what must be learned. See if it does not frighten you; my letters are brief, but they are only concise résumés which speak of much in a few words. I let rather a long time go by between each of my first five lessons in order to leave you time for reflection; I can write to you more often if you so desire.

Please, Sir, believe in my deep desire to be of service to you.

Devotedly, in the name of holy science.

ELIPHAS LEVI

SIXTH LESSON

III

Kind Sir and Brother,

The Bible gives man two names. The first is Adam, meaning drawn from the earth, or man of the earth; the second is Enos or Enoch, meaning divine man or man elevated to the level of God. According to Genesis, it was Enos who first addressed public homage to the source of all beings, and this same Enos or Enoch, it is said, was raised living into heaven, after having engraved the primitive elements of religion and universal science on the two stones which are called the columns of Enoch.

This Enoch is not a personage, but a personification of humanity raised to a sense of immortality through religion and science. At the epoch designated by this name, the cult of God appears on the earth and ritual worship begins. At this same time civilization begins, with the advent of writing and the hieratic movements.

The civilizing force which the Hebrews personify in Enoch was called Trismegistus by the Egyptians, and Kadmos or Cadmus by the Greeks. It was he who, to the strains of Amphion's lyre, saw the living stones of Thebes rise up and take their place.

The primitive sacred text, the book which Postel calls the genesis of Enoch, is the first source of the Qabalah, that tradition at once human and divine, in short, religious. Here, in all simplicity, appears the revelation of supreme intelligence to man's reason and love, the eternal law governing infinite expansion, numbers in infinite expansion, numbers in immensity and immensity in numbers, and poetry in mathematics and mathematics in poetry.

Who would believe that the inspiration for all religious symbols and theories has been preserved and come down to us in the form of a pack of bizarre cards. Nothing, however, is more obvious; and Court de Gebelin, followed since by all those who have seriously studied the symbolism of these cards, was in the last century the first to recognize this.

The alphabet and the ten numerical signs are the most

elementary factors in all sciences. Add to them the signs of the four cardinal points of heaven or of the four seasons, and you have the book of Enoch in its entirety. But each sign represents an absolute, or essential idea.

The form of each number and each letter has its mathematical equivalent and its hieroglyphic significance. Ideas, inseparable from numbers, follow the movement of these latter, through adding, dividing, multiplying, etc., and thus acquire their exactitude. In a word, the book of Enoch is the arithmetic of thought.

Yours in the name of holy science.

ELIPHAS LEVI

SEVENTH LESSON

IV

Kind Sir and Brother,

In the twenty-two figures of the Tarot, Court de Gebelin saw a representation of the Egyptian mysteries and attributes their invention to Hermes or Mercury Trismegistus, also referred to as Thoth. It is certain that the hieroglyphs of the Tarot can be found on ancient Egyptian monuments; it is also certain that these signs, traced in synoptic groupings on stelae or metallic tables, such as the Isaic table of Bembo, were reproduced separately on engraved stones or medallions which later became amulets and talismans. Thus the pages of the infinite book were separated into diverse combinations, assembled and transposed in ways forever new, furnishing the inexhaustible oracles of truth.

I own one of these ancient talismans, brought back from Egypt by one of my friends. It represents the binary of Cycles, or more commonly, the two of coins. It is a symbolic expression of the great law of polarization and equilibrium which produces harmony through the analogy of opposites. This is how the symbol appears in our present day Tarot.

S The medal itself is rather worn, about as wide as a silver five-franc piece, but thicker. The two cyclic polarities are shown exactly as they are in the Italian Tarot, a lotus blossom with an aureole or nimbus.

The astral current which both separates and attracts the two poles is represented on the Egyptian talisman by the goat of Mendes placed between two vipers comparable with the serpents of the caduceus. On the reverse side of the medallion, an adept or Egyptian priest, replacing Mendes between the two poles of universal equilibrium, leads a goat down a tree-lined avenue, the animal having become a docile, ordinary beast beneath the wand of man, imitator of God.

The ten numerical signs, the twenty-two letters of the alphabet, and the four astronomical signs of the seasons are summary of all the Qabalah.

Twenty-two letters and ten numbers give the thirty-two paths of the Sepher Yetzirah; four gives the mercavah and the shemamphorash.

It is as simple as a child's game and as complex as the most arduous problems of pure mathematics.

It is both naive and profound, like truth, like nature.

The four elementary astronomical signs are the four forms of the sphinx and the four animals of Ezekiel and Saint John.

Yours in the name of holy science.

ELIPHAS LEVI

EIGHTH LESSON

V

Kind Sir and Brother,

The science of the Qabalah makes doubt impossible in matters of religion, for it, and it alone, reconciles reason and faith, by showing that universal dogma, variously formulated but, at heart, always and everywhere the same, is the purest expression of the aspirations of the human mind enlightened by a necessary faith. It also causes us to understand the usefulness of religious practices which, by fixing the attention, fortify the will, thereby throwing a superior light equally on all cults. It proves that the most efficacious of all cults is the one which, by tangible means, brings together divinity and man, makes him see it, touch it and in a way, incorporate it into himself. It almost goes without saying that I am speaking of the Catholic religion.

This religion, as it appears to the common man, is the most absurd of all since it is the most *revealed*; and here I am using the term in its literal sense, *revelare*, to re-veil, to veil again. As you know, in the Gospels it is said that at the death of Christ the veil of the temple was rent in two; and the dogmatic work of the Church across the ages has been aimed at weaving and sewing a new one.

It is true that the heads of the sanctuary, themselves, wanting to become its princes, long ago lost the keys to higher initiation. But this does not prevent the letter of dogma from being holy, nor the sacraments from having an effect. In my works I have shown that the Christian-Catholic cult is high magic, organized and regularized by symbolism and hierarchy. It is an assemblage of aids given to human weakness in order that the will might be strengthened in goodness.

Nothing has been left out, not the dark, mysterious temple, nor the incense which both calms and exalts, nor the long, monotonal chants that lull the brain into a state of semi-somnambulism. The dogma, whose obscure formulas seem the despair of all reason, serves as a barrier to the petulant attacks of inexperienced and overbearing criticism. These formulas appear bottomless; all the better to express the infinite. The mass itself, celebrated in a language which the masses cannot understand, gives breadth to the thought of the man who prays, permitting him to find in prayer all which might have a bearing on the needs of his mind and heart. This is why the Catholic religion can be likened to the phoenix which follows itself in succession from century to century, always born again from its own ashes; and the great mystery of faith is quite simply a mystery of nature.

It seems an enormous paradox to say that the Catholic religion is the only one which can rightly be called natural, and yet this is true, since it alone fully satisfies the natural need of man which is his religious sense.

Yours in the name of holy science.

ELIPHAS LEVI

NINTH LESSON

VI

Kind Sir and Brother,

If the Christian-Catholic dogma is fundamentally Qabalistic, the same must be said for the great religious philosophies of the ancient world. The legend of Krishna, as recounted in the Bhagavadam, is a veritable gospel, like ours, but more naive, more brilliant. The incarnations of Vishnu number ten as do the Sephiroth of the Qabalah and constitute a revelation in some ways more complete than our own. Osiris, killed by Typhon, then resurrected by Isis, is Christ denied by the Jews, then honoured in the person of his mother. The Thebaid is a great religious epic which must take its place beside the great symbol of Prometheus. Antigone is a symbol of divine woman as pure as that of Mary. Everywhere good triumphs through voluntary sacrifice, after having been for a time subjected to the wild assaults of forceful fatality. Even rites are symbolic and find their way from one religion to another. Diadems, mitres and surplices belong to all the great religions. From such facts, it is concluded that all are false; but it is the conclusion which is false. The truth is that religion is one, like humanity, and like humanity, forward-going, in transformation and always the same.

If, for the Egyptians, Jesus Christ is named Osiris, for the Scandinavians Osiris is called Balder. He is killed by the wolf, Juris, but Wotan or Odin brings him back to life, and the Valkyries themselves pour him mead in Valhalla. Skalds, druids and bards sing of the death and resurrection of Tarenis or Tetenus, distributing holy mistletoe to the faithful, as we do the sacred palm, during celebrations of the summer solstice, and worship virginity, inspired by the priestesses of the Isle of Seyne.

We can, then, rightly and in all freedom of conscience, perform the duties imposed on us by our parental religion. These practices are collective acts, repeated with direct, persevering intent. Now, such acts are always useful; they can be thought of as exercises for the strengthening of the will; and thus they bring us closer to the spiritual goal we wish to attain. Practices of magic and applied magnetism share this self-same goal, producing analogous, though less perfect, results.

How many men do not find the strength necessary to accomplish what they would like and ought to do? And there are innumerable women who give themselves over without complaint to painfully unpleasant tasks of the hospital and the school! Where do they find such strength? In small, repeated practices. Each day they say their rosary and, on their knees, offer up the prescribed prayers.

Yours in the name of holy science.

ELIPHAS LEVI

TENTH LESSON

VII

Kind Sir and Brother,

Religion is not a servitude imposed on man; it is a help which is offered him. The priestly classes have always attempted to exploit, sell and transform this help into an unbearable yoke, and the evangelical work of Jesus was aimed precisely at separating religion and the priest, or at least in returning the priest to his rightful place as minister or servant of religion. Look at the parable of the good Samaritan and at these precious verses: Law is made for man and not man for the law; Cursed be you who bind the shoulders of others burdens you would not see fit to touch with the tip of your finger; etc., etc. The official Church is spoken of as infallible in the *Apocalypse*, this Qabalistic key to the Gospels; for Christianity has always contained an occult or Johannite strain, which, while respecting the official line of the Church, has preserved an interpretation of dogma quite other than the one given to the common man.

Templars, Rosicrucians and Freemasons of high degree have all belonged to this occult Church; in the last century, prior to the French Revolution, its apostles included Pasqualis Martinez, Saint Martin and even Mme Krudemer.

The distinctive characteristic of this school is to avoid

publicity and anything that would make of it a dissident sect. Count Joseph de Maistre, this radical Catholic, was far more sympathetic than is believed toward the Martinist society and foretold a coming rebirth of dogma, inspired by lights emanating from the sanctuaries of occultism. There still exist fervent priests who are initiate in the ancient doctrines, and one bishop, among others, has recently died who made repeated requests to me for Qabalistic communication. The disciples of Saint-Martin had themselves called unknown philosophers, and those of a contemporary teacher, fortunate enough to be even more unknown, have need of no name whatsoever, since not even their existence is suspected. Jesus said that the yeast should be hidden in the bottom of the trough which holds the dough so that it can work day and night in silence until it has permeated the entire mass that is destined to be bread.

An initiate can, then, simply and sincerely practise the religion into which he was born, since all rites represent in various ways a single dogma; but he should open the heart of his conscience to God alone, accountable to no one for his most intimate beliefs. No priest can judge what the Pope himself does not understand. The exterior signs of the initiate are modest science, unostentatious philanthropy, equanimity and inalterable goodness.

Yours in the name of holy science.

ELIPHAS LEVI

GENERAL THOUGHTS ON THE QABALAH

by Sedir

The Qabalah is one of the most celebrated of the doctrines of traditional occultism; it is the expression of the esoteric philosophy of the Hebrews. Its father, or better, its founder was, according to the rabbis, the patriarch Abraham; and the basic books containing an exposition of all its mysteries are none other than those of Moses. Contemporary scholars assign far less antiquity to the Qabalah. Mr Nicolas finds that it goes back to the century prior to the Christian era[1]. Others claim that it was invented in the thirteenth century B.C., by Moise de Léon; but in his well-known book, M. M. Franck considers it prior to the compilations of the *Misha* and the *Talmud*. This opinion is shared by all initiates who have written on the question, and Fabre d'Olivet expresses it excellently, thus:

> It seems, so say the most noted rabbis, that Moses himself, foreseeing the fate his book was to undergo and the false interpretations which would be given it in time, instigated an oral law which he gave aloud to trustworthy men whose loyalty had been assured, charging them to transmit it in the secret of the sanctuary to other men, who, in their turn, passed it on from age to age, thus bringing it down to a time almost unbelievably distant from its beginnings. This oral law, which modern Jews claim to still possess, is called the Qabalah, from a Hebrew word meaning that which is received, that which comes from somewhere else, that which is passed from hand to hand[2].

A study such as this is intended to present the theories of those who not only accept archaeological testimony, but who also put their whole confidence in the most secret voice of Initiation.

[1] *Encyclop. des Sc. Relig*, LICHTENBERGER. Entry *Kabbale*.
[2] D'OLIVET, *Langue Hébraique Restituée*, p. 92.

As Moses was an Egyptian initiate, the Qabalah should naturally offer a complete exposé of the mysteries of Mizraim; but we must not forget that Abraham played a large role in the constitution of this science; and since the name and legend of this symbolic personage show that he represents a school of Chaldean priests, we can say that the Qabalah also contains the mysteries of Mithras.

I cannot give proof here of all I advance; it would mean re-fashioning the entire science of languages and all of ancient history; I repeat: I intend only to expose as briefly and clearly as possible a certain number of little-known ideas.

Tradition teaches that before the white race there appeared on the earth three other consecutive races, a cataclysm of fire or water marking the end of one and the beginning of the next. Two of these races lived on continents which have today disappeared, situated where now lie the expanses of the Pacific and Atlantic oceans. Geographical, geological, ethnological and historical proof which argues in favour of this theory can be found in the works of Elisée Reclus and Ignatius O'Donnelly. Without going into the ideological history of these extinct peoples, suffice it to say that at the time the young Hebrew was rescued from the waters in his bulrush bark, the temples of Thebes contained the sacerdotal archives of Atlantis and of the Church of Ram. The latter were a synthesis of the esoterism of the black race assembled by ancient India invaded by the whites. In addition, Moses took from the temples of Jithro, the last survivor of the black sacerdotal practices, the pure mysteries of this race. Thus the oral tradition that the early patriarch of the Hebrews left to his seventy chosen men contained the whole of the occult traditions which the world had known since its origin.

That is why the Qabalah is emanationist like Egypt, pantheistic like China; like Pythagoras it knows the power of letters and numbers, it teaches the psychurgic arts, like the Hindu Yogis; it works with the secret properties of herbs, stones and planets, like the Chaldean astronomers and the alchemists of Europe. This is also why archaeologists have often confused it with doctrines which are in fact quite late by comparison and of far more restricted scope.

Thanks to a passage from Exodus, we know that it was Joshua to whom Moses entrusted the keys of the oral tradition; but these keys grew rusty, to use the words of Saint-

Yves, during the period of terrible wars and civil strife which fell upon Israel until the time of Ezra; they were, however, preserved, not by the priestly class of Levi, but in the bosom of secular communities of prophets and seers, of which the best-known today are the Essenes. The reading of the books of Moses took place before the people each Saturday; commentaries on them, the *Tarqumim*, were at first oral, then came to be written down; all this casustic and scholastic literature accumulated from the return from exile until after the destruction of the third temple is called *Midrashim*, commentaries. These are of two types, *Halakha*, the tempo and rhythm of the march, and *Haggada*, saga and legend.

According to Saint-Yves[1], some of the science of the esoteric communities crept into the latter: *Shemata, Qabalah*. This second word, commonly held to signify Tradition, has another etymological root, however.

Commonly the derivation is traced to the Hebrew word *qebil*, meaning receive, collect, and this is translated: tradition. This seems to us to be somewhat forced and inexact. We believe the Hebrew word *Kabbale* to be of Chaldo-Egyptian origin, signifying occult science or doctrine.

The Egyptian root *Khepp, Khop* or *Kheb, Khob*, in Hebrew, *gab*, *Khebb*, or *Khebet*, means hide, enclose, and *al* or *ol* in Egyptian signifies take: so that the word would mean a science taken from hidden principles: *ex arcana*[2].

From Ezra onward, the interpretations of the esoteric texts of Moses advances from triple to quadruple, that is, no longer solar, but lunar, in a sense, polytheistic. And so we have that famous Persian word Paradise, spelled without vowels: P.R.D.S., a key to the Synagogues' teachings far different from the keys given Joshua by Moses.

Molitor characterizes these four degrees as follows:

The lowest, *Pashut*, is the literal sense; the second is called *Remmez*, simple allegory; the third, *Derash*, is a superior form of symbolism communicated under the seal of secrecy; the fourth, finally, *Sod*, secret, mystery, analogy is unsayable; it can only be understood by direct revelation.

The theoretical Qabalah contained:

[1] *Mission des Juifs*, new edition, 1928.
[2] F.-S. CONTANCIN, *Encycl. du XIXe Siècle*.

1. The patriarchal traditions concerning the Holy Mystery of God and of divine personages;

2. Concerning spiritual creation and the angels;

3. Concerning the origin of chaos, matter and the renewal of the world during the six days of creation;

4. Concerning the creation of visible man, his fall and the divine laws pertaining to his reinstatement.

The work of creation is the *Bereschith*.

The heavenly chariot is called the *Mercavah*.

We will now give a resumé, following Molitor, of the theoretical part which is concerned with creation: Cosmogony.

ORAL TRADITION IN THE AGE OF TOHU

The essence of any created being rests on three forces; the median force is the life principle of all creatures and maintains their identity.

A creature is such only by virtue of the real principle which manifests itself through a tendency toward individualization, in order ultimately to act on the exterior.

This action is entirely different from the false action which detached the creature from divine unity.

The act from which the creature derives is, in its primitive essence, only a blind instinct of nature.

This negative contraction of the creature is only an action which has no existence except in its continuity, growing until it reaches its tropic point.

From then on, each creature yearns for the principle in which it had its origin.

Alongside the action of the creature, revelation has a double action called *Shiur Komah* (the measure of being).

The first produces the being, preserves his life, gives him his own individuality (the Son): this is creation.

The second is Redemption, the revelation of the Son in grace and love (the Spirit), directed at the deliverance of the creature from his nothingness and reinforcing his desire to return to the original centre.

The perfection of creature life is this: the moment of the creature's own existence coincides with the moment of its union with God; a voluntary renunciation of one's own existence is necessary.

Beatitude is the fusion of the double joy of Being and non-Being.

Life is comprised of three worlds, *Mercavah*, the chariot:

1. *Neshammah*, The Internal; – the spirit, the mind; includes intelligences so close to God that the eccentric, individual action of the creature is overcome by the divine, these intelligences, then, becoming higher powers capable of losing themselves freely in Him;

2. *Ruach*, The Intermediary; a hierarchy of invisible beings, channels; the soul;

3. *Nephesh*, The Exterior or Revealed, the body of creation, where individual action attains its fullest expression.

Each creature possesses these three; a *Neshammah* which ties him to his superior origin and where he exists as a high ideal, a *Nephesh* which gives the creature its particular existence. These two worlds partake respectively of two force-currents:

Or Hayashor: the unified light of involution.

Or Hashoser: the reflected light of evolution.

Life tends ceaselessly toward unity; elementary beings are not capable of any spiritual life, they ascend, but do not evolve: their exterior never loses itself in their interior, the real, in the ideal.

The crowning being of the whole, he who gives it its initiative, is man, participating in all three worlds alike, a kind of lens, a focus for all beings, casting on the world a concentrated beam of glorification. God uses man to attract each creature to the heart of his love.

Man represents the concentric direction of life.

The interior, spiritual man is *Zelem Alohim*.

The exterior, corporeal man is *Demuth Alohim*.

An angel, as opposed to man, tends to reveal the ideal in a real form.

Man has three parts, twelve organs and seventy members. The development of his parts is the story of creation and of his gradual union with God. When this accomplished, the godly class and the entire world will enter into eternal love.

The double vocation of the creature is to:

1. Freely construct his own unity;

2. Adapt to the conditions of his existence and to the infinite vista of eternal love.

This union of the individual and the infinite is accomplished only through the will which resides in the soul; it has two phases:

Shimush Achorayin, Union from behind. – The state of exteriorization of the creature at the moment of his coming out from God to be lost in the all.

Sivuq Panim Al Panim, Union from the front. – the glorification which supernatural life gives the creature and which assimilates him to God.

The creature draws always nearer the infinite, without ever reaching it: *Ain Soph*, which man can understand only in its external manifestation or its splendour, the *Sephiroth*; these ten make up but three persons.

Adam has a double mission (positive and negative precepts):

1. To cultivate the garden of Eden;
2. To preserve himself from the influence of darkness.

If man had obeyed, the union between the two Adams, the creaturely and the divine, would have been consummated for eternity; and the same unity would have taken effect throughout all nature. Fixed in God, Adam would have continued his development without egoism (Cf. Fabre d'Olivet, *Cain*): his individualization would have been founded on a consciousness of the absolute nothingness of the creature, a factual idea which must at some time be held. The Word would have caused the cultivation of the garden to be an entirely interior one, then the Holy Spirit would have come to proclaim the great *Sabbath*.

But the serpent aroused a love for the creature in the heart of man; the equilibrium of the two poles of life was disturbed; the principle of contraction subsided little by little into dullness and the principle of expansion became chaotic. (Cf. BOEHME, *Passage de la Lumière aux Ténèbres*).

The measure of grace and mercy, *middath-hachesed et Rachmim*, was thus changed into one of stringency and rigour, *middath hadin*.

The man who offers absolute resistance to the means of return afforded him by grace is forever cast into an endless orbit outside the circle of harmony.

Let us recapitulate:

The activities of the supreme Being extend to all levels of creation, growing fainter proportionately to the distance from the source.

But whereas in the *Sepher* the decrescence of the modes of existence or manifestation of Being takes place in three stages, the *Zohar*, remaining closer to the general principle of its system, doubles the second (in the Sepher this is the stage composed of thought and word) and speaks of four different, successive worlds. First there is the world of emanations, *olam essicuth* from the verb *assul*, meaning *emanare ex alio et se ab illo separare certo modo*, that is, the interior working which renders the possible (*ayin* = nihil) becomes real (the thirty-two paths of wisdom).

Next there is the world of creation (*olam beria*, from the verb *bara*, meaning to come out of oneself = excidit); that is, the movement by which the spirit, leaving its isolation, manifests itself as general spirit, without, however, there yet being the slightest trace of individualization.

The *Zohar* calls this word the pavilion which serves to veil the indivisible point, and which, although of a less pure light than the point itself, can still not be looked at directly.

The third world is that of formation.

Olam Yetzirah, from *Yatsar, fingen* (to fashion, but with the passive sense of *formari*), that is, the world of pure minds of intelligible beings, or the movement by which general spirit-mind manifests itself, breaks itself down into a crowd of individual minds.

Lastly, the fourth world is that of production (*Olam assiya*, from the verb *assa*, to make, *conficere*), that is, the tangible universe of world. The Sepher speaks of the evolution of Being in 'an always descending movement' from the highest degree of existence to the lowest. It does not seem to speak of what happens next.

The Zohar teaches us that the expansive movement of Being is followed by a movement of concentration; Being turns inward on itself. This movement of concentration is in fact the definitive goal of all things. Souls (pure spirits) who have fallen from the world of formation into the world of production will return to their primitive state once they have developed perfection, the indestructible seeds of which they carry within themselves. If necessary, there will be several existences. This is what is called the circle of transmigration[1].

According to the Qabalah, which here follows the general tradition of Occultism, the human being is composed of three parts: the body, the soul and the mind. In conformity with the law of creation indicated by the system of the *Sephiroth*, each of these parts is a reflection of the others and thus contains an

[1] *Encyclopédie*, LICHTENBERGER.

image of the other two; and these ternary subdivisions can be extended according to the doctrine of initiate rabbis to include the tiniest physiological details and the most subtle movements of the psychic being. Contrary to the thought of Catholic theologians, atheistic philosophers and the propounders of the Gnostic heresy, who somehow managed to overlook the true sense of the texts they had before them, this ternary division with its implications of the existence of God and the immortality of the soul, is clearly expressed in the books of Moses and particularly in the *Sepher*.

In Hebrew, the lower part of the human being is called *Nephesh*; the median part, the mind, is called *Ruah*; and the upper part, *Neshamah*. Each of these centres-of-being is extracted, so to speak, from the corresponding plan of the Universe: *Nephesh* perceives the physical world, feeds on its energies and there deposits its creatures; *Ruah* does the same on the astral plane, and *Neshamah*, on the divine. All parts of Man are thus in a continual state of interchange with their corresponding parts of the Universe, as well as with the other parts of Man himself. A table will make these correspondences more easily understood.

According to a contemporary Qabalist, Carl de Leiningen[1], these three fundamental parts of man are not completely distinct and separate; on the contrary, they must be thought of as passing gradually from one into the next, like the colours of the spectrum, which although successive, cannot be completely distinguished, since each of them grows out of the preceding one.

From the body, that is, the lowliest power of *Nephesh*, rising through *Ruah* to the highest degree of *Neshamah*, all gradations can be found, just as one passes from darkness to light through an area of shadow; and inversely, from the most elevated parts of mind to the most material of physical levels, one passes through all the nuances of radiance, as one might pass from light to darkness through dusk. And above all, thanks to this interior unity, this fusion of parts one into the next, the number Nine loses itself in the One, producing man, a corporeal spirit which unites these two worlds in a Self.

By adding this information to that which Molitor gave us earlier, we see taking form the analogy of Man, the Universe and God, a theory which is to be found in all traditions. The following table will give a clearer idea.

[1] *Le Sphinx*, April 1887.

10	General	Particular	Concrete
Neshamah	9 *Yehidah*	8 *Haia*	7 Knowledge
Ruah	6 Qualitative	5 Exterior	4 Quantitative
Nephesh	3 Principle	2 Efficient force	1 Wrought matter

This table, which is nothing other than an adaptation of the schema of the *Sephiroth*, brings us to a rapid discussion of the practical part of the tradition.

*
* *

The practical Qabalah is based on the following theory. The Hebrew letters correspond strictly to the divine laws which formed the world. Each letter represents a hieroglyphic Being, an Idea and a Number. To combine letters is thus to approach knowledge of the laws or essences of Creation. Moreover, this system of twenty-two letters which correspond to the divine trinity, the Zodiac and the planets: $3 + 12 + 7 = 22$, develops according to ten modes which are the ten *Sephiroth*. This system, from which Pythagorism borrowed greatly, has been characterized as follows by Eliphas Lévi:

> The Qabalah or traditional science of the Hebrews might be called the mathematics of human thought. It is the algebra of faith. It solves all the problems of the soul as if they were equations, by isolating the unknowns. It gives to ideas the clarity and rigorous exactitude of numbers; its results are infallibility for the spirit (within the sphere of human knowledge) and for the heart, profound peace.[1]

[1] ELIPHAS LEVI, *Initiation*, December 1890, p. 195.

But it is not enough to have discovered an exact mathematical method; to be perfect, this method must be progressively revelatory, that is, it must give us the means of making all possible deductions, of obtaining new knowledge and of developing the mind without leaving anything to the caprice of the imagination.

This is what one obtains through *Gematria* and *Themurah*, which are the mathematics of ideas. The Qabalah has its ideal geometry, its philosophical algebra and its analogical trigonometry. Thus it forces, so to speak, Nature to render up her secrets.

Once such high knowledge is acquired, one passes on to the last revelations of the transcendental Qabalah, studying in the *shemamphorash* the source and reason of all dogma[1].

In an attempt to hold myself to generalities, I will only cite from masters of the science; it is only the horizons of this science which will come into view, far more complicated and involved than is generally believed. The following lines, from the pen of one of the strongest contemporary Qabalists, are proof enough of this:

There are two kinds of Qabalah, and I shall try to dwell on the differences which separate them. One, the literal Qabalah is the one belonging to the domain of the philologists, and which certain of them have classified and analysed. It is the one which, by its precise, mathematical aspect, has struck the imagination of not a few, and which remains a dead science, a skeleton buried in the terrific mass of Talmudic studies. These exists no *Rabbin*, no matter how unlearned, who is not acquainted with certain odds and ends; this is the Qabalah which finds its way into ceremonial incantations, which is inscribed on the talismans of sorcerers, on the parchment amulets of Jews and even, what mockery!, can be found among the typographical conventions of editors of Hebrew works. This Qabalah took its life only from the ideas which it expressed, and formerly, at the time of the *Zohar*, and even at the time of the new Qabalah, in the seventeenth century, an entire mystical doctrine, quite particular and involved, was expressed in this medium, using its language and its symbols.

Those who have studied the books of the *Zohar*, the Qabalistic treatises of all times, know what patience and effort are required, first to arrive at the meaning of the symbols and localize them as to origin, next to follow the comparisons and explanations given by the savant Qabalists themselves.

A few rare scholars among the Jews, a few elite minds, are in

[1] ELIPHAS LEVI, *Initiation*, January 1891, p. 306-307.

full possession of this lengthy science, more difficult than Wronski, more diffuse than Spanish mysticism, more complex than gnostic analysis, but to make it one's own ten years of study and isolation are necessary; one must live for it and within it alone. Thought must continually be affixed on this point, so strongly attached that nothing can break the spell, and furthermore such efforts must eventually be rewarded by the supportive involvement of some protective spirit, evoked by the constant appeal and worth of the researcher. Certainly the Qabalah thus understood and studied merits all the attention and effort of those who wish to succeed; but as most often happens, would-be scholars find themselves near the outset either distracted or weary, and so do nothing more than mark time, discouraged and remaining superficially erudite, capable of impressing the ignorant, but fundamentally inept and of little interest.

A Qabalist should be able to read any rabbinical work at sight, give an explanation in the original language of the Jewish mystic, that is, supporting the work with citations from other authoritative texts, and bring to bear personal contributions garnered from his own reflection and his research. And for the development of such a capacity the student would have about ninety years, since a lifetime would be barely sufficient for such efforts. And the teacher? Where is he to be found?

This great and noble science must not be profaned and made ridiculous by prideful ignorance, and it is as pitiful to see the unlearned reciting several words of Molitor's, or repeating a few formulas of Frank's, as it would be to see children 'adding' a fraction, a circle and a trigonemetric equation and then crying that they know mathematics.

What to do, then? Is there another Kabbala? Yes, and I wish to demonstrate this here. There is always another theological science from that of the official school, for there are always heretics and mystics; there is mystical doctrine other than that of the *Talmud* and other interpretations of the *Torah*, for among the Qabalists themselves there have always been teachers who were proscribed, and who were persecuted and ultimately passed over into Christianity. From one end to the other of the Jewish and Christian worlds, there have come men who have broken every spell and every fetter in order to search out the truth individually and to the best of their ability. The Guillaume Postels, the Keuchlins, the Khunraths, the Nicolas Flamels, the Saint-Martins, the Fabre d'Olivets, what are they? These are the masters of the Qabalah as Stanislas de Guaita has seen it and made it known. These men were conquerors in search of the golden fleece, refusing all sanction and honour from their contemporaries, speaking from on high because they were highly placed, and expecting the honours which one receives only from one's own descendants. These honours are the only ones, since, as we are taught by tradition and Egyptian symbolism, we alone can judge ourselves. When the river has subsided, we appear naked, having left behind our death-clothes with our dreams, and then to each it shall be given in accordance with his living works: Our God is the God of the living and not the God of the dead[1].

Such Qabalistic practice may be intellectual or magical. When it is intellectual, its key is the *Sephiroth*. We will not pause here to give a study of the *Sephiroth*; suffice it to say that their law is the same as that of numbers. An excellent explanation of this can be found in the *Traité Elémentaire de Science Occulte* by Papus.

We will give two adaptations: one is borrowed from the literature of psychurgic training, the other, from psychology and ethics, according to Khunrath.

The following schema refers to the exercise of the thaumaturgical power; the elements can be found in the *Messianic Apodictic* by Wronski, its system being entirely Qabalistic.

According to Boehme, the Qabalah is a kind of Magic, with its centre being the *Tetragrammaton*, which contains the true forces whereby the intelligible acts in the sensible. On this latter plane operates the Law of Moses, whose transgressions receive eternal punishment.

	Wakefulness	
Lethargy		Ecstasy
Sleep		Exaltation
	Dream	
Catalepsy		Epilepsy
	Somnambulism	
	Thaumaturgy	

[1] Marc HAVEN, Stanislas de GUAITA, Qabalist. *Initiation*, January 1898, pp. 33 to 36.

The Qabalah is also the science of mutations possessed by the angels, those of fire as well as those of Light, for they can formally realize their desires by means of the Imagination. This is the beatitude of Science.[1]

This refers, of course, to the magical portion of this science.

*
* *

Here now is some information on the reinstatement of man:

Qabalists call sin an outer shell: the shell, they say, forms like an excrescence, wrinkled on the outside, by the sap which ceases to flow; at last the shell dries out and falls. In this same way, man, who is called to participate in the work of God, to finish his own creation by perfecting himself through an act of free will, should he permit the immobilization of the divine sap given him for the development of his faculties for Good, this man progresses in retrograde fashion, degenerating and falling away like the dead shell. But, according to the Qabalists, nothing in nature comes to its conclusion in evil; always evil is absorbed by good; the dead shells have their use, in that they can be gathered by the labourer who burns them and warms himself, then making of their ashes a fertilizer which nourishes his trees, or by rotting of themselves at the foot of a tree, they give it nourishment and return to the sap through the roots. In Qabalistic thought, the eternal fire which is to burn the wicked is also the regenerating fire which purifies them and by painful but necessary transformations, puts them to the general use, thus giving them over to goodness which must always triumph. God, they say, is the absolute of Goodness, and there cannot be two absolutes; evil is error which will be absorbed by truth, it is the shell, the bark which, putrified or burned, returns to the sap, contributing again to universal life[2].

To burn the outer bark is a long and painstaking work; initiation provides the means of climbing this steep path more rapidly.

'Choose your master,' says the Talmud (*Pir Aboth*. 1,6); and the commentator adds: 'Let him find a single teacher and take the traditional teachings from him alone, not receiving instruction today from one, tomorrow from another.'

A man is not admitted to the sacred mysteries of the Qabalah

[1] *Questions Théos*, III, 34; II, 11.
[2] ELIPHAS LEVI, *Initiation*, November, 1894, pp. 109-110.

SEPHIROTIC CORRESPONDENCES AFTER KHUNRATH

SEPHIROTH	MODES	FACULTIES	DESCENDING ASPECTS OF GOD	ASCENDING VIRTUES
Kether	Fides	Mens	Optimus omnia videns	Castitas
Binah	Meditatio	Intellectus	Multus benignitate	Benignitas
Chokmah	Cognito	Ratio	Solus sapiens	Prudentia
Gedulah	Amor	Judicium superius	Misericors	Misericordia
Geburah	Spes	Judicium inferius	Fortis	Fortitudo
Tiphereth	Oratio	Phantasia	Longanimis	Patientia
Netzach	Conjunctio	Sensus interior	Justus	Justicia
Hod	Frequentia	Sensus exterior	Maximus	Humilitas
Yesod	Familiaritas	Medium	Verax Zelotes	Temperantia
Malkuth	Similitudo	Objectum	Terribilis	Timor Dei

unless he accords a total, unshakable and uninterrupted confidence to his master and the latter's teachings, never combating them nor taking the initiative[1]. This is something that might keep many people away from the holy science, but let us remember that we are not speaking here of the occult sciences in general; none of this is necessary to understand the Od like M de. Roch'as or hermetism like M. Berthelot. This is not a branch of human knowledge, it is the high magic of good and evil, the science of life and death, which the profane wish to possess, and as Eliphas Lévi has said: *Surely we can ask him who desires to become almost a god to be at least a little more than a man.* This apparent passivity, which would offend so many vanities, is only momentary, and in any case, highly personal.

As in the Pythagorean schools (Cf. Aulus-Gellus, *Noct Att.*, I, bh. IX), the disciple must listen and abstain from all discussion or commentary, giving in his words and actions a testimony of his adherence. The revelations transmitted by the Qabalah are divine, of a more elevated order than those which would normally belong to the domain of reason; ordinary faculties are exhausted, nullified, as it were, by the act of receiving mysteries. Thus one has the right to exact this sacrifice; one ought to in fact, for the soul of the neophyte, the sincerity of his aspirations, the force of his desire and will are here put to the test. If he has a low opinion of himself and doubts his own powers sufficiently to see in this weaning-period a kind of individual death, he is not worthy of continuing and will, of himself, withdraw. Certainly he must be weak who would stop so near the beginning, and crassly stinting of himself he who hesitates before so precious a renunciation.

In the second place, the Qabalist must be well-versed in all the worldly sciences and arts, for he who aspires to the honour of Initiation must be equipped with all human powers. *However, and both reason and daily experience show the truth of this, it is not with slight knowledge, nor a vague smattering of the humane sciences, nor with superficial cultivation that the candidate must present himself, he whose work, zeal and will shall henceforth be given over to the contemplation of elevated forms, he who, so to speak, will violate the very sanctuaries of God (Reuchlin).* But this profane knowledge is not to be the matter nor the foundation of absolute knowledge. Emptiness and death must come to the soul, there everything must become shadowy and

---

[1] These rules are traditional. They can be found scattered through various texts and commentaries. Among the texts, the *Shar aorah* of Rabbi Joseph Castebeusis, among the commentaries: Reuchlin, *De Cabbala*, Paul Ricceus, *De Coelesti Agricultura*, Rob. Fludd, *Tractatus apologeticus*, are the principal sources; we will not refer to them again.

untouched again, as with Moses in the wilderness[1], so that the soil, now fertile, will be ready for new harvests.

He who has not studied the sciences of the past and present has no right to speak lightly of them; he who has not let play within himself all the machinery of mathematics, all the springs of the natural sciences, all the cords of the imagination, he who has neither wept nor mused has no right to scorn tears or thought, scientific affirmation or artistic emotion. He is still asleep; he will remain an imitator, unless he becomes a magician. Among the ancients I could cite the names of several men who immersed themselves in erudition before becoming students of lofty science. But perhaps a contemporary example is more valuable: a very great artist, a teacher of literature did not recoil from the many unpleasantnesses and fatigues of the laboratory in order to merit the names of adept[2].

Such examples, if this were necessary, would be sufficient to prove that the chain of tradition has not been broken.

In the third place, the Qabalists desire that their disciples be of mature age; they are persuaded that no one is capable of such sublime and profound religious thought if he has not grown older, if the fires and passions of youth have not waned, if his morals and habits have not grown stronger and purer, if he has not become, as the eighteenth century would say, an honest man.

These were the sentiments of Rabbi Eleazar, answering his teacher Jochanan who, out of kindness, wished to initiate him rather early into the mysteries of the *Mercavah*: 'But my hair has not yet grown white.' For he who meditates and develops the seeds of truth within him, a process of purification takes place, a continual sublimation. This is not a periodic state which Tradition calls for, but a point in individual evolution where troubled and feverish modes of thinking have become calm and clarity reigns, and where the angel of death – who is also the angel of generation – has been dominated by man, where, in a word, action is possible, and man is ready to receive knowledge and realize it.

The fourth condition is an absolute purity; and this follows from the foregoing, implying that maturity varies from individual to individual. But spurning this purity, by sacrificing everything to desire, considering material joys as ends in themselves, man allows himself to partake of the most dangerous of illusions, making all psychic elevation impossible. One must choose, not between voluptuousness and virtues, this is the error of many

---

[1] ZIROLDE DE MOSE, *Introd. ad Histor. Eccles.*, ch. I, p. 26.
[2] Stanislas de Guaita, author of numerous erudite works on the Qabalah, both dogmatic and magical, from his first articles in *Artiste* to his last works.

sects, but between love and victory, recognizing, once the choice is made, that Beauty, a reflection of the crown, lies between these two roads. The thirty-two paths of Wisdom open only to those whose hearts are good[1].

A tranquil soul, free from all wordly preoccupations, is also an important condition; let the mind be a lake where all inspiration and direction from above can be reflected without the danger of there coming a movement from below to trouble the waters. 'Leave wives, parents, children, and follow me,' said the Christ. 'Sell your goods and give your gold to the poor,' said Joachim de Flore to his disciples. 'Beware of the egotism of family and friends, say the teachers; 'Remain alone before the face of God so as to be closer to humanity.' 'This is silence, the sabbatical of authors, so that the voice, stronger and more sonorous, can be raised again. But cursed by those who keep silent forever, cursed by the wordless ones for the crop they have sown, for the painful passions of those who shall come after[2]!'

With these beautiful words let us bring to an end this hurried study which, reading it over, seems to be a juxtaposition of disparate material. We give it, however, as it is; firstly because time and the means are lacking to offer a more worthy idea of this venerable Tradition, and secondly, because we hope to have aroused a certain curiosity, a certain desire for Truth, Beauty and Goodness.

SEDIR

---

[1] Isaak ben Elyakim. Amst. 1700.
[2] Marc HAVEN, *Initiation*, February 1894, pp. 136 to 141.

SYSTEMATIC RÉSUMÉ OF THE QABALAH

CHAPTER I

Preliminary Exposé – Division of the Subject

In the following study we shall do our best to summarize the teachings and traditions of the Qabalah.

The task is a difficult one for the Qabalah contains on the one hand, an entire system, particularly based on the study of the Hebrew tongue, and on the other, a body of philosophical teaching of the highest importance, derived from this system.

We shall be careful to take up these diverse points in an orderly fashion, separating them clearly from one another. Our study will thus include:

1. A preliminary study on the origin of the Qabalah.
2. An exposé of the Qabalistic system and its divisions, a *veritable course in the Qabalah* in several pages.
3. An exposé on the philosophy of the Qabalah and its applications.
4. The principal texts of the Qabalah upon which the foregoing are based.

This is the first time that work of this kind has been presented to the public. Thus we will try to rely always on competent authors whenever the development is not strictly our own.

The Qabalah is the keystone of the whole western tradition. Any philosopher who deals with the highest conceptions of the human mind comes necessarily to the Qabalah, whether his name by Raymond Lulle[1], Spinoza[2], or Leibniz[3].

All the alchemists were Qabalists; all the secret religious or militant societies which have appeared in the West (Gnostics,

---

[1] Adepts of this science (the Qabalah), including several Christian mystics such as Raymond Lulle, Pic de la Mirandole, Reuchlin, Guillaume Postel, Henry Morus, consider it to be a divine tradition as ancient as the human race. (*Dictionnaire Philosophique*, by FRANCK).

[2] The works of Spinosa manifest a profound knowledge of the Qabalah.

[3] Leibniz was introduced to the Qabalah by Mercure van Helmont, son of the celebrated alchemist, himself a great Qabalist.

Templars, Rosicrucians, Martinists or Freemasons) are connected with the Qabalah and the teaching of its theories. Wronski, Fabre d'Olivet and Eliphas Lévi owe their deepest knowledge to the Qabalah and declare this more or less openly.

Where then does this mysterious doctrine come from?

The most superficial study of religions shows us that the originator of a people or race always divides his teaching into two parts:

One part hidden in myths, parables and symbols, and open to the masses. This is the exoteric part.

One part revealed to a few favourite disciples and which, if written down, must never be too clearly described, preferably handed on *orally* from generation to generation. This the esoteric doctrine.

Jesus escapes this general rule no more so than Buddha; the Apocalypse is proof enough; and why should Moses be the only one to have proceeded otherwise?

Moses, preserving the purest of the mysteries of Egypt, chose a people to keep his book and a tribe, Lévi, to keep his cult; is it feasible that he would not have given the key to his book to a certain number of trustworthy disciples?

We will see that the Qabalah teaches above all the manipulation of Hebrew letters considered as ideas or even effective powers. This is to say that in this way Moses pointed out the true meaning of his Sepher.

Those who claim that the Qabalah comes from *Adam* simply recount the symbolic history of the transmission of tradition from one race to another, without insisting on any special one.

Several contemporary scholars, ignorant of all there is to know about antiquity, are surprised to find in the Qabalah certain profound ideas concerning the sciences; they place the origin of all such knowledge in the second century of our era; others deign to carry these origins back to the school of Alexandria.

Some critics even claim the Qabalah was *invented* in the thirteenth century by Moise de Léon. M. Franck, a true savant worthy of all our admiration, has had no trouble in correcting these critics, beating them, as it were, on their own ground[1].

---

[1] Upon examining the Qabalah in itself, upon comparing it to analogous doctrines and reflecting upon the immense influence it has exercised, not

We choose to share the opinion of Fabre d'Olivet, placing the origin of the Qabalah at the very time of Moses.

*
* *

It appears, according to some of the most illustrious rabbis, that Moses himself, foreseeing the fate which would befall his book and the false interpretations which would be given it in later times, resorted to an oral law which he gave aloud to a few trustworthy men whose loyalty he had tested, charging them to transmit it in the secret of the sanctuary to other men, who, in their turn, would pass it on from age to age, bringing it down thus to a time enormously distant from that of its origins. This oral law, which modern Jews still claim to possess, is called the Qabalah, from a Hebrew word meaning that which is received, that which comes from elsewhere, that which passes from hand to hand.

The most famous books which they possess, such as those of the *Zohar*, the *Bahir*, the *Midrashim*, the *Gemara* which make up the *Talmud*, are almost entirely Qabalistic.

It would be very difficult today to say whether Moses actually did leave behind this oral law, or if, having left it, it was not considerably changed over the years, as the scholar Maimonides gives us to understand, writing that those of his nation have lost the knowledge of an infinite number of things without which it is almost impossible to understand the Law. Whatever the truth of the matter, one cannot ignore the likelihood of such an institution being present in the minds of the Egyptians, whose proclivity for mysteries is quite well known.

The Qabalah such as we know it is thus the most complete embodiment which has come down to us of the teaching of the mysteries of Egypt. It contains the key to the doctrines of all those who had themselves initiated, at the peril of their lives, as philosopher-legislators and theurgists.

---

only on Judaism but on the human mind in general, it is impossible not to regard it as a system of great seriousness and originality. Without it, it is equally impossible to explain the numerous texts of the *Misha* and the *Talmud* attesting to the existence of a secret doctrine, proper to the Jews, concerning the nature of God and the universe, and belonging to the time in which we have placed the beginnings of Qabalistic science. (Ad. FRANCK).

As with the Hebraic language, this doctrine has no doubt been subject to numerous alterations due to the long, long passage of time; what remains, however, is still worthy of serious consideration.

Such as we have it today, the Qabalah comprises two major parts. The first constitutes a sort of key based on the Hebrew language and susceptible to numerous applications; the second exposes a philosophical system analogically drawn from these technical considerations.

In most treatises on the question, the first part alone is designated by the name *Qabalah*, the other being developed in the books fundamental to the doctrine.

There are two of these: 1. the SEPHER YETZIRAH, the book of formation, containing in symbolic form a history of Genesis, *Maaseh Bereschith*.

2. The ZOHAR, the book of light, containing also in symbolic form all the esoteric developments synthesized under the name of History of the heavenly chariot; *Maaseh Mercavah*[1].

The two cabala of the Jews, the cabala *Mercavah*, the cabala *Bereschith*, must be regarded symbolically. The cabala *Mercavah* brought the illuminated Jew into the most profound and intimate mysteries of the essence and qualities of God and the angels; the cabala *Bereschith* showed him in the choice, arrangement and numerical relation of the letters which made up the words of his language, the great designs of God and the elevated religious teachings which God had placed there.

(DE BRIERE)

Mercavah and Bereschith, these are the two great classic divisions of the Qabalah, adopted by all authors.

In order to take up the teachings of the *Mercavah*, a knowledge of the *Bereschith* is necessary, and for this, one must be acquainted with the Hebraic alphabet and the mysteries of its formation.

Beginning with this alphabet, we will deal successively with the various parts which constitute this general key, then we will speak of the philosophical system.

The Qabalists can be divided into two categories. Those who apply the principles of doctrine without stopping to develop the elementary foundations, and those who, to the contrary, have made classic treaties on the Qabalah.

---

[1] FABRE D'OLIVET, *Langue Hebraique*, p. 29.

Among the latter we can cite Pic de la Mirandole, Kircher and Lenain.

Pic de la Mirandole divides the study of the Qabalah into a study of numbers (or *Sephiroth*) and a study of divine names (or *Shenroth*). The entire key can in fact be reduced to these two points.

Kircher, a Jesuit father, gives us some of the most complete works on this question; he adopts the general division of three major parts:

1. *Gematria*, or study of transpositions.
2. *Notaria*, or the study of the art of signs.
3. *Themurah*, or the study of commutations and combinations.

Lenain, author of Qabalistic Science, treats above all the divine names and their combinations.

We will speak further of these various divisions, since as it stands, they cannot be easily understood.

CHAPTER II

The Hebrew Alphabet

The twenty-two letters and their meanings

The point of departure for the entire Qabalah is the Hebrew alphabet.

The alphabet of the Hebrews is composed of twenty-two letters; however, the letters are not placed in an arbitrary series. Each corresponds to a number according to its rank, to a hieroglyph according to its form, and to a symbol according to its relation to the other letters.

All the letters derive from one among them, the *yod*, as has been mentioned elsewhere[1]. The *yod* produced them in the following manner (See *Sepher Yetzirah*):

1. Three principals:

B	(Aleph)	א
M	(Mem)	מ
Sh	(Shin)	ש

2. Seven doubles (doubles because they indicate two sounds, one positive and strong, the other negative and weak):

(B)	(Beth)	ב
G	(Gimel)	ג
D	(Daleth)	ד
K	(Kaph)	כ
P	(Pe)	פ
R	(Resh)	ר
T	(Tau)	ת

---

[1] See the study on the word *yod, he, vau* (p. 115).

NUMERICAL ORDER	HIEROGLYPH	NAME	CORRESPONDING ROMAN LETTER	TYPE	NUMERICAL CORRESPONDENCE
1		aleph	A	principal	1
2		beth	B	double	2
3		gimel	G	double	3
4		daleth	D	double	4
5		he	E	single	5
6		vau	V	single	6
7		zayin	Z	single	7
8		cheth	CH	single	8
9		teth	T	single	9
10		yod	I	single & primary	10
11		kaph	K	double	20
12		lamed	L	single	30
13		mem	M	principal	40
14		nun	N	single	50
15		samekh	S	single	60
16		ayin	GH	single	70
17		pe	P	double	80
18		tzaddi	TZ	single	90
19		qoph	Q	single	100
20		resh	R	double	200
21		shin	SH	principal	300
22		tau	TH	double	400

3. Lastly, twelve singles formed by the other letters.

For the sake of clarity, the preceding table has been given.

Each Hebrew letter thus represents three things.

1. A letter, or hieroglyph.

2. A number, that of the order which the letter occupies.

3. An idea.

To combine Hebrew letters is thus to combine numbers and ideas; this is the origin of the *Tarot*[1].

As each letter is a *force*, it is more or less closely aligned with the creative powers at work in the Universe. These powers evolve in three worlds, physical, astral and psychic; therefore each letter is the point of departure as well as the destination of a crowd of correspondences. To form Hebrew words is to act upon the Universe itself; thus the rôle of Hebrew words in magical ceremonies.

Now that we are acquainted with the alphabet in general, we must turn our attention to the meanings and relations of each of the twenty-two letters of this alphabet. In this study, based on the work of Lenain, we will be able to see the correspondence of each letter to divine names, angels and sephiroth.

*
* *

Ancient rabbis, philosophers and qabalists explain, according to their method, the *order, harmony* and *celestial influences on the world* of the twenty-two letters that make up the mystical alphabet of the Hebrews[2].

Explanation of the mysteries of the Hebrew alphabet

This alphabet designates:

1. From the letter aleph א to the letter י yod, *the invisible world*, that is, *the angelic world* (sovereign intelligences receiving the influences of the primary eternal light attributed to the Father from whom everything emanates).

2. From the letter כ kaph to the letter tzaddi צ , different orders of angels who inhabit the *visible* world, that is, the astrological world attributed to God the Son, signifying the

---

[1] and [2]. See *The Tarot of the Bohemians* by PAPUS.

divine wisdom which created this infinity of spheres circulating in the immensity of space, each under the safeguard of an intelligence especially charged by the creator to preserve it and maintain it in its orbit, so that no planet or star can trouble the order and harmony. He has established.

3. From the letter tzaddi צ to the final letter ת tau, the elementary world is indicated, that attributed by philosophers to the Holy Spirit. This is the sovereign Being of beings who gives soul and life to all creatures.

Individual explanation of the 22 letters.

1	א	*Aleph*

Corresponds to the first name of God, Eheieh אהיה, which is interpreted as the divine essence.

Qabalists call him he whom eye has not seen because of his great elevation.

He resides in the world called Ensoph which signifies the infinite; his attribute is Kether כתר, interpreted as crown or diadem. He rules the angels which the Hebrews call Haioth-Hakodesh חיות הקודש, that is, animals of sainthood. He gathers together the first choirs of angels, the seraphim.

2	ב	*Beth*

Second divine name corresponding to this letter: Bashur בהור (clarity, youth), designating angels of the second order. Ophanim אופנים.

Forms or wheels.

Cherubim (through their ministry, God will make order out of chaos).
Numeration חכמה Hokma, wisdom.

3	ג	*Gimel*

Name Gadol גדול (maguus) designates the angels Aralym אראלים, that is *great and strong*, thrones (through them God tetragrammaton Elohim maintains *the form of matter*).

Numeration Binah בינה, providence and intelligence.

| 4 | ד | *Daleth* |

Name Dagul דגול (insignes), angels Hasmalim חשמלים.

Dominations

It is through them that God EL אל produces the images of bodies and all the diverse forms of matter.

Attribute חסד (hoe sed), mercy and goodness.

| 5 | ה | *He* |

Name Hadom הדום *(formosus, majestuosus). Seraphim* שרפים, *powers (by their ministry God Elohim Lycbir brings forth the elements).*

Numeration פחד *(pachad), fear and judgement, the left hand of the Father.*

Attribute נבורה Geburah, force and power.

| 6 | ו | *Vau* |

Formed חיו Vezio (cum splendore), the sixth order of angels מלאכים Malakim, the choir of virtues (through their ministry God Eloah *produces metals and all that exists in the mineral kingdom*).

Attribute תפארת Tiphereth, Sun, splendour.

| 7 | ז | *Zayin* |

Formed זכאי Zakai (purus mundus), the seventh order of angels, principalities, children of Elohim (through their ministry God tetragrammation Sabahot produces plants and all *that exist in the vegetable world*).

Attribute נצח netzach, triumph, justice.

| 8 | ח | *Cheth* |

Designates Chased הסיד (misericors), angels of the eighth order, Beneh Elohim, sons of God (*choir of archangels*) (*Mercury*); through their ministry God Elohim Sabahot produces *the animals and the animal kingdom*.

Attribute הוד Hod, praise.

| 9 | ט | *Teth* |

Corresponds to the name טהור Tahor (mundus purus), angels
of the ninth order which preside at the birth of men (through
their ministry Sadai and Elhoi send guardian angels to
mankind).
Attribute יסוד Yesod, foundation.

| 10 | י | *Yod* |

From which comes Yah יה (Deus).
Attribute: kingdom, empire and temple of God or influence
through heroic beings. It is through their ministry that men
receive intelligence, industry and a knowledge of divine things.
Here ends the angelic world.

___

| 11 | כ | *Kaph* |

Name   כביר   (potens).   Designates   the   first   heaven,
corresponding to the name of God י expressed in one letter,
that is, the primary cause which sets all that is mobile in
movement. The primary sovereign intelligence which governs
the first heaven of the astrological world attributed to the
second person of the Trinity, is called מטטרון Mittatron.

His attribute signifies prince of faces; his mission is to
introduce all those who are to appear before the face of God.
Below him is the prince Orifiel with an infinity of subordinate
intelligences; qabalists say that it is through the ministry of
Mittatron that God spoke to Moses. It is also through him
that all the lower powers of the sensible world receive their
properties from God.

The final letter, represented thus ך, corresponds to the two
great names of God, each composed of two Hebrew letters, El
אל, Yah יה . They rule the intelligences of the second order
which govern the sky of fixed stars, notably the twelve signs of
the Zodiac which the Hebrews call Galgol hamnazeloth; the
intelligence of the second heaven is called Raziel. His attribute
signifies the vision of God and the smile of God.

| 12 | לְ | *Lamed* |

Source of Lumined לִמֻד (doctus), corresponds to the name Sadai, name of God in five letters, called the emblem of Delta, and ruling over the third heaven and the intelligences of the third order which govern the sphere of Saturn.

| 13 | מ | *Mem* |

Meborak מְבָרֵךְ (benedictus), corresponds to the fourth heaven and to the fourth name Jehovah יהוה, ruling the sphere of Jupiter. The intelligence which governs Jupiter is called Tsadkiel.

Tsadkiel receives the influences of God through the intermediary of Shebtayel so as to transmit them to the intelligences of the fifth order.

Mem מ, an *essential* letter, corresponds to the fifth heaven and to the fifth name of God; in Hebrew, the fifth princely name. Rules over the sphere of Mars. Intelligence governing Mars: Samael. Samael receives the influences of God through the intervention of Tsadkiel and transmits them to intelligences of the sixth order.

| 14 | נ | *Nun* |

Name Nora נורא (formidabilis) corresponds also to the name Emmanuel (nobiscum Deus), the sixth name of God; rules the sixth heaven, *Sun*; primary intelligence of the Sun: Raphael.

The name thus represented נ refers to the seventh name of God Ararity, composed of seven letters (immutable God). Rules the seventh heaven and Venus. Intelligence of Venus: Haniel (the love of God, justice and grace of God).

| 15 | ס | *Samekh* |

Name Samekh סומך (fulciens, firmans), eighth name of God; planet Mercury. Primary intelligence of Mercury, Mikael.

16   עَ   *Ayin*

Name עזז Hazaz (fortis); corresponds to Jehovah-Sabahot.
Rules the ninth heaven; Moon; intelligence of the Moon:
Gabriel.
Here ends the archangelic world.

---

17   פ   *Pe*

There is a correspondence with the 18th name; פודה Phodeth
(redemptor, *intellectual soul* (*Kircher*, II 227).
   This letter designates *Fire*, the element of the salamanders.
The intelligence of Fire: the Seraphim and several subordinate
orders. *In summer its influence is on the south.*
   The final thus represented ף designates *air*, the habitation
of the Sylphs, Intelligences of the air, the Cherubim and several
subordinate orders. In the spring the intelligences of the air rule
over the west.

18   צ   *Tzaddi*

Universal matter (K). Name צדק Tsedek (justus). Designates
Water, habitation of the nymphs. Intelligence: Tharsis. In
autumn, governs the west.
   The final ץ forms the elements (air, earth, fire, water) (K).

19   ק   *Qoph*

Derived name קדש Kodesh (sanctus). *Earth*, habitation of the
Gnomes. Intelligence of the earth: Ariel. In winter governs the
north. *Minerals*, inanimate matter (Kircher).

20   ר   *Resh*

Name רדה (imperans) Rodeh, plant kingdom (Kircher);
attributed to the first principle of God which applies to the
animal kingdom and gives life to all animals.

21   ש   *Shin*

Name Schaday שדי (omnipotens) which signifies God all-powerful, attributed to the second principle of God (animals), that which has life (Kircher) and quickens all vegetable substances.

| 22 | ת | *Tau* |

Name Thekhinah תחנה (gratiosus), Microcosm (Kircher), third principle of God which gives existence to all that exists within the mineral kingdom.

This letter is the symbol of man, for it designates the end of all that exists, just as man is the end and the perfection of all creation.

Division of the alphabet

	9	8	7	6	5	4	3	2	1
Units	9	8	7	6	5	4	3	2	1
First world	ט	ח	ז	ו	ה	ד	ג	ב	א
Tens	90	80	70	60	50	40	30	20	10
Second world	צ	פ	ע	ס	נ	מ	ל	כ	י
Hundreds	900	800	700	600	500	400	300	200	100
Third world	ץ	ף	ן	ם	ך	ת	ש	ר	ק

The following table shows the arrangement and mystic significance of these letters.

1st CONNECTION	2nd CONNECTION	3rd CONNECTION
אלף aleph, chest breast. בית beth, house. ג gimel, plenitude, retribution. ד daleth, table and door. Indicating the house of God which in divine books is called plenitude.	ה he (ista), this one. ו vau (uncinus), hook, corner. ז zayin (Haec), that one, weapons. ח cheth, life. Indicating analogically the one and the other life, and what other life can be as portrayed in the scriptures through which Christ himself speaks of the life of believers.	ט teth, well, good, declension. י yod, principle. Indicating analogically that although we are now aware of the universality of written things, we in fact know only a part and can prophesy in relation to only a part; when, however, we take our deserved place with Christ, then the doctrine of books will cease and we will be face to face with the good principle in its essence.

Angelic World

4th CONNECTION	5th CONNECTION	6th CONNECTION
כ kaph, hand, conduct. ל lamed (discipline), heart. Indicating that the hands are a part of works, that the heart and conduct (behaviour) are a part of the senses, for we can do nothing without first knowing what it is we must do.	מ mem, ex ipsis. נ nun, sempiternum. ס samekh, adjutorium. Indicating analogically that it is from the scriptures alone which man must draw the sources necessary for eternal life.	ע ayin, source, eye. פ pe, mouth. צ tzaddi, justice. Indicating analogically that scripture is the source and eye and mouth of justice, containing the origin of all works proceeding from the mouth of divinity.

World of Spheres

7th CONNECTION

ק	qoph	Vocation, voice.
ר׳	resh	Head.
שׁ	shin	Teeth.
ת	tau	Sign, microcosm.

As if one were to say: the vocation of the head is the sign of the teeth; the voice in articulation issues from the teeth and it is by these signs that one arrives at the head of everything, which is Christ and the Eternal Kingdom.

World of the 4 Elements

CHAPTER III

The Divine Names

If the reader has understood the foregoing, grasping that each letter has a triple significance and expresses a hieroglyph, a number and an idea, then he is in possession of the fundaments of the Qabalah. Now we must turn our attention to various combinations.

If each of the letters is an effective force, grouping them according to certain mystic rules gives rise to active centres of power, productive of actual effects when set into motion by the will of man.

Thus the *ten divine names*. Each of these names expresses a particular attribute of God, that is, an *active law of Nature* and a universal centre of action.

Since all divine manifestions, that is, all acts and all beings, are linked among themselves, just as the cells of man are linked together and to man, to set one of these manifestations in motion is to create a current of real action whose repercussions will be felt in all the Universe; in the same way as a sensation perceived by man at any point in his body reverberates throughout the entire organism.

The study of divine names thus includes:

1. On the one hand, special qualities attributed to the name;

2. On the other, the relation the name bears to the rest of Nature.

We will touch on these points successively.

At the outset, let us enumerate these names, which are to be found on all talismans and in all the formulas of evocation.

The Roman letters have been placed under the Hebrew letters, *in reverse*, to indicate their sense.

1	אהיה AIEB	*Eheieh.*
2	יה AI	*Yah.*
3	יהוה IEVE	*Jehovah.*
4	אל JA	*El.*
5	אלוה ELOE	*Eloha.*
6	אלהים ALEIM	*Elohim.*
7	יהוה ' IEVE	*Tetragrammaton*[1].
	צבאות TOABST	*Tsabaoth.*
8	אלהים ALEIM	*Elohim.*
	צבאות TOABST	*Tsabaoth.*
9	שדי IDS	*Shaddai.*
10	אדני INDA	*Adonai.*

The Qabalah is so wondrously constructed that all the terms which make it up are merely various facets of one another. Thus we are obliged, due to the poverty of our Western languages, in dealing with abstractions, to study separately the meaning and relations of the ten divine names, then the meaning and relations of the ten numbers, all of this in its diverse acceptations. It must be remembered, however, that all of this, *name, idea* and *number* is synthesized in each of the hieroglyphs, whether in speaking of a divine name or in enumerating the Sephiroth.

These names deserve our very special attention. All of them have a secret sense developed in detail in Qabalistic writings.

1st Divine Name

The first, Eheieh, is often written with the single letter *yod.* In

[1] As the name IEVA or IOHA can never be pronounced, it is replaced by the word *tetragrammaton* or the word *adonai* (lord).

TABLE

Summarizing the Symbolism of all the major Arcana and allowing for the immediate definition of the meaning of any one of these Arcana

Creative principle (י) Active י	God the Father 1	Will 4	The Father 7
Creative principle Passive ה	Adam	Power	Realization
Creative principle Equalizing ו	Nature as cause	creator Universal fluid	Astral light
Preserving principle (ה) Active י	God the Son 2	Intelligence 5	The Mother 8
Preserving principle Passive (ה)	Eve	Authority	Justice
Preserving principle Equalizing ו	Nature as effect	Universal life	Elementary existence
Realizing principle (ו) Active י	God the Holy Spirit 3	Beauty 6	Love 9
Realizing principle Passive ה	Adam-Eve Humanity	Love	Prudence
Realizing principle Equalizing ו	The Cosmos	Universal attraction	Astral fluid (AOUR)
	Himself (י) + GOD (21)	Manifested —	Himself (ה) + MAN HUMANITY

Necessity 10	Universal trans-forming principle 13	Destruction 16	The Elements 19
Potential force	Death	The Adamic fall	Nutrition
Display of magic power	Universal plastic force	The visible world	Mineral kingdom
Freedom 11	Involution 14	Immortality 17	Movement 20
Courage	Corporeal life	Hope	Respiration
Reflective and temporary life	Individual life	Physical force	Vegetable kingdom
Charity 12	Destiny 15	Chaos 18	Movement of limited duration 0
Hope	Fate	The material body	Innervation
Counterbalancing force	Nahash Astral light in circulation	Matter	Animal kingdom
Manifested — (21)	Himself (ו) +	Manifested —	Return (ה) to Unity
	UNIVERSE (21)		

this case it signifies simply I.

Lacour, in his book on the Elohim or Gods of Moses, shows that this word gave birth to the Greek *aei* (*always*). *Eheieh* thus signifies precisely THE ALWAYS, and it is understandable that the letter *yod*, expressive of the beginning and the end of everything, should represent it.

This name mystically written in a triangle thus:

represents the three principal attributes of divinity manifest in creation, of the *Always* giving birth to temporal measures.

The first *yod* shows Eternity giving birth to Time in its triplicity: Past, Present and Future.

This is *Number*.

This is the *Father*.

The second *yod* shows *Infinity* giving birth to *Space* in its triplicity: Length, Depth and Breadth.

This is the *Measure*.

This is the *Son*.

The third *yod* represents eternal substance giving birth to *Matter* in its triplicity: Solid, Liquid and Gas.

This is the *Weight*.

This is the *Holy Spirit*.

Unite Time, Space and Matter and the *eternal and infinite Substance* and THE ALWAYS is made manifest.

Thus the Qabalistic represent the divine name as follows:

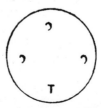

The correspondences of this name are given by Agrippa, one of the finest Qabalists known[1].

1. Eheieh, the name of divine essence:

Numeration: kether (crown, diadem), signifying the very simple being of divinity; is called what eye has not seen. Attributed to God the Father and influencing the order of Seraphim or, as the Hebrews call them, *Habth Hakadosh*, in Latin *animalia sanctitatis*, the famous animals of saintliness. Gives, through the prime mover, the name of being of all things with which the Universe is filled, from its outermost edge to its very centre. The particular intelligence is named Mithraton (Prince of Faces) whose duty it is to present others before the face of the Prince, and it is through his ministry that the Lord spoke to Moses.

2nd Name

2. Name *Yah*:

Yod or tetragrammaton together with Yod; numeration: Hokhma (*sapientia*).

Signifies divinity filled with ideas and first born and is attributed to the Son. Through the order of Cherubim (which the Hebrews call Ofanim), influences the forms of wheels and thence, the starry heavens, producing as many substantial forms as it contains ideas, ordering chaos or the confusion of matter through the ministry of its particular intelligence *Raziel* who was the celestial tutor of Adam.

3rd Name

3. Name YEVE (Jehovah) – יהוה.

This name, one of the most mysterious of Hebrew theology, expresses one of the most astonishing natural laws with which we are acquainted.

Thanks to the discovery of some of its properties we have been able to give a complete explanation of the Tarot[2], something not previously accomplished.

---

[1] H.C. AGRIPPA, *Occult Philosophy*, v. II, p. 36.
[2] See the meanings of letters previously given.

Here is our analysis of this divine name:

THE QABALISTIC WORD יהוה (*yod-heh-vav-heh*).

If one believes the ancient oral tradition of the Hebrews, the Qabalah, there exists a sacred word which gives to the mortal discovering its true pronunciation the key to all divine and human sciences. This word, which the Israelites never pronounce and which the high priest would say once a year amid the cries of the uninitiated people, is the one which is found at the summit of all initiations, the one which shines in the centre of the flaming triangle of the thirty-third Masonic degree of Scotch Rites, the one inscribed above the doors of our ancient cathedrals, formed of four Hebrew letters, reading: *yod-he-vau-he* יהוה..

In the *Sepher Bereschith* or Genesis of Moses, it serves to designate the Divinity, and its grammatical construction is such that by its very constitution[1] it recalls the attributes which man has always given to God.

Now, we shall see that the powers attributed to this word are, up to a certain point, real, seeing how easily it opens the symbolic door of the ark containing the account of all ancient science. Thus it is essential that we enter into a fair amount of detail in this regard.

The word consists of four letters, *yod* (·) *he* (ה) *vau* (י) *he* (ה).

The last letter *he* is repeated twice.

A number is attributed to each letter of the Hebrew alphabet. Let us consider these letters in particular.

---

[1] 'First of all this name offers the sign indicative of life, doubled, and forming the essentially living root EE (הה). This root is never used as a noun and is the only one to enjoy this prerogative. From its very formation it is not only a verb, but a unique one, from which all others derive; in a word, the verb הוה (EVE), to be being. Here, as can be seen and as I took care to explain in my grammar, the sign of intelligible light י (Vau) is placed in the middle of the root of life; Moses, taking this fundamental verb in order to give a proper name to the Being of Beings, adds the sign of the potential manifestation of eternity י) and thus obtains יהוה (YEVE) in which being is placed between a past without origin and a future without end. This admirable name thus means exactly Being-which-was-and-which-shall be.'

(FABRE D'OLIVET, *La Langue hébraïque restituée*.)

י yod   = 10
ה he   = 5
ו vau   = 6

The total numerical value of the word יהוה is thus

$$10 + 5 + 6 + 5 = 26$$

Let us examine each of the letters separately.

YOD

Yod, represented by a comma or by a period embodies the *principle* of things.

All the letters of the Hebrew alphabet are only combinations resulting from various assemblings of the letter *yod*[1]. The synthetical study of nature led the ancients to believe that there existed only *one single law* governing natural productions. This law, the basis of analogy, posed a unity-principle at the origin of all things and considered these things as mere *reflections* of the various degrees of this unity-principle. Thus the *yod*, foundation of all letters and hence of all words and sentences, was understandably the image and representation of this *Unity-Principle*, knowledge of which was hidden from the profane.

Therefore the law which presided over the creation of the Hebrew tongue was the same as that which presided over the creation of the universe, and to know one is to implicitly know the other. This is demonstrated in one of the oldest books of the Qabalah: the *Sepher Yetzirah*[2].

Before proceeding, let us clarify the foregoing with an example. The first letter of the Hebrew alphabet, *aleph* (   ), is formed of four *yod*, in opposing pairs (   ), Similar arrangements pertain to the other letters.

The numerical value of *yod* leads to other considerations. The UNITY-PRINCIPLE, according to Qabalistic doctrine,

---

[1] See *la Kaballa denudata*.

[2] Recently (c. 1850) translated into French for the first time, editions Carré.

is also the UNITY-END of beings and things; from this point of view, eternity is only an eternal present. Thus ancient symbolists represented this idea by a dot in the centre of a circle, an image of the Unity-Principle (the dot) at the centre of eternity (the circle, a line without beginning or end)[1].

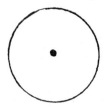

Accordingly, Unity is considered as the *sum* and all created beings are only *constituent parts*; just as the Unity-Man is made up of the sum of millions of cells which constitute this being.

At the origin of all things, then, the Qabalah poses the absolute affirmation of being in itself, the I-Unity, represented symbolically by the *yod* and numerically by the number 10. This number 10 represents the *All-Principle*. 1 joined to the O of *Nothing* is a most adequate symbol[2].

HE

But the I can only be conceived in opposition to the Non-I. As soon as the affirmation of the I is established, it is necessary to suppose an immediate reaction of the Absolute-I against itself, from which is drawn the notion of existence by a sort of division of Unity. Such is the origin of *duality*, of opposition, of the Binary, an image of femininity, just as unity is the image of masculinity. Ten divided so as to stand in opposition to itself gives $\frac{10}{2} = 5$, the exact number of the letter *he*, second letter of the great sacred name.

Thus the *he* represents *the passive* as against *the active*

---

[1] See KIRCHER, *Oedipus Aegyptiacus*;

    LENAIN, *La Sciéence Kabbalistique*;

    J. DEE, *Monas Hiéroglyphica*.

[2] See SAINT-MARTIN, *Des rapports qui existent entre Dieu, l'Homme et l'Univers*;

    LACURIA, *Harmonies de l'etre exprimées par les nombres*.

symbolized by the *yod*, the *non-I* in opposition to the I, *woman* in opposition to *man*, *substance* contrasted with *essence*, *life* contrasted with *soul*, etc. etc.

VAU

But the opposition of the *I* to the *Non-I* gives immediate rise to another factor, the *relationship* between this I and the Non-I.

Now, *Vau*, sixth letter of the Hebrew alphabet, produced by 10 (yod) + 5 (heh) = 15 = 6 (1 + 5), signifies *book, relation*. It is the book which unites all opposites in nature, constituting the third term of this mysterious trinity.

I – Non-I. Relationship of the I to the Non-I.

THE 2nd HE

Beyond the Trinity, considered as law, nothing more exists.

The Trinity is the synthetic and absolute formula in which all sciences have their end; and this formula, its scientific value aside, has been integrally handed down to us by all religions, unconscious depositaries of the SCIENCE WISDOM of primitive civilization[1].

Thus three letters alone make up the great sacred name. The fourth element of this name is the second letter, *He*, again repeated[2].

This repetition indicates the passage of the Trinitary law into a new application, that is to say, a *transition* from the metaphysical world to the physical world or, more generally speaking, from any world to the world immediately inferior[3].

Understanding of this property of the second *He* is the key to the entire divine name in all the applications of which it is

---

[1] See ELIPHAS LEVI, *Dogme et Rituel de haute magie; la clef des grands mysteres*; – LACURIA, *op. cit.*

[2] See FABRE D'OLIVET, *La Langue hébraïque restituée.*

[3] See Louis LUCAS, *Le Roman alchimique.* Præter hæc tria numera non est alia magnitudo, quod tria sunt omnia, et ter undecundque, ut pythagorici dicunt; omne et omnia tribus determinata sunt. (Aristotle, quoted by Ostrowski, p. 24 of his *Mathesis.*)

capable. Proof of this will be clearly given in succeeding pages[1].

SUMMARY OF THE WORD YOD-HE-VAU-HE

Now that we are acquainted with each of the separate terms which make up the sacred name, let us draw a synthesis and total the results we have obtained.

The word *yod-he-vau-he* is composed of four letters, each signifying:

Yod   Pre-eminent active principle.
       The I = 10.
       He   Pre-eminent passive principle.
       The Non-I = 5.
Vau   Median term, *the hook*, joining the active to the passive.

The Relationship of the I to the Non-I = 6.
These three terms express the absolute trinitary law.
2nd He Passage from one world to another. Transition.
The second *He* represents complete Being enclosing within an absolute unity the three terms of which it is composed, I-Non-I-Relationship.
It indicates the passage from the noumenon to the phenomenon or the reverse, the transition from one level of existence to another.

FIGURATION OF THE SACRED WORD

The word *yod-he-vau-he* can be represented in various ways, each having its particular effectiveness.
It can be written in a circle as follows:

---

[1] Malfatti saw this clearly: 'The passage of 3 to 4 corresponds to that of Trimurti into Maya, and as this latter opens the second ternary of the pre-genetic decade, so the number 4 opens the second ternary of our genetic decimal system.

(*Mathesis*, p. 25)

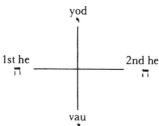

But since the second *He*, a term of transition, becomes the active entity of the following level, that is, since this *He* actually represents a germinal *yod*[1], the sacred word can be set down with the second *He* under the first *yod*, thus:

> *yod*　　1st *he*　　*vau*
> 2nd *he*

Finally, a third way of representing the word consists in surrounding the trinity, *yod he vau*, with the transitional term or second *he*:

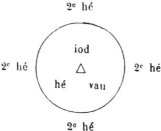

The study of the Tarot is nothing more than a study of the transformations of this divine word, as is shown in the following synthetic figure.

If in fact we wished merely to summarize Qabalistic deductions concerning this 3rd name, an entire volume would be necessary. *Eliphas Lévi* furnishes in all his works quite

---

[1] This second *he*, whose importance we have expressly emphasized, can be compared to *a grain of wheat* as contrasted with the stalk. The stalk, the manifested trinity, *yod he vau*, channels all its activity into the production of the grain of wheat or 2nd *He*. But this seed is only the *transition* between the stalk which has given birth to it and the stalk to which it, in turn, will give birth in the following cycle. It is the transition between one generative process and another which it contains in germinal form; this is why the second *He* can be spoken of as a germinal *yod*.

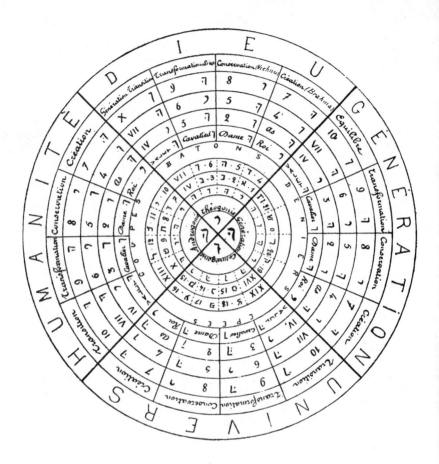

THE TAROT

Cycle of the Revolutions of YEVE (יהוה)
Complete Key to Occult Science
by
PAPUS

exceptional developments on the subject. *Kircher* also extensively develops the divers interpretations of the word. Let us cite the hieroglyphic relationships of יהוה according to this latter author.

The following figure is thus explained by Kircher:

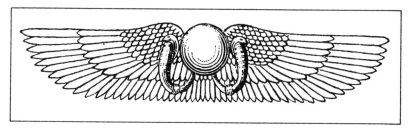

The central globe represents the essence of God, inaccessible and hidden.

The X, image of the denary system, indicates the *yod.*

The two serpents emerging from the bottom of the globe are the two *he.*

Lastly, the two wings symbolize the spirit, the *vau.*

*
* *

The name of 72 letters. The 72 spirits

It is also from this divine name that the qabalistic name of 72 letters can be drawn in the following fashion:

The name YEVE is written in a triangle, so:

The sacred word. First representation.

Here is the explanation of these two manners of writing the 72-letter name:

For the first:

Add the numbers corresponding to each Hebrew letter and you will obtain the following results:

$$
\begin{array}{llr}
\text{י} & = 10 & = 10 \\
\text{יה} & = 10 + 5 & = 14 \\
\text{יהו} & = 10 + 5 + 6 & = 21 \\
\text{יהוה} & = 10 + 5 + 6 + 5 & = 26 \\
\hline
& \text{Total} & 72
\end{array}
$$

For the second:

Count the number of crowned circles making up the word written in this way and you will find them to be 24 (the 24 old ones of the Apocalypse).

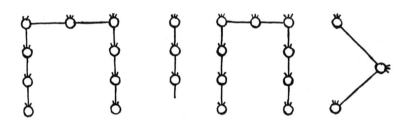

The sacred word. — Second representation.

Each crown having 3 points, one has only to multiply 24 by 3 to obtain the 72 mystic letters:

$$24 \times 3 = 72$$

*   *

*

In the *practical Qabalah* (universal magic), use is made of the 72 names of Spirits drawn as follows from the Bible:

The names of the 72 angels are based on the three mysterious verses of the 14th chapter of Exodus, verses 19, 20 and 21, which, following the Hebrew text, are each composed of 72 letters.

How to arrive at the 72 names.

First write down these verses separately, making three lines, each composed of 72 letters taken from the Hebrew text. Take the first letter of the 19th and 21st verses beginning from the left; then take the first letter of the 20th or middle verse, beginning from the right; these three letters form the attribute of the spirit. By following this same procedure on through to the end, you will obtain the 72 attributes of the divine virtues.

If you add to each of these one of the two great divine names, Yah יה or El אל, you will have the 72 names of the angels composed of three syllables and each containing in itself the name of God.

Other Qabalists take the first letter of the verses as orally rendered.

But we must not forget that our aim is to give only a summary of the Qabalah; thus let us finish with matters pertaining to this third name in order to pass on to the remaining seven.

3rd name: *Tetragrammaton Elohim*:

Numerata Binah (*providentia et intelligentia*) signifies jubilee, remission and rest, attonement or redemption of the world and the life of the era to come; this applies to the Holy Spirit and maintains its influence through the order of Thrones (those which the Hebrews call *Arabim*, that is, angels of great height, health and strength), and thereafter through the sphere of Saturn, furnishing the form of fluid matter. Its particular intelligence is Zafohiel, protector of Noah, and another intelligence is named Jofiel, protector of Shem. These sovereign and exalted numerations are like the Thrones of the divine personages, by whose commandments all things come into being; but the execution of this divine will is accomplished through the ministry of the seven other numerations called, for this reason, the numerations of works.

4th Name

4th name *El*:

Numeration *Hæsed* (Clementia, bonitas) signifies grace, mercy, piety, magnificence, sceptre and right hand. Its influence is channelled through the order of Dominations (which the Hebrews call *Hasmalim*) within the sphere of Jupiter, and forming the images or material representations of bodies, giving to all men mercy, peaceful justice, and having as its particular intelligence, Zadkiel, guardian of Abraham.

5th Name

5th name *Elohim Gibor* (*Deus robustus puniens culpas improborum*):

Numeration *Beburah* (power, gravity, force, purity, judgment, inflicting punishment through catastrophes and wars). Associated with the judgment-seat of God, with the girdle, the sword and the left hand of God. Also called Pahad (awe) and having influence through the order of Powers (called by the Hebrews *Seraphim*) within the sphere of Mars, propagator of force, sender of war, afflictions and controller of the elements.

The particular intelligence is Kamael, guardian of Samson.

6th Name

6th name *Eloha* (or the 4-letter name) joined to Vaudahat:

Numeration *Tiphereth* (ornament, beauty, glory, pleasure), signifies Wood of life. Influence through the order of Virtues (which the Hebrews call Malakhim, that is, angels) within the sphere of the Sun, giving both light and life, and producing metals. Particular intelligence: Raphael, who was the protector of Isaac and the young Tobias, together with the angel Feliel, guardian of Jacob.

7th Name

7th name *Tetragrammaton Tsabaoth* or *Adonai Tsabaoth*, that is, God of armies:

Numeration *Netzach* (triumph, victory). Associated with the right-hand column and signifying eternity and the justice of a vengeful God. Influence through the order of Principalities (those which the Hebrews call *Elohim*, that is, Gods) within the sphere of Venus, source of zeal and love of justice, producer of plants. Intelligence: *Haniel*, together with the angel *Cerirel*, guardian of David.

8th Name

8th name *Elohim Tsabaoth*, also interpreted as the God of armies, but not of wars and justice, rather of piety and peace; for each of these two names, this one and the preceding, embody an 'army' element:

Numeration *Hod* (praise and confession, seemliness and great renown). Associated with the left-hand column. Influence extended through the order of the Archangels (those which the Hebrews call *Bene Elohim*, that is, sons of God) within the sphere of Mercury, and giving brilliance and the properties of adornment, and producing the animals. Intelligence: Michael, protector of Solomon.

9th Name

9th name *Shaddai* (all-powerful and of a fitness for everything) or *Elhai* (living God):

Numeration *Yesod* (foundation). Signifies accord, alliance, redemption and rest. Influence exerted through the order of Angels (called by the Hebrews *Cherubim*) within the sphere of the Moon, which gives growth and decline to all things, presiding over the spirits of men and distributing guardian angels and protectors. Particular intelligence: Gabriel, under whose tutelage lived Joseph, Joshua and Daniel.

10th Name

10th name *Adonai Meleh* (Lord and King):

Numeration *Malkuth* (kingdom and empire), signifies Church and Temple of God and gate. Influence through the animastic order, that is, the order of most happy souls (to which the Hebrews give the names *Issim*, that is, nobles, *Eliros* and *Prince*); these, operating from below the Hierarchies, breathe understanding into the children of men, giving them wondrous knowledge of things and the gift of prophecy, or as it is sometimes called, the intelligence *Metalhin*, which bears the name of first creation or soul of the world. This was the protector and guide of Moses.

THE QABALAH

Moses divided his teaching into two parts, connected by a third.

1. A written part: the letter, formed of ideographic characters having three significations and constituting *the body*.

2. An oral part: *the spirit*, constituting the key to the preceding division.

3. Between the parts, a code of regulations relative to the scrupulous preservation of the text, forming *the life* of the tradition, with jurisprudence as its animating principle.

The body of tradition took the name of *Massorah*.

The life of tradition was divided into the *Mishna* and the *Gemara*, reunited to make up the TALMUD.

Finally, the spirit of tradition, the most secret part, constituted the *Sepher Yetzirah*, the *Zohar* with the *Tarot* and the *Keys* as annexations.

The whole taken together forms the QABALAH.

The Qabalah (or oral tradition) is therefore the illuminative part of a mystic being-type, constituted by Moses and based on the scheme of created beings. To our knowledge, this is the only tradition which has been given up with such lofty and synthetical character; this accounts for its unity and for its relatively easy adaptation to the exigencies of the occidental mind.

The Qabalah is the science of the Soul and of God in all their correlations and correspondences. It teaches and proves that ALL IS IN ONE and that ONE IS IN ALL, allowing one, thanks to analogy, to move from image to principle, or contrastingly, from principle to form. For the Qabalist, a Hebrew letter is a miniature universe, with all its levels of correlation, just as the Universe is a qabalistic alphabet with its interlinking chains of living correspondences. Thus nothing is easier to understand, nor more difficult to study than the Holy Qabalah, veritable nucleus of all occidental initiation.

There are three levels of existence, called the three Worlds, in which creative Unity manifests itself. These three worlds can be found everywhere, in God as well as in the Universe or in Man, for each of these is constituted according to this triple plan of existence. We will find them as constituent parts of a grain of wheat or a planet, of a lowly earthworm or in the sun, in every human word or written character.

Thus it is not surprising that throughout the ages the Qabalists have been considered by pedants and the uninformed to be nothing more than ingenious dreamers, whereas the initiated have seen in them the prodigious savants which they in fact were.

Possession of the Qabalistic key opens the gateway to the future, the success and even the heaven of all religions or initiate fraternities.

The loss of these keys is a condemnation to death for those who have allowed the precious light to be extinguished.

In the time of Ptolemy, the Jews were no longer able to translate the Sepher of Moses; they were about to lose their independent existence, and only the Essenes, with the keys of the Qabalah in their possession, could perpetuate the tradition, thanks to Christianity.

Today, the Apocalypse is closed for the Roman Catholic as well as for the evangelical Protestant, for the orthodox as well as for the Armenian; the keys have been lost.

In Masonic lodges the acacia is no longer known, the heart of Hiram has not been preserved in the mystic urn; atheists and ignorant power-seekers say INRI and inscribe YEVE on the fronts of their temples. They are more to be feared even than the clergy which receive their abuse, for at least the latter have kept the devotion which makes saints, even though they have lost the tradition which makes initiates.

And so it is necessary to speak further of the Qabalah, although we have traced certain over-all lines in an earlier chapter.

Let us examine, then, successively: Several details concerning the three worlds themselves, that is, in their constituent Principles as well as in their triple manifestations, the ideal images of these laws, relations and Principles as figured in the ideographic letters of the Hebrew alphabet, the ten secret numerations or Sephiroth, and the operations of sacred Arithmetic.

*

*   *

The Qabalah establishes, as a basis, a general law, of which all of creation is only an application. This law is the trinity, derived from a primordial unity if one studies origins, aspiring to fusion within Unity if one studies ends, or developing in a quaternary cycle if one studies life or temporal existence.

This trinity first exists as the original Principle of all creation and is thus represented:

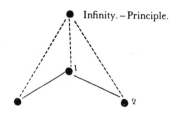

Each of the elements which constitute this Trinity possesses the power of creation and generation held by the Original Principle; but in each derived element, this power is coloured by a particular character which will be called affinity or sex, according to successive levels of actions.

There are indeed only three levels of action on which any creature can exercise activity. These three levels, planes or hierarchies are called by the Qabalah *the three worlds* and present within the most insignificant creature as well as the most immense.

Thus, a Hebrew letter is an intellectual creature containing the three worlds under the aspect of three hierarchic significations; a blood cell is a living creature, manifesting the three worlds through three constituent elements (envelope, median substance, nucleus); man's physical body is a physical creation also manifesting the three worlds in its constitution (head, breast, stomach).

These three worlds are made up:

1. Of an upper world;
2. Of a median world;
3. Of a lower world,

which will take on altogether different names depending on the creature in which they are to be considered. This is the source of a great number of obscurities and errors for students, errors, however, which the Qabalists have attempted to dispel.

Thus, in a blood cell, the worlds are represented by the soul of the cell acting within the nucleus, the life of the cell acting within the median substance, and the body of the cell limited by its envelope.

In man, the worlds are the spirit or immortal Being, utilizing the conscious nervous system, Life or the animating principle, utilizing the sympathetic nervous system and the blood vessels; and lastly the material body with its regenerative and supportive functions.

But it can easily be seen that the body is itself a representation of the three worlds. Life too is three-fold in its make-up. And so also is the immortal Spirit. How can all this be represented so as to avoid obscurity and possible errors of interpretation?

Let us represent each world by a space limited by two horizontal lines. The upper horizontal line contiguous to the world above, the lower horizontal line contiguous to the world immediately below, the three worlds come to be superimposed thus:

. . . .

_____Upper World_____
=====================
_____Median World_____
=====================
Lower World

. . . .

But each world has in the others a reflection or representation of itself. Thus, the conscious nervous system, although centralized in the head, is not without emanations in the Breast and Stomach. The sympathetic nervous system, although centralized in the Breast, sends out arteries and veins into the other human worlds, just as the lymphatic and digestive system, although centralized in the Stomach, provides the entire organism with a network of vessels and cells.

With the addition of three subdivisions to each world this can be clearly indicated.

	Localization of the Upper
UPPER WORLD	Reflection of the Median
	Reflection of the Lower
	Reflection of the Upper
MEDIAN WORLD	Localization of the Median
	Reflection of the Lower
	Reflection of the Upper
LOWER WORLD	Reflection of the Median
	Localization of the Lower

But to better demonstrate that these worlds and their reflections interpenetrate one another, Qabalists have adopted vertical lines or columns, each of which cuts through the other three worlds, thus indicating at first glance the relation of these various hierarchic centres one with another, as can be seen in the following figure:

		UPPER	
UPPER WORLD	Upper reflection	Localization	Upper reflection
MEDIAN WORLD	Median reflection	Median reflection	MEDIAN Localization
LOWER WORLD	Localization LOWER	Lower reflection	Lower reflection

This is the field of action in which creatures operate, and it is obvious that this field will change names according to the kind of creature functioning there.

Taking man as an example, in the upper world or level (head) we find:

1. The Spirit-Mind which is localized there.
2. Life which is reflected there.
3. The body which is also reflected there.

On the middle level (chest) we find:

1. The reflection of conscious spirit-mind.
2. The localization of Life.
3. The reflection of the material body.

At the lower level (stomach), we find again this triple division. This is easily figured thus:

Head Nerves	MIND	Psychic Being Intellectual Life
Breast Blood	FEELING	Organic Life
Stomach Lymph	INSTINCT	Cellular Life

Let us not forget, however, that these nine centres emanate from a great Principle, which gave birth to the original trinity. Our figure, therefore, cannot be complete unless it includes above the upper world, this first creative Principle, and below the lower world, the direct reflection of this principle, that element through which a second creation or generation can take place. Taking man still as an example, this gives the following schematic representation:

	Creative Principle GOD	
Head	MIND	Psychic being
Breast	FEELING	Organic life
Stomach	INSTINCT	Cellular life
	GENERATION Reflection of the Creative Principle in Matter	

It must be noted that this figure which applies to mankind in its entirety is also applicable to any one man. This shows that this figure is an absolute expression of the general law of constitution, and one has only to change the names of the various elements in order to obtain the names of the corresponding levels or worlds. Thanks to this figure, one can analyse, on a system of ten (three ternaries with the 2 annexations), the finest divisions of a cell, even as we have systematized those of a whole man.

	Mesoderm	Endoderm Fertilized Egg Ectoderm	
HEAD ectoderm {	Nerves	Brain	Nervous fluid
BREAST mesoderm {	Vessels	Heart	Blood
STOMACH { endoderm	Intestines	Stomach	Lymph
		Generative Organs	

Having determined this general law, the Qabalists gave to each of the constituent terms a name general enough to allow for any particular application; thus each of these terms was called a NUMERATION, for nothing is more general than the concept of number.

Such is the origin of what the Qabalah calls:

THE TEN SEPHIROTH OR NUMERATIONS

Each of the Sephiroth or Numerations was applied to one of the qualities of God in the first representational Example. This gave the classic Sephirotic table, for which we have provided in the preceding pages (and to our knowledge this has never been done before), the origin and key to its construction.

The Ten elements of analysis, applicable as they are to any reality, are in no way isolated from one another. In addition to their relationship as members of the same column, there exist among them *paths of communication*, called CHANNELS, and uniting the various elements with one another.

Each of these channels is made up of a *created reality*, produced by an intellectual, vital or material being, according to the world to which the creature under consideration belongs.

As the *Numerations* indicated the elements which compose

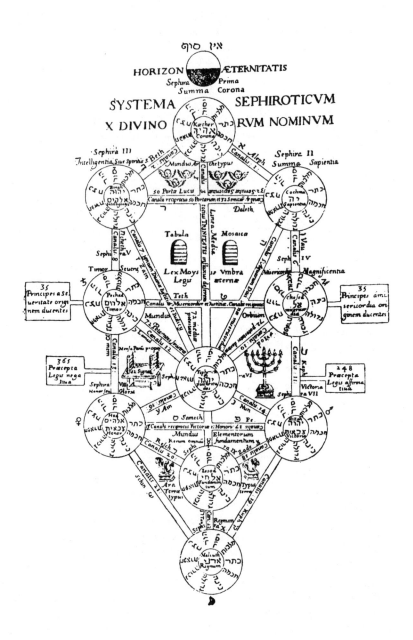

(Sephirotic table in Latin & Hebrew)

(IN HOC SIGNO VINCES)

our general figure, so the *Hebrew letters* indicate each of the mysterious paths which unite these elements.

Once again it was necessary to follow the trinitary law, and Qabalists did not fail to do so in composing the wondrous instrument which is the Hebrew alphabet.

The Hebrew alphabet contains twenty-two hieroglyphic letters, each of which is an intellectual creature, open to profound interpretations. These letters correspond to the three worlds in the following fashion:

Three principal letters, Aleph, No. 1, Mem, No. 13 and Shin, No. 21, represent the upper world.

Seven double letters represent the median world.

Twelve single letters represent the inferior world.

Since each of the worlds is present in the others, we find that each of the types of letters exists in each world. Thus:

The upper world contains a principal letter, three doubles and four singles, constituting the channels.

The median world has one principal, two doubles and six singles.

The lower world has one principal, two doubles and two singles.

The names and numbers of each of these letters are to be found on page 98.

Such is the law of the static constitution of the system of the Sephiroth.

The triple ternary, with its upper and lower annexations, and the mystic channels manifested through the Hebrew letters and joining these various centres.

But this is only a static representation of the system, and one must not forget that the system is an exact figure of the Law of Life which extends throughout the entire Universe; thus the divers elements which we have just given will give way, in their various combinations, to an infinity of new laws governing the detailed distribution of central force in the ultimate divisions of the various worlds.

Each time the great Sephirotic schema is applied to a new system of realities, all the meanings of the centres and paths change character, and it is in moving along these lines that the Qabalists have put off the lazy and the profane.

The symbolic significance of the Hebrew letters has been considered *within several different systems, diversely applied to realities from various levels*; and this is why certain letters refer to man, such as *Ooph*, indicative of a circumscribed point, while others refer to Nature, such as *Samekh*, which designates the astral serpent. In actuality there exists *no complete written key* giving the real value of the Hebrew letters in any one sphere of application, and each student must himself work out a key by beginning personally and anew for each reality-system; for it is in so doing that the serious researcher learns to employ analogy and open the mysterious book closed with the seven seals.

How must one study the Qabalah?

Understandably in this short exposé we cannot enter into the multiplicity of detail concerning the Qabalah which forms the real basis of occidental initiation. We have just given a rather clear explanation of the Sephirotic system, we have touched upon the Hebrew letters, and now there remains only to give what advice we can to those desirous of furthering their studies. The following is a list of the fundamentals of the question.

1. *The ten Sephiroth* in their application to divine manifestation.

2. *The 22 letters*, their name, placement, number and hieroglyph in the traditional alphabet.

3. *The Shemoth* or Divine Names which form the *soul* of the Sephiroth considered as divine virtues.

4. It is useful to study the book of formation, the analogical key to the Law of life, the *Sepher Yetzirah*[1].

5. Then one can understand, first in Agrippa (*Occult Philosophy, Vol. 2*), then in the classics, the art of transpositions, *Gematria*, the art of determining the character of written signs, *Notaria*, and the art of substitutions and combinations, *Themurah*.

6. These preparatory studies are necessary in order to take up the reading of the sublime and mysterious book, *the book of Light, the book of the celestial chariot, The Zohar*, which initiates us into the mysteries of the Digestion of Universes by the

[1] Our French translation of this book can be found in the *Traité méthodique de Science occulte* and a new translation, still more fully developed in our review, *Initiation*.
TRAITE METHODIQUE DE SCIENCE OCCULTE. In-octavo, 1128 pages. 400 engravings. 2nd edition. 1928, ed. Dorbon.

Celestial Man and the constitution of Adam Kadmon.

7. The works of *Eliphas Lévi* and also those of *Louis Michel de Figanières* (*Key to Life, Universal Life*) are particularly indicated as commentaries and summaries of all Qabalistic teachings.

It can now be seen why the study of the Qabalah has always been considered to be one of the finest efforts to which human intelligence can be devoted. Elements of the above are to be found in the following tables, and certain developments are given in our *Methodical Treatise of Occult Science* as well as in the remarkable and highly personalized works of Stanislas de Guaita.

THE SEPHIROTH

in their application to divine manifestation

ENSOPH
The Absolute

KETHER
The Crown

BINAH
Intelligence
PECHAD
Awe

CHOKMAH
Wisdom
CHESED
Mercy

TIPHERETH
Beauty

HOD
Honour

NETZACH
Victory

YESOD
Foundation
MALKUTH
Kingdom

———

The 22 Letters

Place in the alphabet and type		Name	Figure	Usual Hieroglyph	Value
PRINCIPAL	1	Alpeh	א	Man	1
Double	2	Beth	ב	Man's mouth	2
Double	3	Gimel	ג	The hand taking	3
Double	4	Daleth	ד	The breast	4
Single	5	He	ה	Breath	5
Single	6	Vau	ו	The eye — The ear	6
Single	7	Zayin	ז	Arrow	7
Single	8	Cheth	ח	A field	8
Single	9	Teth	ט	A rooftop	9
Single & primary	10	Yod	י	The index finger	10
Double	11	Kaph	כ	The hand clasping	20
Single	12	Lamed	ל	Outstretched arm	30
PRINCIPAL	13	Mem	מ	Woman	40
Single	14	Nun	נ	A fruit	50
Single	15	Samekh	ס	Serpent	60
Single	16	Ayin	ע	Materialized link	70
Double	17	Pe	פ	Mouth and tongue	80
Single	18	Tzaddi	צ	Roof	90
Single	19	Qoph	ק	Hatchet	100
Double	20	Resh	ר	Man's head	200
PRINCIPAL	21	Shin	ש	Arrow	300
Double	22	Tau	ת	The breast	400

The 10 Divine Names (Shemoth)

1. Eheieh
2. Yah
3. Jehovah
4. El
5. Eloha

6. Elohim
7. Tetragrammaton
8. Elohim Tsabaoth
9. Shaddai
10. Adonai

SOME NOTES ON THE HIGH QABALAH

The Qabalistic treatise, *The Revolution of Arms*, a heretofore unpublished translation with commentaries by Dr Marc Haven, one of the greatest contemporary Qabalists, elucidates certain higher points of these doctrines, points which in the past have often been incompletely presented by commentators of the Qabalah. By summarizing these teachings, following Dr

Haven's manuscript, we will leave certain questions in an obscurity which only the patience and personal endeavour of the student clarify.

THE WORLDS[1]

The Qabalistic worlds are three in number, to which is appended a fourth.

The world of emanation: ATZILUTH
The world of creation: BRIAH
The world of formation: JETZIRAH
The world of action: ASSIAH

THE PERSONS

In each of these worlds exist five mystical persons, thus disposed:

MACROPROSOPUS
or Long-suffering

THE FATHER   THE MOTHER

MICROPROSOPUS   THE SPOUSE
  or Irascible

The reflexion, from highest to lowest, of these mystic persons, generates the ten Sephiroth.

In Man, the Persons are represented thus[2]:

HAIA   YEHIDA
NESHAMAH   RUAH
(Soul proper)   (Living spirit)

NEPHESH
(Psyche)

---

[1] See in this regard the preceding study on the *Mondes Kabbalistiques*.

[2] This is why David said (Psalms 103-104): *Let my soul praise the Lord five times.*

ADAM

Adam is manifested in three ways:

ADAM KADMON
ADAM BELIAL
ADAM PROTOPLASTES

Adam Kadmon is the Adam of before the Fall. *Adam Belial* is the Adam of Cortices, and *Adam Protoplastes* is the Principle of differentiated souls (he whom Fabre d'Olivet calls Universal Man).

Adam Kadmon is manifest in the five Principles re-established and Adam Belial in the five Principles overthrown (this is a mystery).

SOULS

Souls issue from the differentiation of Adam Protoplastes: they number sixty myriads and are generated in accordance with the following mystic numbers:

$$3 - 12 - 70 - 613 - 60 \text{ myriads}$$

Here and nowhere else is the origin of the 613 precepts of the Law.

The Embryonic state of souls or Ibbur (עיבור) is double according to whether the soul is new or reincarnate.

The Revolution of souls or Gilgul (גילגול) completes the mystery of human destiny. Those who know this mystery can identify the man of thirteen years and a day.

CHAPTER IV

THE SEPHIROTH (*after Stanislas de Guaita*)

Tables of correlation

The Sephiroth – Exposé of Stanislas de Guaita

In order to conclude matters pertaining to this part of the
Qabalah it remains for us to speak of the *numerations* or
Sephiroth. In an extremely noteworthy work, one of the most
learned of contemporary Qabalists, *Stanislas de Guaita*, had
condensed the important fundamentals touching the divine
names and the Sephiroth.

This work is only the analysis of certain Qabalistic extracts
made by *Khunrath*. Let us begin with these, after which the
reader can follow de Guaita's developments.

KHUNRATH'S EXTRACTS CONCERNING THE ROSY-CROSS

NOTE ON THE ROSY-CROSS

These Qabalistic extracts are taken from a small folio, most
singular and rare, and well known to collectors of old books of
engravings. It is especially sought after by all those who, for
whatever reason, busy themselves with the study of esoteric
religions, of the tradition of secret doctrine veiled within the
symbolism of Christianity, in short, *the transmission of sacerdotal
magic* in the West.

'AMPHITHEATRUM SAPIENTIAE AETERNAE,
SOLIVS VERAE, christiano-kabalisticum, divino-magicum,
necnon physico-chemicum, tertriunum, katholikon
instructore HENRICO KHUNRATH, etc., HANOVIAE,
1609, folio.'

Though unique and invaluable for researchers eager to acquaint themselves further with these troublesome questions, this book is unfortunately incomplete in a great number of its published copies. Thus the reader may take it kindly if we pause here to give a few pertinent details concerning the total publication as it should appear.

*
* *

The twelve engravings, made from copper plates, are generally grouped together at the beginning of the work. They are arbitrarily arranged, their. author having neglected – perhaps purposely – to specify their true order. The essential is to procure a complete set, since their order varies from specimen to specimen.

Three of them are of simple format: 1. the allegorical frontispiece framing the title; 2. the author's portrait, surrounded by allegorical attributes; 3. a sea-hawk wearing a pair of spectacles, perched majestically between two lighted torches, surmounting two smaller torches placed crosswise to each other. Above this is inscribed a short verse in rather dubious High German, which can be thus translated:

To what purpose torches, spectacles and lighted flames
For those whose eyes remain closed so that they may not see?

These are followed by nine superb magical figures, very carefully engraved on double-spread, thumb-indexed pages. These are:

1. *The great hermetic androgyne*; 2. Khunrath's *Laboratory**; 3. *Adam-Eve* within the verbal triangle; 4. the pentagram of the *Rosy-Cross*[1] (about which we will speak in detail further on); 5. the *Seven grades of the sanctuary and the seven rays*; 6. the *Alchemical Citadel* with its twenty blind gates*; 7. the *Gymnasium naturæ*, a synthetical and very learned figure with the appearance of a simple landscape; 8. the *Emerald Table*, engraved on the igneous, mercurial stone; 9. the *Pentacle of Khunrath**, encircled by a satirical caricature after the manner of Callot, in fact,

---

[1] This figure, as well as that of the *Hermetic Androgyne*, has been reproduced by means of copper-plate engravings, commented upon in detail, at the beginning of the re-edition, considerably augmented, of our work of 1886: *Essais des sciences maudites: 1. Au seuil du mystère.*

wholly his style. (See in this connection: Eliphas Lévi, *Histoire de la magie*, p. 368).

This last plate, of biting irony and executed with a deliciously savage art, is missing from almost all available copies. The numerous enemies of the Theosoph, seeing themselves there caricatured, have no doubt taken great pains to suppress so scandalously fascinating an engraving.

Of the other plates, those which are followed by an asterisk are commonly found to be missing as well.

*
* *

Now let us turn our attention to the text, divided into two sections. The first sixty pages, numbered separately, contain a royal charter (dated 1598), then divers pieces: discourses, dedication, poems, prologue, polemic writings. Then is given the text of the proverbs of Solomon, together with an esoteric commentary on them, this section constituting the remainder of the *Amphitheatrum*.

This commentary forms the body proper of the work, seven chapters long, and followed by a number of curious elucidations, entitled: *Interpretationes et Annotationes Henrici Khunrath*. There are 222 pages in this second section. The final page gives the name of the printer: G. Antonius, and the date: Hanoviae, M DC. IX.

We will conclude this description with an important note from the learned bibliophile G.-F. de Bure, who says in the second volume of his *Bibliography*: 'It is to be noted that in the first part of this work, sixty pages in length, there ought to be found, between pages 18 and 19, a particular table headed *Summa Amphitheatri sapientia*, etc ..., and in the second part, another, likewise to be printed on a double thumb-indexed page, numbered 151, both figures being referred to and starred in the body of the text. – We noticed that these two tables were missing from all the copies we examined; their absence should not be overlooked ...' (page 248).

Let us now pass on to the study of the Qabalistic plate, which has been made available to the subscribers to *Initiation* by that review.

ANALYSIS OF THE ROSY-CROSS

after HENRY KHUNRATH

This figure is a wondrous pentacle, a hieroglyphic resumé of an entire doctrine: here, as the review has pointed out, are to be found synthesized all the representational mysteries known to adepts of the Rosy-Cross.

*
* *

First, we have the central point with its three concentric degrees, showing the three circular regions symbolic of the process of *Emanation*.

* *
*

In the middle, a Christ in the form of a cross within a rose of light: this is the brilliant outpouring of the Word or of *Adam-Kadmon* אדסקדמין; it is the emblem of the Great Arcana; never has the essential identity of Man-in-Synthesis and God-made-manifest been so audaciously revealed.

(It is not without the profoundest reasons that the hierographer has reserved the middle of the figure for his symbolic rendering of the incarnation of the eternal Word. For it is *through* the Word, *in* the Word and *by* the Word (itself indissolubly united to Life) that all things, spiritual as well as corporeal, are created. – '*In principle erat Verbum*, (says Saint John), et Verbum erat apud Deum, et Deus erat Verbum ... *Omnia per ipsum facta sunt* et sine ipso factum est nihil quod factum est. *In ipso vita erat ...*' If note is taken of that part of the human figure occupying the central point, and thereby originating from the circumference, one can clearly understand the hieroglyphic power with which the Initiator was able to express this fundamental mystery.)

A luminous radiance spreads outward from this point: the

full-blown rose with five petals, the five-pointed star of the Qabalistic *Microcosm*, the *Flaming Star* of Freemasonry, the symbol of omnipotent will, armed with the fiery sword of the Kirubi.

In the terminology of exoteric Christianity, this is the sphere of *God the Son*, placed between that of *God the Father* (the Sphere of shadow from on high, cut through by the luminous characters: *Ain Soph*) and that of *God the Holy Spirit, Ruah Hakkadosh* (the luminous sphere from below, cut through by the hierogram *Œ meth* אמת in characters of shadow).

These two spheres appear as if hidden in the clouds of *Atziluth* אצי֫לות , indicating the occult nature of the first and third persons of the holy Trinity; the Hebrew words expressive of them stand out boldly, on the one hand full of light against a dark background, on the other, full of darkness against a background of light, giving to understand that our mind, incapable of penetrating such principles in their essence, can only glimpse their antithetical relationship according to the analogy of opposites.

*

* *

Above the sphere of *Ain Soph* the sacred wood *Jehovah* or *Yaweh* is inscribed in a flaming triangle as follows:

Without entering into an analysis of this sacred name nor an examination of the secrets of its generation – which would require interminable expositions – we can, however, say that *from a particular point of view Yod* י symbolizes the Father, *Yah* יה the son, *Yaheh* יהו the Holy Spirit, *Yaheweh* יהוה the living Universe; and that this mystic triangle is attributed to the sphere of the ineffable *Ain Soph*, or God the Father. By this attribution Qabalists have wished to show that the Father is the source of the entire Trinity, and furthermore, that He contains, in occult potentiality, all that is, was or will be.

*

*   *

Above the sphere of *Œmeth* or of the Holy Spirit, within the very radiance of the Rosy-Cross and under the feet of Christ, a dove wearing the pontifical diadem takes its luminous flight: emblem of the double current of love and light which comes down from the Father to the Son – from God to Man – and re-ascends from the Son to the Father – from Man to God – its two outspread wings corresponding exactly to the pagan symbol of the two intertwined serpents of the caduceus of Hermes.

Only initiates are capable of an understanding of this mysterious correspondence.

*

*   *

Let us return to the sphere of the *Son*, which requires further commentary. Above we pointed out the impenetrable character of the essence of the *Father* and the *Holy Spirit*.

Alone the *second person* of the Trinity – represented by the central Rosy-Cross – can penetrate the clouds of *Atziluth*, sending forth its ten sephirotic rays.

These are like so many windows open onto the great secret of the Word, and through which one can contemplate its splendour from ten different points of view. In effect, the Zohar compares the ten *Sephiroth* to so many transparent vases of different colours, through which shines in its various aspects the heart and centre of the Unity-Synthesis. Or let us imagine a tower with ten windows, in the centre of which there burns a five-branched candlestick; this luminous quinary will be visible through each of them; anyone approaching and looking through them successively will see ten candlesticks in all ... (Multiply the pentagram ten times, making the five points of light radiate through each of the ten apertures, and you will have the *Fifty Gates of Light*.)

He who aims at synthesis must enter the tower; he who circles it from outside is bound to remain a pure analyst. And such a one cannot of course fail to err, should he begin to reason as to the whole.

*
*   *

Later on we will have more to say regarding the sephirotic
system; now, let us conclude the matter of the central emblem.
Reduced to the geometric proportions of a simple schema, it
might be thus drawn:

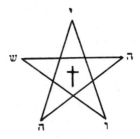

A cross enclosed in the flaming star. It is the quaternary
finding its expansion in the quinary; it is Mind which
multiplies and weakens itself in order to descend into the
cesspool of matter where it will wallow for a time, but its
destiny is to find in its very abasement the revelation of its
personality, and already – a presage of salvation – at the
lowest point of its decline it feels welling up within the great
force of Will. This is the *Word* which becomes incarnate as the
Mournful Christ, corporeal man יהשוה, against the day when,
assuming with man a human nature reborn, it will return to
glory.

This is the meaning of the adept Saint-Martin in the first
volume of his *Erreurs et Vérité* when he teaches that the fall of
man originated from his transposition of the pages of the
Great Book of Life, substituting the fifth page (that of
corruption and degradation) for the fourth (that of
immortality and spiritual eternity).

By adding the quaternary of the cross and the pentagram of
the star, one obtains 9, mysterious number whose detailed
explanation would cause us to stray from the limits we have
here imposed upon ourselves. Elsewhere (*Lotus*, vol. II, No. 12,
pp. 327-328) we have given such details and shown through a
process of qabalistic calculation that 9 is the *analytical* number
of man. May we then simply refer the reader to these pages.

Let us note, however – for all holds together in High Science and the analogical concordances are absolute – let us note that in the sephirotic figures of the *Rosy-Cross* the rose is traditionally represented by *nine* interlinking circles, in the manner of the links of a chain. Again we have the analytical number of man: 9!

*

* *

And now for an important remark and a new confirmation of our theory. For those who possess some notion of esoterism, it is obvious that the four branches of the interior cross (represented by the figure of Christ with extended arms) must be marked by the letters of the tetragram: *Yod, he, vau, he.* This is not the place to recapitulate what we have said elsewhere[1] concerning the hieroglyphic and grammatical composition of this sacred word; the most extensive and most complete commentaries can be found in the works of all serious qabalists. (See, preferably: ROSENBROTH, *Kabbala denudata*; LENAIN, *la science Kabbalistique*; FABRE D'OLIVET, *Langue hebraïque restitituée.* ELIPHAS LEVI, *Dogme et Rituel, Histoire de la magie, Clef des grands mystères*; and PAPUS, *Traité élémentaire de la science occulte.*) But let us consider a moment the hierogram Yeshua יהשׁוה of what elements is it composed? Certainly anyone can ascertain the famous tetragram יהוה divided in the middle יה-וה by the Hebrew letter *Shin* שׁ. Now here the יהוה is expressive of Adam-Kadmon, Man in his integral synthesis, in short divinity made manifest through the *Word* and symbolizing the fertile union of universal Spirit and Soul. To cut this word in two is to symbolize the disintegration of its unity and the resultant divisional offspring of the generation of submultiples. *Shin* שׁ, which unites the two truncated elements, represents (Arcana 21, or 0 of the Tarot) the subtle, generative fire, the vehicle of undifferentiated life, the universal plastic Mediator whole rôle it is to effect incarnations by allowing Spirit to descend into matter, penetrating it, working it, using it for its end. The forming a kind of hyphen between the two sections of the broken tetragram is then a symbol of the fall and the taking up of residence in the elementary, material world of יהוה, its unity in a state of disintegration.

[1] *Au seuil du mystère*, vol. I, p. 12, 1886. – *Lotus*, vol. II, No. 12, pp. 321-347, *passim* ...

It is ש , finally, whose addition to the holy quaternary engenders the quinary or number of decline. Saint-Martin saw this very well. But 5, which is the number of the fall, is also the number of will, and the will is the instrument of reintegration.

Initiates know that the substitution of 5 for 4 is only transitorily disastrous; that, in the mire to which he has fallen, the human submultiple learned to win a personality, both free and conscious at last. Felix culpa! From his fall, he rises again stronger and greater; thus *evil* never follows after *good* but temporarily and in order that the *best* may be finally realized.

This number 5 contains the profoundest secrets; but we are obliged to bring our discussion of it to a close for fear of finding ourselves involved in an interminable tange of digressions. What we have said of 4 and 5 in their connection to the Rosy-Cross is sufficient for those seeking Initiation. And after all these pages are destined only for them.

*

* *

Now let us turn our thoughts to the ten rays which penetrate the cloudy region of *Atziluth*. This is the denary of Pythagoras which, in Qabalistic terms, is called the sephirotic emanation. Before giving our readers a clear classification of the Qabalistic Sephiroth, let us draw up a table of the traditional correspondences existing among these ten numerations and the ten principal names given to the divinity by Hebrew theologians. These names, which Khunrath has engraved in circles in the unfolding of the flaming rose, each correspond to one of the ten Sephiroth. (See the table on page XXX.)

As to the divine names, after having given their translation in ordinary language, we will attempt as briefly as possible to deduce from a hieroglyphic examination of each of them the esoteric significance which can be attributed to them.

אהיה. — That which constitutes the innaccessible essence of absolute Being, origin of life.

יה — The indissoluble union of the universal Spirit and Soul.

יהוה. Copulation of the male and female Principles, eternally engendering the living Universe (Great arcana of the Word).

אל. The outpouring of the Unity-Principle. – Its diffusion in Space and Time.

אלהים גבור. Gods-of-Gods of the giants or man-gods.

SEPHIROTH				DIVINE NAMES			
כתר	Kether	. . .	The Crown	אהיה	Eheieh	. . .	Being
חכמה	Chokmah	.	Wisdom	יה	Yah	. .	Yah
בינה	Binah	. .	Intelligence	יהוה	Yaweh	. .	Jehovah the Eternal
חסד	Chesed	. .	Mercy	אל	El .	. .	El
גבורה	Geburah	.	Justice	אלהים גבר	Elohim Ghibbor	. .	Elohim Ghibbor
תפארת	Tiphereth.		Beauty	אלה	Eloha	. .	Eloha
נצח	Netzach	.	Eternity	צבאות אלהים	Elohim Tsabaoth	. .	Elohim Tsabaoth
הוד	Hod	. .	The Foundation	יהוה צבאות	Yaweh Tsabaoth	. .	Jehovah Tsabaoth — God of the Armies
יסוד	Yesod	. .	Victory	שדי	Shaddai	. .	The All-Powerful
מלכות	Malkuth	.	The Kingdom	אדני מלך	Adonai Melek	. .	The Lord King

אלוח. God reflected in one of the gods.

יחוח צבאות. The *Yod-he-vau* (see above) of the septenary or of triumph.

אלחים צבאות. Gods-of-gods of the septenary or of triumph.

שדי. Fecundation by means of quaternized astral Light in expansion, then its return to the forever hidden principle from which it emanates. (Masculine ofשדח, the Fecundated, Nature.)

ארני. The quaternary of cubic multiplication of the Unity-Principle for the production of ceaselessly changing Becoming; then the final eclipse of the concrete objective by a return to the potential subjective.

בלך.Maternal death, pregnant with life: a fatal law spreading throughout the entire Universe, and whose perpetual movement of exchange is interrupted forcefully each time a being is objectified.

Such is one aspect of the secret significance of the hierograms.

*
*   *

Note that each of the ten Sephiroth (aspects of the Word) corresponds in the pentacle of Khunrath to one of the angelic choirs; a sublime idea, providing one can develop it deeply enough. In the Qabalah the angels are not beings of a particular and unchanging essence; everything lives, moves and is transformed in the living Universe! By applying to the celestial hierarchies the beautiful comparison whereby the authors of the Zohar attempted to explain the nature of the Sephiroth, we can say that the angelic choirs are comparable to transparent coverings of various colours where Spirits, definitively freed from temporal forms, come to shine by turns with an ever purer and more splendid light, as they climb the supreme steps of Jacob's ladder, the summit of which is the seat of the Ineffable יהוה .

To each of the angelic choirs Khunrath relates one of the verses of the Decalogue: it is as if the governing angel of each step opened his mouth to utter one of the precepts of divine law. But this seems somewhat arbitrary and less worthy of our attention.

*
*   *

A more profound idea of the theosoph of Leipzig is to have the letters of the Hebrew alphabet come out of the cloud of Atziluth, riddled with the Sephirotic beams.

To cause the twenty-two letters of the sacred hieroglyphic alphabet to be born from the opposites of Light and Shadow — letters which correspond, as is perhaps known, to the twenty-two arcana of absolute Doctrine, translated into pentacles in the twenty-two keys of the Samaritan Tarot — is this not to condense in a single, striking image the entire doctrine of the Book of Formation, the Sepher Jetzirah (ספר יצירה)? These emblems, by turns radiant and lugubrious, mysterious figures symbolizing so well the Joyful and the Baneful of eternal Destiny, Henry Khunrath sees them as born from the fecund union of Shadow and Light, Error and Truth, Evil and Good, Being and Non-Being! In such a way unforeseen phantoms spring up suddenly on the horizon, their faces smiling or sad, splendid or threatening, whenever Phoebus, from the bank of dense and sombre shadows and once again victor over the Python, sends forth his golden arrows.

*
* *

The following table will furnish, along with the real sense of the Sephiroth, the correspondences which the Qabalah establishes between them and the spiritual hierarchies.

To round out the basic notions we have given touching the Sephirotic system, we will conclude this study with the well-known schema of the triple ternary; this classification is, to our mind, the richest and most precious in corollaries.

The three ternaries represent the trinity as it is manifested in the three worlds.

The first ternary — that of the intellectual world — is alone the absolute representation of the holy Trinity; there Providence balances the two sides of the Scales of the divine order: Wisdom and Intelligence.

The two lower ternaries are only reflections of the first in the denser middle area of the moral and astral worlds. This is why they appear in reverse, like the image of an object mirrored in the surface of a liquid.

In the moral world, Beauty (or Harmony or Rectitude) balances the sides of the scales: Mercy and Justice.

In the astral world, Generation, instrument of the stability

THE SEPHIROTH		CORRESPONDING TO	
כתר Kether	Equilibrating Providence	חיות הקדש Haioth Hakkadosh	Providential intelligences
חכמה Chokmah	Divine Wisdom	אופנים Ophanim	Activators of the starry wheels
בינה Binah	Ever active Intelligence	אראלים Aralim	The Powerful
חסד Chesed	Infinite Mercy	חשמלים Chasmalim	The Lucid
גבורה Geburah	Absolute Justice	שרפים Seraphim	Angels burning with zeal
תפארת Tiphereth	Ineffable Beauty	מלאכים Malachim	Kings of splendour
נצח Netzach	Victory of Life over Death	אלהים Elohim	Gods (sent by God)
הוד Hod	Eternity of Being	בני אלהים Beneh-Elohim	Sons of God
יסוד Yesod	Generation, corner stone of stability	כרובים Cherubim	Ministers of astral fire
מלכות Malkuth	Principle of Forms	אישים Ishim	Glorified Souls

of beings, assures Victory over death and nothingness, nourishing Eternity with the inexhaustible succession of ephemeral things.

Finally there is Malkuth the kingdom of forms, which actualizes at the base the total synthesis of the sephiroth, fully realized and perfect, the same synthesis which is germinal, potential form is the uppermost domain of Kether, Providence (or the crown).

There remains much that could be said of the symbolic Rosy-Cross of Khunrath, but time and space do not permit a more extensive development than that which we have given.

In fact an entire volume would not be over-sufficient for the logical development of the matters we have touched on so cursorily in these few pages. If the reader has found what we have said too abstract, or even obscure, this is the result of necessary brevity, and we offer our deepest apologies.

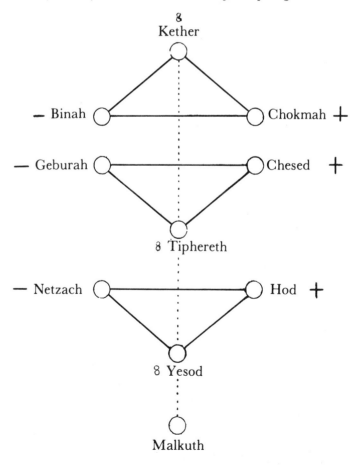

Should he wish to take the trouble to study the very sources of the Qabalah, certainly he will find the end-product of this massive and fatiguing reading to be a satisfactory acquisition of a great number of remarkable and transcendent secrets.

Like algebra, the Qabalah has its equations and its technical vocabulary. Reader, this is a language worthy of being learned, and its marvellous precision and accustomed use will most surely reward you for the mental efforts expended during your period of study.

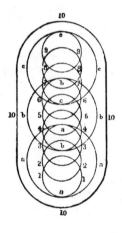

Interlinking circles summarizing the teachings of the Qabalah (see Chapter VI)

*
*   *

DERIVATION OF THE CHANNELS

Here are shown only the divine appellations which the channels indicate. Their terminal points are given on tables showing the sephirotic tree (see page 134).

1	א	God of Infinity	איה
2	ב	God of Wisdom	ביה
3	ג	God of Retribution	גיה
4	ד	God of the Gates of Light	דיה
5	ה	God of God	היה
6	ו	God the Founder	ויה
7	ז	God of Thunder and Lightning (fulgoris)	זיה
8	ח	God of Mercy	חיה
9	ט	God of Goodness	טיה
10	י	God the Principle	ייה
11	כ	God the Immutable	כיה
12	ל	God of the 30 Paths of Wisdom	ליה
13	מ	God the Arcane	מיה
14	נ	God of the 50 Gates of Light	ניה
15	ס	God the Destroyer	סיה
16	ע	God of Adjuration	עיה
17	פ	God of Discourse	פיה
18	צ	God of Justice	ציה
19	ק	God of Rectitude	קיה
20	ר	God the Head	ריה
21	ש	God the Saviour	שיה
22	ת	God the End of All	תיה

All the names have the same ending יה. Their sense depends solely on the initial letter and, as a result, can serve to establish the meaning of this letter itself.

SUMMARY

There exist then strict relationships among the divine names, the numbers, the letters and the Sephiroth; *Stanislas de Guaita* has just enumerated some of them; the following tables, one taken from *Kircher*, the other from *R.P. Esprit Sabbathier*, will further develop these correspondences, summarizing all we have said up to this point. Not only do these tables show the

TABLE OF THE QABALISTIC DENARY BY KIRCHER

10 PRECEPTS OF THE LAW	MEMBERS OF TERRESTRIAL MAN	MYSTIC MEMBERS OF CELESTIAL MAN	MYSTIC MEMBERS OF ARCHETYPAL MAN	MYSTIC MEMBERS ACC. TO ORTHODOXY	NAMES OF GOD	CORRESPONDING SEPHIROTH
1	Brain	Empyrean heavens	Haroth	Seraphim	אהיה Sum qui sum	Crown
2	Lung	First mobile	Ophanim	Cherubim	יה Essentializing essence	Wisdom
3	Heart	Firmament	Aralim	Thrones	יהוה God of Gods	Intelligence
4	Stomach	Saturn	Chasmalim	Dominations	אל God, Creator	Grandeur
5	Liver	Jupiter	Seraphim	Virtues	אלה God, Powerful	Force
6	Gall	Mars	Malachim	Powers	אלים God, Strong	Beauty
7	Spleen	Sun	Elohim	Principalities	יהוהצבאות God of Armies	Victory
8	Kidneys	Venus	Ben Elohim	Archangels	אלהים Lord of Armies	Glory
9	Genitals	Mercury	Cherubim	Angels	שדי All-Powerful	Foundation
10	Womb	Moon	Ishim	Souls	אדני Lord	Kingdom

Sephiroth and the divine names, they furnish a total view of the Qabalah at a glance.

We promised to conclude our exposition with outlines of the two principal treatises which have been written on the question: one by *Kircher* and one by *Lenain*. Thanks to the foregoing exposition, the reader can understand these outlines, and he will see that we have done our utmost to summarize this part of the Hebrew Qabalah.

OUTLINE OF KIRCHER'S STUDY

Ch. 1. The divine names. – The divisions of the Qabalah.
Ch. 2. History and origins of the Qabalah.
Ch. 3. Foundation of the Qabalah. – The alphabet, the mystical order of its characters.
Ch. 4. Names and surnames of God.
Ch. 5. The tables of Zruph or combinations of the Hebrew alphabet.
Ch. 6. The Divine Name of 72 letters (יהוה) and its use.
Ch. 7. The tetragrammatical Divine Name in pagan antiquity.
Ch. 8. Most secret mystic theology of the Hebrews. – Qabalah of the ten Sephiroth or divine numeration.
Ch. 9. The various representations of the Sephiroth, their realms of influences and their channels.
Ch. 10. Concerning the natural Qabalah called Bereschith[1].

OUTLINE OF LENAIN'S STUDY

Ch. 1. On the name of God and his attributes.
Ch. 2. On the origin of the divine names, their attributes and their influence on the Universe. (Alphabet and meaning of its letters).
Ch. 3. Explanation of the 72 attributes of God and of the 72 angels governing the Universe.
Ch. 4. The 72 names.

---

[1] For a development of this subject see p. 272, no. 179.

M.S.	INTELLIGENCE OF THE SPHERES	ORDER OF THE BLESSED
ד ע	Prince of the World מטטרון: Metatron	Seraphim Holy Animals חיות הקודש Hayyoth Hakadosh
ה פ	Herald of God רציאל: Radziel	Cherubim Wheels אופנים: Ophanim
ו ħ צ	Contemplation of God צפקיאל Tasaphkiel	Thrones Powerful אראלים: Aralim
ז ♃ ק	Justice of God צדקיאל Tsaphkiel	Dominations Brilliant חשמלים Hasmalim
ח ♂ ר	Punishment of God סמאל Samael	Powers Fiery שרפים Seraphim
ט ☉ ש	Like unto God מיכאל Michael	Virtues Kings מלכים Melachim
י ♀ ת	Grace of God חבניאל Haniel	Principalities Gods אלהים Elohim
כ ☿ ך	Divine Physician רפאל Raphael	Archangels Children of God אלהים בני: Elohim Beni
ל ☽ ם	Man-God גבריאל Gabriel	Angels Seat of Sons כרובים Kerubim
מ ן	Messiah מטטרון: Metatron	Blessed souls Men אשים Ishim
נ ף	NO NAME OF 11 LETTERS, 11 BEING AN EVIL NUMBER	
ס ע		

(Ideal shadow of Universal wisdom)

SEPHIROTH	NAMES OF GOD ACCORDING TO NUMBER OF LETTERS		QABALISTIC NAMES OF GOD	
Crown כתר: Kether		I יׄ Yod	I shall be אהיה Eheieh	
Wisdom הכמה Chokmah	God אל El	Being, itself יה Yah	Being of Beings יהוה Jehovah	I יׄ Yod
Intelligence בינה Binah	Jesus ישׁוׄ; Jeshua	Omnipotent שדי Shaddai	God אלהים Elohim	Being of Beings יהוה Being of Beings
Mercy חסד: Chesed	Sav	Being of Beings יהוה: Jehovah		God אל: El
Strength גבורה: Geburah	Saviour God Most high יהשׁוה אלהים עליון Jehoshua Elohim Helion		Strong גבור Gibor	God אלהים Elohim
Beauty תפראת Tiphereth		Strong God אל-גבור El Gibor		God אלוה Eloha
Victory נצח Netzach		Immutable אראריתא Ararita	Of armies צבאות Tsabaoth	Lord יהוה Jehovah
Praise הוד Hod		Science of God יהוה Jehovah	Of armies צבאות Tsabaoth	God אלהים Elohim
Foundation יסוד Yesod	Of armies צבאות Tsabaoth	Lord יהוה Jehovah	Omnipotent שדי Shaddai	
Kingdom מלכות Malkuth	Of armies צבאות Tsabaoth	God אלהים Elohim	Lord אדני Adonai	
ACCORDING TO THE HEBREWS			God מקום Makom	
Holy Spirit הקדש ורוח Hakkodesh Veruah	Son בן Ben	Father אב Ab	God Uni-Trinity אגלא Agla	

Ch. 5. Explanation of the sacred calendar.
Ch. 6. The influences of the 72 Spirits, their attributes and their mysteries.
Ch. 7. The mysteries of Magic (the practical Qabalah).

CHAPTER V

THE PHILOSOPHY OF THE QABALAH

The soul according to the Qabalah

2. – The philosophy of the Qabalah

The systematic part of the Qabalah has been set out in the preceding section. It remains for us to speak of the philosophical part.

At the time of the re-edition of M. Ad. Franck's excellent book we gave a critique of the work in which to the best of our ability we summarized the doctrinal teachings of the Qabalah, relating these teachings to certain points of contemporary science, as is our custom.

We cannot do better than to reproduce this material here, following it with the letter in which M. Franck gives his reactions. Then, in order to show the depth of Qabalistic thinking concerning man and his transformations and the identification of this thinking with oriental tradition, we will conclude this section with a study by the contemporary German Qabalist, Carl de Leningen.

1

ANALYSIS OF M. FRANCK'S BOOK

THE QABALAH

M. Franck has made a very serious and thorough study of the Qabalah, but from the particular point of view of contemporary philosophy and academic criticism. Thus we will do our best to summarize his opinions on the subject, while supplementing them with those of contemporary

Qabalists more or less acquainted with the Esoteric tradition. These two somewhat different points of view cannot fail to shed new light on a question so important to the Occult Sciences.

The foregoing considerations indicate the plan we will follow in our study. We will successively summarize the opinions of M. Franck on the Qabalah itself, on its antiquity and its teachings, each time comparing them with those of contemporary occultists.

We must, however, limit ourselves to the most general questions, given the restrictive framework within which we are obliged to operate.

*

*   *

First let us look at the plan of construction of M. Franck's book.

His method of disposing the material is remarkable for the clarity with which such difficult subjects are presented to the reader.

Three parts, an introduction and an appendix form the structure of the work.

The introduction and the preface give a general idea of the Qabalah and its history.

The first part treats of the antiquity of the Qabalah, based on its two fundamental books, the Sepher Yetzirah and the Zohar, whose authenticity is admirably discussed.

The second part, the most important without any doubt, analyses the doctrines contained in these books, the basis of Qabalistic studies.

The third part compares the philosophical system of the Qabalah with various schools of thought bearing some likeness to it.

The appendix is given over to an examination of two Qabalistic sects.

In summary fashion all this material can be contained within the answers to the following questions:

1. *What is the Qabalah and what is its antiquity?*
2. *What are the teachings of the Qabalah regarding*
   God
   Man
   The Universe?

3. *What influence has the Qabalah had on philosophy through the ages?*

Worthy treatment of such a subject would require an entire volume; we must be content with limiting ourselves to the most strictly necessary information.

I

WHAT IS THE QABALAH AND WHAT IS ITS ANTIQUITY?

Basing his thesis on the established facts of sound learning M. Franck thus defines the Qabalah:

> A doctrine having more than one point of resemblance with those of Plato and Spinoza; which, by its form, sometimes rises to the majestic tone of religious poetry; which was born on the same ground and almost at the same time as Christianity; which, for a period of twelve centuries, without other proofs that the hypotheses of ancient tradition, without other evident motive than the desire to intimately penetrate the sense of holy books, has developed and spread in the shadow of the deepest mystery; this is what one finds, having purged them of all alloy, in the original and most ancient works of the Qabalah.

All occultists are in agreement as to the first part of this definition: the Qabalah is in fact a *traditional doctrine*, as its very name so indicates[1].

But we differ entirely with M. Franck on the question of the *origin* of this tradition.

Academic criticism cannot stray too far afield from certain established rules, the principal one of which is to base the

---

[1] 'It seems, according to the most famous rabbis, that Moses himself, foreseeing the fate which his book was to have and the false interpretations which were to be given it through the ages, resorted to an oral law which he proclaimed aloud to a certain number of trustworthy men, charging them to transmit it to others in the secret of the sanctuary, and that these men in turn transmitting it from age to age, succeeded in passing it on to a present immensely distant from its origins. This oral law, which modern-day Jews claim still to possess, is called the Kabbala, from a Hebrew word signifying that which is received, that which comes from elsewhere, that which is passed from hand to hand.' (FABRE D'OLIVET, *Langue hébraïque restituée*, p. 29)

origin of whatever doctrine it is studying only on the most authentic documentation, leaving aside the unverifiable affirmations of the partisans of this particular doctrine.

This is of course the method which M. Franck has followed in his historical research on the subject of the Qabalah. He determines the origin of the two fundamental works of the doctrine, the *Sepher Yetzirah* and the *Zohar* (and in a way which could not possibly be improved upon), and then infers from this point of origin that of the Qabalah in its entirety.

The occulist is not obligated to take these unfortunate restrictions into consideration. For him, an ancient symbol is as authentic and valuable a piece of evidence as a book, and oral tradition can only transmit formulas in dogmatic form, which reason and science must needs inspect and verify at a later date.

Wronski defines the dogma of *porisms*, that is, *problems to be demonstrated*[1]; this is why we must first deal with traditional dogmas, but never ascribing to them without having verified them scientifically.

Thus we will see what occult tradition teaches us on the subject of the origins of Esoterism, and consequently of the Qabalah itself, while posing as a *problem to be demonstrated* that which science has not yet been able to explain, and yet indicating the points where this tradition confirms the conclusions of the oral and written tradition of Occult Science.

*

* *

Each continent has seen the progressive development of a flora and a fauna, culminating in the generation of the human race. The continents were successively born in such a way that the one containing the human race destined to succeed the existing race came into being at precisely the moment when the latter was in full flower and civilization. On our planet several great civilizations thus succeeded each other in the following order:

1. The colossal civilization of Atlantis, created by the *Red Race*, evolving on a continent which has since disappeared, but which occupied the place of the Atlantic Ocean.

[1] WRONSKI, *Messianisme ou réforme absolue du Savoir humain*, vol. II, Introduction.

2. At the moment when the Red Race was in full flower of civilization, a new continent was born, constituting *Africa as we know it* and generating as its ultimate evolutionary element the *Black Race*.

When the cataclysm which swallowed up Atlantis came about, a cataclysm designated by all religions as the *universal Flood*, civilization quickly passed into the hands of the Black Race, to which the few survivors of the Red Race transmitted their principal secrets.

3. Finally, when the Blacks had themselves arrived at the apogee of their civilization, a new continent (Europe-Asia) was born with its *White Race*, to which eventually supremacy over the entire planet was to be given.

*

*   *

The subject matter we have just summarized is not new. Those who can esoterically read the Sepher of Moses will find the key in the first words of the book, as Saint-Yves d'Alveydre has shown. But without going this far, Fabre d'Olivet, in 1820, unveiled this doctrine in *l'Histoire philosophique du Goure humain*. Moreover, the author of *Mission du Juifs* himself shows us the application of this doctrine in *Ramayana*.

Geology, along with Archaeology and Anthropology, has proven the reality of several elements of this tradition.

In addition, certain unsolved problems of evolutionary theory, among others that of the *diversity of colours* of the Human Race, here find more valuable solutions, as yet unrecognized by official Science.

Thus it is that the *tradition* comes originally from the Red Race, and if one remembers that *Adam* signifies *red clay*, it is not difficult to see why the Qabalists take Adam himself as the source of their science.

The principal seats of this tradition were then: *Atlantis, Africa, Asia* and finally *Europe*.

Oceania and America are vestiges of Atlantis, and of an anterior continent: Lemuria.

Since many of these dogmatic observations are for the contemporary scholar nothing more than *porisms* (problems to be demonstrated), let us only posit them without discussion and so pass on to what official science has affirmed to be the origin of Humanity: *Asia*.

*
* *

All traditions, that of the *Bohemians*[1], the *Freemasons*[2], the *Egyptians* and the *Qabalists*[3], and in this they are not opposed by official science, agree in their consideration of India as the origin of our religious and philosophical knowledge.

The myth of *Abraham*, as Saint-Yves d'Alveydre has shown, marks the passage of the Hindu or oriental tradition to the Occident; and since the Qabalah which we today possess is nothing more than this tradition adapted to the western mind, one can understand why the oldest known Qabalistic book, the *Sepher Tetzirah*, bears as a heading the following notice:

THE QABALISTIC BOOK OF CREATION

IN HEBREW, SEPHER YETZIRAH
by ABRAHAM

Transmitted orally to his sons; then, given the unfortunate state of affairs in Israel, entrusted by the wise men of Jerusalem to written documents of the highest secrecy.[4]

To prove the truth of our affirmation, we must then find the fundamental principles of the Qabalah and particularly the *Sephiroth* in the Hindu esoteric tradition. This point, which escaped M. Franck's attention, will allow us to place the origin of the continuous line of tradition well before the first century of our era. We will undertake this shortly.

Meanwhile let us say a few words regarding the existence of this esoteric tradition in antiquity, a tradition which actually exists in spite of Littré's opinion[5] which is partially shared by one of the authors of Ad. Franck's philosophical dictionary[6].

Every religious or philosophical reformer of antiquity divided his doctrine into two parts: one veiled and destined for the masses (*exoterism*) and one clear, destined for initiates (*esoterism*).

Not to mention the Orientals, Buddha, Confucius or

---

[1] See *la Kabbale des Bohémiens*, No. 2 of *l'Initiation*.
[2] See RAGON, *Dithodoxie Maçonnique*.
[3] See SAINT-YVES D'ALVEYDRE, *Mission des Juifs*, new edit., 1928.
[4] PAPUS, *le Sepher Jesírah*, p. 5.
[5] Preface to the 3rd edit. of *Salverte* (Occult sciences).
[6] Article: *Esotérisme*.

Zorastre, history shows us Orpheus unveiling esoterism to initiates through the creation of the *mysteries*, Moses selecting a tribe of priests or initiates, the tribe of Lévi, from which he chose those to whom the *tradition* could be entrusted. But the esoteric transmission of this tradition unquestionably can be traced to Pythagoras in approximately the year 550 A.D. when he was initiated into the self-same mysteries as Orpheus and Moses in Egypt.

The secret education of Pythagoras was principally based on numbers, and the few remains of this education that have been handed on to us by the alchemists[1] demonstrate its absolute identification with the Qabalah of which it is merely a translation.

This tradition remains especially alive among the disciples of the great philosopher who reinforced it either by returning to its original source in Egypt or by becoming involved with the Grecian mysteries. Such is the case for Socrates, Plato and Aristotle.

The letter which Alexander the Great addressed to his teacher accusing him of having unveiled the esoteric teaching proves that this traditional and oral teaching was very much alive at the time.

We also find some mention of it in Plutarch when he says that certain vows have sealed his lips and that he cannot speak. But there is in fact no need to prolong our work with all the references we might make, for these are well known among occultists.

Let us only mention the continuation of this oral tradition in Christianity, for we see Jesus disclosing the veritable sense of the parables to his disciples and confiding the entire secret of esoteric tradition to his favourite disciple, John.

The Apocalypse is wholly Qabalistic in nature and represents the true Christian esoterism.

The antiquity of this tradition can then be doubted and the *Qabalah* is most assuredly older than M. Franck makes out. In addition, it was born in a land quite far away from the one which saw the rise of Christianity, as is shown by the existence of the *Hindu Sephiroth*.

But now it is time to have done with the answer to our first

---

[1] See Jean DEE, *Monas Hieroglyphica in Theatrum Chemicum.*

question and to turn our attention to the *teachings of the Qabalah*.

II

TEACHINGS OF THE QABALAH

The manner in which M. Franck presents the teachings of the Qabalah is open to a certain amount of ciriticism. Although the Qabalistic information pertaining to each particular subject is analysed brilliantly, no over-all information is given on the system considered as a synthetic whole. For example, after reading Chapter IV, entitled *Opinions des Kabbalistes sur le monde*, the reader has been acquainted with certain points of the tradition touching Angels, Astrology, the unity of God and the Universe, but he has not been sufficiently instructed to form a general idea of the constitution of the Cosmos.

We will attempt then to present our readers with as clear as possible a summary of these Qabalistic traditions, so well analysed, as has been said, by our author. Since these subjects are quite difficult, we will begin in more familiar territory with a study of Man, leaving until last the metaphysical considerations about God.

1. Teachings of the Qabalah on Man

The first teaching of the Qabalah in this respect is that man represents in himself an exact constitution of the entire Universe. This is the origin of the name *Microcosm* or Little World assigned to man as opposed to *Macrocosm* or Great World given to the Universe.

To say that Man is the image of the Universe is not to say that the Universe is a verterbrate animal. It is the constitutive principles, *analogous* but not *identical*, of which we wish to speak.

Thus cells of quite varied form and constitution combine in Man to make up the *organs*, stomach, liver, heart, brain, etc. A group of organs also combines to form an *apparatus*, giving rise to certain *functions* (the group: lungs, heart, arteries and veins makes the *circulatory apparatus*; the group: cerebral lobes, spinal fluid and sensory and motor nerves makes up the *apparatus of the nervous sytem*, etc.).

Now according to *analogy*, the fundamental method of Occult Science, elements of the Universe are analogous to the organs and apparatuses of Man, providing they *obey the same law*. Nature shows us certain beings of quite varied constitution (mineral beings, vegetable beings, animal beings, etc.) which come together to make up *planets*. These planets combine in their turn to make up *solar systems*. The *interplay of Planets* and their satellites produces the *Life of the Universe*, just as the *interplay of organs* produces the *Life of Man*. An organ and a planet are therefore analogous beings since they act according to *the same law*; how evident it is, however, that the Heart and the Sun are beings of very different form. These examples show the application of Qabalistic data to our exact sciences, constituting part of a comprehensive effort underway now for nearly five years and far from being over. And so let us leave the question of analogy and limit ourselves to the constitution of the Microcosm, since we now can understand why man is so named.

The Qabalah considers Matter to be an adjunction created at a later time than all beings, due to the Adamic fall. This idea has been sufficiently developed by Jacob Boehme and Saint-Martin, among other contemporary thinkers, to require our giving it too much space here. The fact, however, must be mentioned so as to explain why none of the given principles represents our body's *matter*.

According to the Qabalists, Man is composed of three essential elements:

1. *A lower element*, not the material body, since essentially matter does not exist, but a determining principle which accounts for the appearance of the material form:

NEPHESH

2. *A higher element*, the divine spark, the soul of the idealists, the spirit of the occultists.

NESHAMAH

These two elements are like oil and water of such different essence that they could never interrelate without a *third factor*, participating in their two natures and uniting them[1].

3. *This third element*, mediator between the two preceding, is what the scholars call life, the philosophers, the spirit-mind, the occultists, the soul:

RUAH

Nephesh, Neshamah and Ruah are the three *essential* principles, the ultimate factors to which analysis leads, but each of these elements is itself *composed of several parts*. These correspond more or less to what modern scholars designate as:
Body, Life and Will.

The three elements, however, are so thoroughly synthesized in *the unity of being*, that man can be schematically represented by three dots (the three elements given) enclosed within a circle:

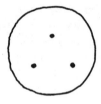

Now that we are acquainted with Qabalistic opinion regarding the constitution of Man, let us take up the two following points: From where does he come? And where is he going?

M. Franck's development of these two important points is very good indeed. Man comes from God and this is also his destination. We must therefore consider three principal phases of this evolution:

---

[1] As in chemistry the alkaline carbonates unite oil and water through the process of saponification.

1. The point of Departure
2. The point of Arrival
3. What occurs in between Departure and Arrival.

1. *Departure.* The Qabalah teaches the doctrine of Emanation. Man thus emanates from God originally in the state of pure Spirit. Made up, in the image of God, of Force and Intelligence (Chokmah and Binah), that is, of positive and negative, he is both male and female, Adam-Eve, at the outset *a single being.* Because of the fall[1] two phenomena occurred:

1. The decomposition of the single being in a series of androgynous beings, Adam-Eves.

2. The materialization and subdivision of each of these androgynous beings into two material beings of different sex, a man and a woman. This is the terrestrial state.

It must be noted, however, as the Tarot teaches us, that each man and each woman contains in him and herself an image of their primitive unity. The Brain is Adam, the Heart is Eve, and this is true for each and every one of us.

2. *Transition from Departure to Arrival.* Materialized man, subject to the passions' influence, must *freely and voluntarily* recover his primitive state; thus he must recreate his lost immortality. To accomplish this he *reincarnates* as many times as necessary in order to redeem himself through the universal force, powerful above all others: Love.

The Qabalah, like the Hindu sources of the Neo-Buddhist movement, teaches *reincarnation*, and resultantly, *pre-existence*, as M. Franck points out; but it diverges completely from the Hindu theosophical conclusions as to the means of redemption. We can do no better here than to reproduce the words of one of France's most learned occultists, *F. Ch. Barlet*:

If I may hazard a personal opinion, I will say that the Hindu doctrine seems truer to me from a *metaphysical* and abstract point of view, the Christian doctrines from a *moral*, and concrete point of view. Christianity, the Zohar, the Qabalah with their admirable symbolism leave more room for uncertainty and vagueness in the philosophical mind (for example, when they represent *the fall* as the source of *evil*, without defining either one,

[1] The limited framework of our study does not permit a deeper or more scientific analysis of these metaphysical considerations. For further detail, see *Cain*, Fabre d'Olivet.

for such a definition would give an entirely different intellectual turn to the question.)

But Indian Pantheism whether it be materialistic as in the school of the South, or idealistic as in that of the North, manages to neglect, misunderstand and even reject all sentiment, especially that of *Love* with its immense mystical and occult bearing.

One doctrine speaks only to the intelligence, the other only to the soul.

One cannot then come into complete possession of the theosophical doctrine without interpreting the symbolism of the one by the metaphysics of the other. Then and only then can the two poles, animated the one by the other, cast the light of divine splendour on the incredible richness of symbolic language, the only language capable of rendering for mankind the pulse and movement of absolute Life!

3. *Arrival.* So man must first reconstitute his primitive androgynous state in order to synthetically reproduce the original being which came from the division of the great Adam-Eve.

These reconstituted androgynous beings must in turn synthesize themselves so thoroughly as to identify with their original source: God. Thus the Qabalah and India both teach the theories of involution and evolution and the final return to *Nirvana*.

Despite my reluctance to lengthen this summary with quotations, I cannot resist citing here a most instructional passage of M. Franck's (p. 189):

Among the various degrees of existence (also called the seven tabernacles), there is one, designated by the name holy of holies, where all souls will be reunited to the supreme soul, mutually completing one another. Everything returns to unity and to perfection; everything comes together in a single thought which extends throughout the universe and fills it entirely. But the heart of this thought, the light hidden within it, can never be grasped, understood or known. Only the thought emanating from it can be taken in. Finally, in this state, creature can no longer be distinguished from creator. The same thought enlightens them; the same will enlivens them; and the soul as well as God governs the Universe. Its orders are those of God, who executes them.

To summarize, the metaphysical considerations regarding the

fall and ultimate rehabilitation are exactly reducible to laws which we can daily and experientially observe, laws that are made up of three factors:

I. Unity
II. Departure from Unity; Multiplicity
III. Return to Unity

In his Eureka, Edgar Poe applies these laws to Astronomy. Had we sufficient space, we might also apply them to Physics or experimental Chemistry; but our study is already a long one and it is time to take up the question of Qabalistic opinion concerning the Universe.

2. Teachings of the Qabalah on the Universe

We have seen that the Planets are the organs of the Universe and their interplay makes up the life of this Universe.

In man life is maintained by the bloodstream which bathes all the organs, keeps them in good repair and carries away useless elements.

In the Universe life is maintained by currents of light which bathe all the planets, diffusing to them in abundant streams the principles of generation.

But in man each of the blood cells, receiver and transmitter of life, is an actual being, constituted *in the image of* man himself. Thus the vital human current contains an infinite number of beings.

So it is with the currents of light and this is the origin of *the angels*, the *personified forces* of the Qabalah and of an entire segment of the tradition on which M. Franck has not touched at all: *the practical Qabalah*.

The practical Qabalah includes the study of these invisible beings, receivers and transmitters of the Life of the Universe, contained within the currents of light. Qabalists attempt to act upon these beings and to learn their respective powers; hence all the information concerning Astrology, Demonology and Magic which the Qabalah contains.

But in Man the vital force transmitted by the blood and its

channels is not the only one which exists. Beyond this force and governing its progress is another: the nervous force.

Nervous fluid, whether it acts independently of individual consciousness in the system of Organic Life (the Great-Sympathetic, Astral Body of Occultists) or whether it acts consciously through the exercise of the Will (brain and rachidian nerves), always plays a dominant role in the production of vital phenomena.

This nervous fluid is not, like Life, carried by particular beings (the blood cells). It has its beginning in a being situated in a mysterious quarter (the nerve cell) and its end in a centre of reception. Between the origin and the receipt of the impulse there is only a conducting channel.

And so it is, according to the Qabalah, in the Universe. Beyond, or rather within, these currents of light there exists a mysterious fluid as independent from the creator-beings of Nature as nervous energy is independent from the blood cells. This fluid emanates directly from God; moreover it is the very body of God. It is the *spirit of the Universe*.

Thus the Universe like Man appears to be constituted of:

1. *A Body*. The Astral spheres and their contents.

2. *A Life*. The currents of light bathing the spheres and containing the *Active Forces* of Nature, the Angels.

3. *A Will* which is transmitted everywhere by means of the invisible (in a material sense) fluid called by Occultists: Universal Magnetism, and by Qabalists *Aour* אור. This is the gold (*Or*) of the Alchemists, the cause of universal Attraction or *Love of the Spheres*.

Let us mention as well that, like Man, the Universe is subject to periodic involution and that ultimately it will be reintegrated in its origin: God.

To conclude this résumé on the Universe, let us show how *Barlet*, moving along other lines, arrives at the same conclusions on the subject as the Qabalah:

As an ultimate formula for the tangible world our positive sciences give:

No matter without force; no force without matter.

An incontestable formula, but an incomplete one, unless the following commentary is added:

1. The combination of what we call *Force* and *Matter* in all dimensions from what we might name *Materialized Force* (the rock, the mineral, the simply chemical body) to *Germinal Force*

or *Matter-Force* (the grain of pollen, the spermatazoon, the electrical atom), Matter and Force, although they cannot be separated, are thus seen to the extreme and opposite mathematical limits (contrary signs) of a series of actualities whose median elements are the only ones visible to us, abstract limits to be sure, but indubitable.

2. The factors in this series, that is, the individuals of nature, are never stable. *Force*, of which infinite mobility is the prime characteristic, activates, as if across a continuous current from one pole to the other, essentially inert *Matter* which exhibits a countercurrent of return. Thus, for example, an atom of phosphorus ingested by a vegetable substance from mineral phosphates may become an element in the constitution of a human cerebral cell (germinal matter) only to fall again through the process of disintegration into the inert mineral kingdom.

3. Movement, the result of this unstable equilibrium, is not chaotic or disordered. It offers a series of interlinking and harmonious phenomena which we call *Laws* and which find their synthesis in the supreme law of *Evolution*.

We are compelled to this conclusion: this harmonious synthesis of phenomena is the obvious manifestation of what we call *Will*.

Thus, according to positive science, the tangible world is the expression of a will which manifests itself through instability in equilibrium, the ever-progressing union of Force and Matter.

This is summarized by the following quaternary:

I. WILL (simple unified source)
II. FORCE (Elements of polarized will)
III. MATTER   IV. THE TANGIBLE WORLD
(Result of their dynamic equilibrium in fluctuation)[1]

3. Teachings of the Qabalah on God

Man is made in the image of the Universe, but both Man and the Universe are made in the image of God.

God in himself is unknowable for Man. This is affirmed by Qabalists and their *Ain Soph* as well as by the Hindus with

[1] F.-Ch. BARLET, *Initiation*.

their *Parabrahm*. But God can be grasped in his manifestations.

The first Divine Manifestation, whereby 'God creating the principle of Reality must needs create his own eternal immortality, is the Trinity[1].

This primary Trinity, prototype of all natural laws, absolute scientific formula as well as fundamental religious principle, is to be found in various guises in all sects and the metaphysical thinking of all peoples.

Whether it be *the Sun, the Moon and the Earth*; *Brahma, Vishnu and Shiva*; *Osiris-Isis, Horus* or *Osiris, Amen, Ptah*; *Jupiter, Juno, Vulcan*; *the Father, the Son and the Holy Spirit*; always its constitution is the same.

The Qabalah designates it by the three following names:

CHOKMAH   BINAH

KETHER

These three names make up the first trinity of the Ten *Sephiroth* or Numerations.

These ten Sephiroth are expressions of the attributes of God. In a moment we will deal with them in greater detail.

If we bear in mind that the Universe and Man are each composed essentially of a Body, a Soul or Mediator and a Spirit-Mind, we will be led to seek the source of these principles in God Himself.

Now the three elements given above, *Kether, Chokmah* and *Binah* are representations of God, but the *Spirit-Mind of God*, just as consciousness represents the whole man and yet not the whole man.

What then is the *Life of God*?

The Life of God is the ternary we first looked at, the ternary which constitutes Humanity, with its two poles, Adam and Eve.

The *Body of God* is made up of this Universe in its triple manifestation.

In short, by uniting all these elements we obtain the following definition of God:

God is *in his essence unknowable*, but *knowable in his manifestations*.

---

[1] See WRONSKI, *Apondictique Messianique*, or PAPUS, *le Tarot* where the passage from Wronski is quoted *in extenso*.

The Universe constitutes HIS BODY. *Adam-Eve* constitutes HIS SOUL. And *God himself* in his double polarization constitutes HIS SPIRIT. This is indicated by the following figure:

	-	oo	+	
Spirit of God	Binah	KETHER	Chokmah	*Divine World* / *The Father* / BRAHMA
Soul of God	Eve	ADAM-EVE Humanity	Adam	*Human World* / *The Son* / VISHNU
Body of God	Nature as Cause	THE UNIVERSE (1)	Nature as Effect	*Natural World* / *The Holy Spirit* / SHIVA

These three ternaries, fused into Unity, form the *Ten Sephiroth*.

Or rather, they are the image of the Ten Sephiroth, *which represent the development of the three first principles of Divinity in all its attributes*.

Thus, God, Man and the Universe are each in the final analysis made up of *three elements*; but in the development of all their attributes, they are each composed of Ten factors, or of One ternary with its Septenary development $(3 + 7 = 10)$.

Thus the Ten Sephiroth of the Qabalah can be taken in several acceptations:

1. They can be considered as representing God, Man and the Universe, that is, the Spirit, Soul and Body of God.

2. They can be considered as expressing the development of

---

[1] This figure is taken from *The Tarot of the Bohemians* by PAPUS, where it is accompanied by supplementary explanation.

any one of these three great principles.

It is the confusion among these various acceptations which is at the origin of the apparent obscurities and so-called contradictions of Qabalists in regard to the Sephiroth. However, it calls for little attention to see through this confusion to the truth.

Numerous details regarding the Sephiroth are to be found in M. Franck's book (Ch. III) and especially in the remarkable Qabalistic work of Stanislas de Guaita, published in No. 6 of *Initiation* (pp. 210-217). Lack of space obliges us to refer the reader to these important sources.

It must not be thought, however, that the concept of a ternary developing through a septenary is particular to the Qabalah. The same idea grew up in ancient India, a significant proof of the antiquity of the Qabalistic tradition.

*
* *

In order to study the Hindu Sephiroth, one must not hold solely to the teachings of recent years given out by the Theosophical Society. These teachings are in fact almost always lacking in any over-all method, and although they are occasionally quite brilliant in point of detail, they are most vague when attempting to present a solid synthesis. Authors who attempted to introduce a certain method into theosophical doctrine, Soubba-Rao, Sinnet and Dr Hartmann, have been able only to take up very general, albeit interesting, questions, and their works, along with those of Mme H.P. Blavatsky, do not furnish sufficient data for the establishment of the relationships between the Qabalistic Sephiroth and the Hindu Doctrines.

In our opinion, the best work on occult Theogony in India was published in Germany around 1840[1] by Dr Jean Malfatti de Montereggio. This author succeeded in isolating the mystic Organon of the ancient Indians, and, in so doing, obtaining the key to Pythagorism and the Qabalah itself. Thus he manages to arrive at a veritable synthesis, a marriage of Science and Faith, which he designates under the name of MATHESIS.

---

[1] The date of this work accounts for the orthogrophy of the Hindu names used by the author. This orthography has since changed.

According to this author then, this is the constitution of the divine decennary (p. 18):

> The first act (yet self-contained) of revelation accomplished by Brahma was that of the Trimurti, the metaphysical trinity of divine forces of creation (leading to the creative act), of preservation and of destruction (that is, change), which has been personified under the names of Brahma, Vishnu and Shiva, regarded as having a mystic interior union (e circulo triadicus Deau egreditur).
>
> This first divine Trimurti then passed into an exterior revelation, that of the seven pre-creative powers, or that of the first metaphysical and septuple development personified by the allegories Maya, Aum, Harangherbeha, Purusha, Pradiapata, Prakriti and Prana.

Each of these principles is analysed in its acceptations and relationships with Pythagorian numbers. In addition the author examines and analyses ten symbolic Indian statues representing each of these principles. The antiquity of these symbols is proof enough of the antiquity of the tradition itself.

For the time being we can only outline the relationships of the Hindu and Qabalistic Sephiroth with numbers. Perhaps before long we will embark upon a special study devoted to so important a subject.

An interesting comparison could be made between the alphabetic trinity of the Sepher Yetzirah EmeS במש and the Hindu alphabetic trinity AUM. But these subjects require too great a development for our limited space.

QABALISTIC SEPHIROTH	NUMBERS	HINDU SEPHIROTH
Kether	1	Brahima
Chokmah . . .	2	Vishnu
Binah	3	Shiva
Chesed	4	Maya
Geburah . . .	5	Aum
Tiphereth . . .	6	Harangherbeha
Hod	7	Purusha
Netzach	8	Pradiapata
Yesod	9	Prakriti
Malkuth . . .	10	Prana

One final consideration can be made, drawn from the definition of God given above, a definition corroborated by the teachings of the Tarot, which is in fact the Egyptian Qabalah.

Materialistic philosophy studies the body of God or Universe and unknowingly worships the lower manifestation of the divinity in the Cosmos: Destiny.

Materialism attributes the primitive grouping of atoms to Chance, thus proclaiming, in atheistic terms, a creative principle.

Pantheistic philosophy studies the Life of God or the collective being which the Qabalah calls Adam-Eve[1] (יהוה). Thus we have humanity worshipping itself in one of its constituent members.

Theists and Religions study above all the Spirit of God. Hence their many subtle discussions on the three persons and their manifestations.

But the Qabalah occupies a position above each of these philosophical or religious beliefs. It synthesizes Materialism, Pantheism and Theism into a whole, analysing its parts, but without being able to define the totality other than through the mysterious formula of Wronski:

X.

III

INFLUENCE OF THE QABALAH ON PHILOSOPHY

As might be expected, this section of M. Franck's book is quite remarkable. The author's profound erudition could not fail to furnish him with valuable sources and instructional comparisons regarding the influence of the Qabalah on later philosophical systems.

The doctrine of Plato is the first to be taken up in this regard. After discussing certain similarities, M. Franck concludes that the Qabalah could not possibly have been created by the disciples of Plato. But might not the reverse be true?

If, as we have said about the antiquity of the tradition, the

---

[1] In this regard, see the work of Stanislas de Guaita in *le Lotus* and Louis Lucas, *Chimie nouvelle*, introduction.

Qabalah is only a Hebrew translation of traditional truths taught in all temples and especially those of Egypt, is it so unthinkable that Plato might have drawn inspiration, not from the Jewish Qabalah itself, but from the primordial philosophy in which the Qabalah had its origins?

What after all did all those Greek philosophers do in Egypt? And what did they learn from Initiation into the mysteries of Isis? This is a point which academic criticism ought to clarify.

Convinced that the Qabalah dates from the beginning of the Christian era, M. Franck compares the tradition with *the neo-platonic philosophy of Alexandria* and concludes that these are sister doctrines emanating from the same origin.

The study of *the doctrine of Philo* and its comparison with the Qabalah does not indicate that this doctrine was the origin of the tradition (Ch. III).

Gnosticism, analysed in the following chapter, offers remarkable similarities with the Qabalah, but also cannot be taken as its origin.

For M. Franck it is *the religion of the Persians* which turns out to be the long-looked-for *rara avis*, point of departure for the Qabalistic doctrine.

To look through Chapter IX of a book all too little known by our scholars, *la Mission des Juifs* by Saint-Yves d'Alveydre, is sufficient to gain a summary but thorough understanding of the application of esoteric tradition in various ancient cults, including that of Zoroaster. But these historical points are not likely to find acceptance in the universities before the next twenty years; thus we must patiently await this time.

We have already spoken of the opinion of contemporary occultists on the origins of the Qabalah. Need we then repeat ourselves in this regard?

Let us simply recall the influence of the esoteric tradition on Orpheus, Pythagorus, Plato, Aristotle and the entire body of Greek philosophy on the one hand, and on the other, its shaping effect on Moses, Ezekiel and the Hebrew prophets, not to mention the school of Alexandria, the gnostic sects and the esoteric Christianity disclosed in the *Apocalypse* of Saint John. Having reminded our readers of these connections, let us quickly say a few words on the influence of the tradition upon modern philosophy.

The Alchemists, the Rosicrucians and the Templars are too well-known as Qabalists to be spoken of from any other point of view. It is sufficient in this regard to point out the great philosophical reform produced by the *Ars Magna* of Raymond Lully.

Spinoza studied the Qabalah extensively and his system reflects this study to the highest degree, as M. Franck has so well seen.

A less well-known point of historical fact is that Leibniz was initiated into the esoteric tradition by Mercurius Van Helmont, son of the celebrated occultist, and himself a remarkable scholar. The originator of Monadology was also closely connected with the Rosicrucian movement.

German philosophy shares many common elements with Occult Science, a fact to which nearly all critics testify.

And let us conclude by mentioning Freemasonry which exhibits numerous Qabalistic factors.

*
* *

CONCLUSION

In analysing the remarkable and henceforth indispensable work of M. Franck, we have attempted to summarize the opinions of contemporary Qabalists touching these important questions.

Our own opinions do not differ from those of M. Franck except in regard to the origin of the tradition. Contemporary scholars tend to place the beginnings of all branches of Occult Science at the beginning of the second century of our era. Our author is of this persuasion as regards the Qabalah; another eminent scholar, M. Berthelot, dates the origins of alchemy from about the same time[1]. These opinions come from the difficulty critics meet with in consulting the true sources of Occultism. A symbol is not considered as valuable a piece of evidence as a manuscript; but let us be patient, for before long one of the most interesting fields of Science, Archaeology, will furnish serious researchers with consequential and creditable information in this area.

Whatever one may say, there is a need for our scholars to investigate Occultism. Their study is generally not entirely free from prejudice and certain settled opinions, but it also

[1] BERTHELOT, *Des Origines de l'alchimie*, 1886.

demonstrates several precious qualities: a solid erudition and love of method.

It is disappointing for conscientious researchers to note the strange ignorance of the exact sciences manifested by many partisans of the Occult. Such does not apply, however, to contemporary Qabalists of the stature of Stanislas de Guaita, Joséphin Péladan and Albert Jhouney. Occult Science is actually nothing more than the synthetical, metaphysical extension of the positive sciences, and cannot exist without their support.

The re-publication of M. Franck's book is a significant event in the revelation of the doctrines which are dear to all of us, and we can only give the author our deepest thanks for the courage and patience he has demonstrated in the study of such arduous material, while advising our readers to reserve a place in their libraries for The Qabalah of Ad. Franck, one of the fundamental volumes of Occult Science.

LETTER FROM M. AD. FRANCK, OF THE INSTITUTE

To Monsieur Papus, director of *Initiation*.

Sir,

I am most grateful to you for the way in which you have reviewed my old book on the Qabalah. I was all the more sensitive to your words of praise for the profound learnedness and deep love of the subject to which they testify.

But what especially pleased me about your article was not only the personal place you assigned me but the manner in which you attach my modest volume to an entire body of science founded on symbolism and the esoteric method. Reading you, I could not help but think of Louis XIV maintaining at Versailles the modest hunting retreat of his father and surrounding it with an immense palace.
palace.

Although my mind, which you qualify as academic, but which simply desires to remain faithful to the rules of criticism, cannot always accord itself to your magnificent development of the subject, I find it most agreeable that against the positivism and evolutionism of our time there has formed and continues to form a vast gnosis in the heart of which are united, along with the fundamental ideas of Jewish and Christian esoterism, Buddhism, the philosophy of Alexandria and the metaphysical pantheism of several modern schools.

Such a reaction is necessary to combat the decadence and dessication of thought of which we are both victims and witnesses. *La Mission des Juifs*, from which you quote so often in your Review, is one of the leading elements in this movement.

I would recommend only, as a product of my long experience, that you do not go too far. Traditions and symbols ought not to be neglected as they so often are by philosophers; but genius, the spontaneous life of consciousness and reason must also be counted for something. Without this the whole history of humanity is nothing more than a sterile book of records.

In fullest sincerity,

AD. FRANCK

*

*   *

We have given an exposition of the Qabalistic doctrine without at all entering into detail.

Thus we give *in extenso* the following study in order to show that in the very midst of the 19th century there still exist eminent Qabalists and that their work is consistent with the best principles of esoteric tradition.

CHAPTER VI

THE SOUL ACCORDING TO THE QABALAH
(See Fig. on p. 156)

LECTURE DELIVERED TO THE PSYCHOLOGICAL SOCIETY OF MUNICH AT THE SESSION OF 5 MARCH 1887, BY C. DE LEININGEN

1. — The soul during life.

Among all the questions which occupy philosophy as an exact science, that of our own essence, the immortality and spirituality of our interior I, has never ceased to preoccupy humanity. In all times and everywhere systems and doctrines on this subject have displaced one another in rapid succession, varied and contradictory, and the word Soul has been used to designate forms of existence or nuances of being of a most divers nature. Of all these mutually antagonistic doctrines, without contradiction the most ancient – the transcendental philosophy of the Jews – the Qabalah[1] is also perhaps the closest to the truth. Transmitted orally – as its name implies – it harkens back to the very cradle of the human race, and thus it is perhaps partially at least a product of the as yet

[1] We have adopted this spelling as the most authentic solution among the dubious and often quite fantastic forms which have been proposed, such as Cabbala, Cabala, Kabbalah, etc. It is a Hebrew word composed of the consonants *q, b, 1* and *h*. Now the letter which in Greek names corresponds to *k* and in Latin names to *c*, seems in this Hebrew word to be the letter *q*. This same spelling was also recently introduced into English literature by Mathers in his *Kabbala Denudata*, published by George Redway in London.

untroubled mind, that penetrating spirit in quest of truth which, according to tradition, man possessed in his original state.

If we take human nature to be a complex whole, we find, according to the Qabalah, three distinct parts: the body, the soul and the mind. They are mutually distinguishable as are the concrete, the particular and the general, so that one is a reflection of the other, and each one partakes in itself of this triple distinction. Next, a new analysis of these three basic parts reveals still other nuances which extend successively one upon the other from the deepest, most concrete, most material parts of the external body to the highest, most general, most spiritual.

The first fundamental part, the body, with the vital principle and which includes the first three subdivisions, bears in the Qabalah the name of *Nephesh*. The second, the soul, seat of the will and which constitutes properly speaking the human personality, embodying the three following subdivisions, is called *Ruah*. The third, the mind with its three powers, receives in the Qabalah the name of *Neshamah*.

As we have already noted, these three fundamental parts of man are not entirely distinct and separate. On the contrary, one must try to imagine them as passing gradually from one to the next like the colours of the spectrum, which although successive, cannot be entirely isolated, blending as they do from one into the other. Upward from the body, that is the lowest power of Nephesh, passing through the soul – Ruah – to the highest degree of spirit – Neshamah – one traverses all gradations, just as one passes from darkness to light through an area of gradually lightening shadow. Or in reverse, from the most elevated parts of the spirit to the most material of physical elements, one passes through all the gradations of illumination, as one might move from light into darkness through an area of lowering dusk. And above all, thanks to the interior unity, this fusion of the parts one into the other, the number Nine loses itself in the One, producing man, a corporeal spirit, uniting within himself the two worlds.

Attempting to represent this doctrine in schematic form, we obtain the figure given on page 156.

The circle, *a a a*, designates Nephesh, and 1, 2, 3 are its subdivisions, with 1 corresponding to the body, the lowest, most material part of man. Ruah (the soul) is *b b b* and 4, 5, 6

are its powers. Lastly, *c c c* is Neshamah (the spirit-mind) with
the degrees of its essence, 7, 8, 9. As to the exterior circle 10,
this represents the totality of the living human being.

Let us now consider more closely the various fundamental
parts, beginning with the lowest degree, NEPHESH. This is
the principle of life or form of concrete existence. It constitutes
the exterior part of the living man. The principal dominant
factor is a passive sensitivity to the exterior world. On the
other hand, ideal activity is the least present here. Nephesh is
in direct contact with the concrete beings which are exterior to
him and it is only by their influence that he produces a vital
manifestation. But at the same time he works in the exterior
world, thanks to his own creative power, calling forth new
vital forces from his concrete existence, thus ceaselessly giving
back what he receives. This concrete degree constitutes a
perfect whole, complete in itself and in which the human
being finds his exact exterior representation. Considered as a
perfect whole in itself, this concrete life includes three degrees
related as are the concrete, the particular and the general, or
yet again, created matter, creating force and ultimate
principle, and which are at the same time the organs in which
and by which the interior, spiritual element operates and
manifests itself externally. These three degrees then are each
more elevated and interiorized and each of them embodies
within itself particular nuances. The three powers of Nephesh
under examination are so disposed and so act as will be seen
in a moment when we take up the three subdivisions of Ruah.

This second element of the human being, RUAH (soul) is
not as sensitive to the exterior world as Nephesh. Passivity and
activity exist here in equal proportion. It consists of an
interior, ideal being in which all that the concrete corporeal
life manifest externally is to be found in a state of virtuality.
This second human element alternates between passivity and
activity or interiority and exteriority. In its objective
multiplicity, it appears clearly neither as something real,
passive and exterior, nor something interior, intellectual and
active, but rather as something continually changing, which
from within to without manifests itself as active although
passive, or as giving although of a receiving nature. Thus
intuition and conception do not coincide exactly in the soul,
though they cannot be distinctly separated, blending as they
do into each other.

The mode of existence of each being depends exclusively on the more or less elevated degree of his cohesion with nature, and on the greater or lesser passivity resulting therefrom. The perceptive faculties of a being grow in proportion to his activity. The more he is active, the higher he is and the more it is possible for him to look into the intimate depths of his being.

This Ruah, composed of forces which are the basis of objective material being, possesses the property of distinguishing itself from all the other parts as a special entity, of disposing of itself and manifesting itself externally through free and voluntary action. This 'soul' which represents equally the throne and the organ of mind is an image of the whole man, as we have said. Like Nephesh, it is made up of three dynamic degrees which are inter-related in the fashion of the Concrete, the Particular and the General, or of activated matter, activating force and central principle. The consequence of this is an affinity not only between the concrete in Ruah, being its lowest and most exterior degree (circle 4 of the diagram), and the general in Nephesh, the highest sphere of the latter (circle 3), but also between the general in Ruah (circle 6) and the concrete in the spirit (circle 7).

While Ruah like Nephesh contains three dynamic degrees, these have their three correspondents in the exterior world, as can be seen more clearly from a comparison of the Macrocosm and the Microcosm. Each particular form of existence in man lives its own life in the sphere which corresponds to it, and with which it is in a continual state of exchange, giving and receiving, by means of its special senses and individual interior organs.

In addition, this Ruah, by reason of its concrete part, needs to communicate with the concrete which is below, just as its general part gives it a tendency toward the general parts which are above. Nephesh could not be attached to Ruah if there were no affinity between them, no more so than could Ruah be joined to Nephesh and Neshamah if there were no kinship among them.

Thus on the one hand the soul draws the fulness of its own objective reality from the concreteness which precedes it, and on the other, from the corresponding generality, its pure interiority, the Ideality which forms itself in its own independent activity. Ruah is thus the link between the

General or Spiritual and the Concrete or Material, uniting in man the intelligible, internal world with the external, real world. It is at the same time the support and the seat of human personality.

In this way the soul may be said to be in a double relation to its three objects, that is: 1. to the concrete which is below it. 2. to the particular which corresponds to its nature and which is outside it. 3. to the general which is above it. In the soul there occurs, moving in two contrary directions, a circulation of three intermingling currents, for: 1. it is enlivened by Nephesh which is below it and in its turn acts upon this latter by inspiring it; 2. it behaves both actively and passively with the exterior corresponding to its nature, that is, the Particular; 3. and this influence which it transforms having once received it either from below or outside then gives it the power to rise sufficiently in order to stimulate Neshamah in the upper regions. Through this active operation, the upper faculties thus excited produce a vital influence of a higher, more spiritual nature, which the soul, re-assuming its passive role, then receives and passes on to zones outside or below it.

Thus although Ruah has a particular form of existence and its own individual consistency, it is nonetheless true that the first impulse toward its vital activity comes from the excitation of the concrete body which is inferior to it. And as the body, through an exchange of actions and reactions with the soul, is penetrated by the soul, while the latter becomes a sort of participant in the life of the body, so the soul, through its union with the Spirit, is filled by the spirit and finds there its source of inspiration.

The third fundamental part of the human being, *neshamah*, can be designated by the word Spirit, in the sense with which it is used in the New Testament. In it the passive sensitivity to external nature is no longer present; activity dominates receptivity. The spirit lives of its own life and only for the General or spiritual world with which it maintains a constant relation. However, like Ruah, Neshamah with its ideal nature has need of more than the absolute General or divine Infinite; for its nature is also real, and this calls for some relationship with the particular and the concrete which exist below it. Thus it is attracted to the two.

The Spirit also possesses a double relation to its triple object: down, out and up; and there occurs within it, as has been described for Ruah, a triply intertwined current running in opposite directions. Neshamah is a purely interior being, but passive and active at the same time, and represented in the exterior images of Nephesh with its vital principal and its body, and of Ruah with its power. The quantitative elements of Nephesh and the qualitative elements of Ruah come from the spirit – Neshamah – purely interior and ideal.

Now just as Nephesh and Ruah contain three different degrees of existence or spiritualization in potential, in such a way that each is a diminishing image of the entire human being (see the schema), so the Qabalah distinguishes three such degrees in Nephesh.

What was said at the beginning, that the different forms of existence of the human constitution are not distinct, isolated, separate beings, but rather inseparable gradations, is particularly applicable to this higher element; for here everything becomes more and more spiritual, tending more and more toward unity.

Of the three upper forms of man's existence, taking Neshamah in its widest acceptation, the lowest might be called Neshamah proper. Here there is still some kinship with the higher elements of Ruah, consisting of an interior, active consciousness of the quantitative and qualitative levels below. The Qabalah names the second power of Neshamah, the eighth element to man, *Chayah*. Its essence consists of the consciousness of the higher, interior, intelligible force which serves as a basis for the objective manifested being and which, consequently, cannot be known by Ruah or Nephesh, nor even by Neshamah proper. The third power of Neshamah, the ninth element in man, is *Yechidad* (Unity in itself). Its essence consists of the consciousness of absolute fundamental Unity in all its various manifestations, of the absolute primary One.

Now, the relationship indicated from the outset, among Concrete, Particular and General, linking Nephesh, Ruah and Neshamah in such a way that each offers an image of the whole, can be used to summarize our entire exposé. The first degree of Nephesh, the body, the concrete in the concrete. The second degree, the particular in the concrete. The third, the general in the concrete.

And so for Ruah. First power, the concrete in the particular. Second, the particular in the particular. Third, the general in the particular.

Likewise for Neshamah. First degree: the concrete in the general. Second degree (Chayah), the particular in the general. Third (Yechidad), the general in the general.

It is thus that the divers activities and qualities of each of the being's elements are manifested.

The soul (Ruah) of course has its own existence, but it is incapable of independent development without the participation of corporeal life (Nephesh), and the same is true vis-à-vis Neshamah. In addition Ruah exists in double relationship to Nephesh. Under its influence, it is at the same time turned toward the outside where it exercises a free reaction in such a way that concrete corporeal life participates in the development of the soul. The same can be said of the spirit in connection with the soul, or of Neshamah in relation to Ruah. Through Ruah, Neshamah in fact maintains a double relationship to Nephesh. However, Neshamah finds within its own constitution the source of its action, whereas the actions of Ruah and Nephesh are only free and living emanations of Neshamah.

In the same way, Neshamah exists to a certain extent in double relation to the Divinity; for the vital activity of Neshamah is in itself a stimulus to Divinity for the preservation of the former, procuring it the influence necessary to its subsistence. Thus the spirit or Neshamah, and through it Ruah and Nephesh, all draw involuntarily from the eternal divine source, the work of their life perpetually radiating upward; while Divinity constantly penetrates Neshamah, giving it (and through it to Ruah and Nephesh as well) life and duration.

Now according to the doctrine of the Qabalah, instead of living in Divinity and constantly receiving from it the spirituality he needs, man has sunk more and more into love of himself and of the world of sin, dating from the moment of 'his fall' (see Genesis 3: 6-20) when he left his eternal centre to dwell on the periphery. This fall and the ever-growing estrangement from Divinity which resulted from it have brought about a decline in the powers of human nature and in humanity as a whole. The divine spark has withdrawn further and further from man, and Neshamah has lost its intimate

union with God. Likewise Ruah has withdrawn from
Neshamah and Nephesh has lost its intimate union with
Ruah. Due to this general decline and to the weakening of the
links among the elements, the lowest part of man, Nephesh,
which was originally a luminous ether-body, has become the
material body as we know it. Thus man has become subjected
to the dissolution of the three principal parts of his
constitution.

This is treated in the doctrine of the Qabalah concerning
the soul *during and after death.*

2. – The soul in death

According to the Qabalah, the death of man is only the
passage from one form of existence to a new one. Man's
ultimate vocation is to return to the bosom of God, but this
reunion is not possible for him in his present state, due to the
gross materiality of his body. This state, as well as the
spiritual side of man, must undergo a necessary purification in
order to obtain the degree of spirituality required for the new
life.

The Qabalah distinguishes two causes which bring about
death. The first occurs when the Divinity gradually
diminishes or abruptly suppresses its continual influence upon
Neshamah and Ruah, so that Nephesh loses the force which
animates the material body, and this body dies. In the
language of the Zohar, we might call this first type of death
'the death from on high, or from within to without.'

In contrast with this, the second cause of death might be
called 'the death from below, or from without to within.' Here
the body, the lower and exterior form of existence, entering a
state of disorganization through the appearance of some
disorder or injury, loses the dual property of receiving
necessary influence from above and of stimulating Nephesh,
Ruah and Neshamah sufficiently to call them down to it.

Moreover, as each of the three degrees of man's existence
has its particular seat in the human body and its sphere of
activity corresponding to the degree of its spirituality, and as
all three are linked to the body at different periods of life[1], it is

---

[1] This is not the place to explain how the spiritual principles are united to
matter through the act of generation, a subject which the Qabalah treats
explictly.

also at different moments, and in reverse order, that they abandon the cadaver. Thus the period of death is much longer than is commonly held.

Neshamah, whose seat is in the brain and who, in its quality of principle of spiritual and higher life, is the last to unite with the body – this union beginning at the age of puberty – Neshamah is the first to leave the body; generally before the moment which we commonly call 'Death'. In its *Mercavah*[1] it leaves only a kind of after-glow; for as it is said in the Esarah Maimoroth, human personality can subsist without the effective presence of Meshamah.

Before the moment of apparent death, man's essence is heightened by a more elevated Ruah which allows him to see what in life remained hidden from his eyes; often his vision cuts through space, and he can distinguish his defunct relatives and friends. Upon the arrival of the critical moment, Ruah spreads through all the members of the body and takes its leave from them; the result is a shock, the *agony*, often quite painful. Then all the spiritual essence of man withdraws into the heart where it takes shelter from the Masikim (evil spirits) who hurl themselves on the cadaver, as a hunted dove may take refuge in its nest.

The separation of Ruah from the body is very painful because Ruah or the living soul floats, as the Ez-ga-Chaiim says, between the high and infinite spiritual regions (Neshamah) and the lower corporeal concrete levels (Nephesh), leaning sometimes more towards one, sometimes more towards the other. For Ruah is the organ of will and thus constitutes the human personality. Its seat is in the heart, and the heart then can be taken to be the root of life. It is מלך (Melekh, King), the central point, the connecting link between the brain and the liver[2]. And since it is with this organ that vital activity is manifested at the outset, so it is here that such activity finishes. Thus at the moment of death Ruah escapes, and according to the teachings of the Talmud, leaves the heart by the mouth in the final breath.

[1] Mercavah literally means *chariot*; thus it is the organ, the instrument, the vehicle through which Neshamah acts.

[2] The Qabalah says: 'In the word מלך(King) the heart is as the central point between the brain and the liver.' We must interpret this by the mystic sense of letters: the brain, מ is represented by the first letter of the word מלך; the liver כבד, by its final letter, and the heart לב, by ל, which is in the middle. The letter כ at the end of a word gives ך).

The Talmud distinguishes nine hundred kinds of different deaths, all of which are more or less painful. The quietest of all is the one which is referred to as 'the kiss'; the most painful is the one in which the moribund experience a sensation like that of having a thick rope of hair torn from the throat.

When Ruah is gone, as far as we can see the man is dead. Nephesh, however, is still present within him. This is the corporeal life of the Concrete, the soul of elementary life, and has its seat in the liver. Nephesh, the lowest spiritual power, possesses a huge affinity, and therefore much attraction, for the body. This is the principle which is the last to take its leave, just as it was the first to be united to the flesh. Immediately upon the departure of Ruah, however, the Masikim take possession of the cadaver (according to Loriah, they accumulate above the dead body to a height of some 45 feet). This invasion together with the decomposition of the body soon obliges Nephesh to withdraw. Yet it remains quite a long time near the corpse, mourning its loss. Ordinarily it is only when total putrefaction has occurred that Nephesh rises to a plane above the terrestrial sphere.

This consecutive disintegration of man occurring at death is not, however, a complete separation. For what has at one time been a single whole can never be entirely disunited. Some relation always remains among the component parts. Thus a certain connection lingers between Nephesh and its body, even in a state of putrefaction. After the material, external container has disappeared with its vital forces, there yet remains something of the spiritual principle of Nephesh, something imperishable which descends even into the tomb, into the very bones, as the Zohar says. This is what the Qabalah calls *the breath of the bones* or *the spirit of the bones*. This intimate, imperishable principle of the material body, which completely preserves its form and aspect, constitutes the *Habal de Garmin*, which we can translate approximately as 'the body of the resurrection' (the luminous astral body).

After the various component parts of man have been separated by death, each goes to the sphere to which it is attracted by its nature and constitution, accompanied by similar beings which surrounded the death-bed. As in the entire Universe everything is in everything, being born, living and perishing according to a single law, as the smallest element is a reproduction of the largest, as the same principles govern equally all creatures from the lowest to the most spiritual, the highest of powers, so the entire Universe, which the Qabalah names ATZILUTH, containing all the degrees from the grossest matter to the highest spirituality – to the One – this Universe is divided into three worlds: ASSIAH, YETZIRAH and BRIAH, corresponding to the three fundamental divisions in man: *Nephesh, Ruah* and *Neshamah.*

Assiah is the world in which we live. However, what we perceive of this world with our bodily eyes is only the lowest sphere, the most material plane, just as we perceive with our sense organs only the lowest, most material principles of man: his body. The figure given earlier[1] is thus a diagram of the Universe as well as of man, for according to the doctrine of the Qabalah, the Micrososm is absolutely analagous to the Macrocosm; man is the image of God manifested in the Universe. Thus the circle *a a a* represents the world *Assiah* and 1,2,3 are the spheres corresponding to those of Nephesh.

b b b represents the world *Yetzirah*, analogous to Ruah, and 4,5,6 are its powers.

Lastly the circle *c c c* stands for the world *Briah* whose spheres 7,8,9, like those of Neshamah, attain the highest power of spiritual life.

The enveloping circle, 10, is the image of the All of *Atziluth*, as it was also the image of the totality of human nature.

The three worlds which, according to their nature and the degree of their spirituality, correspond to the three constituent principles of man represent the various dwelling-places of these principles. The body, as the most material form of man's existence, remains in the lower spheres of the world Assiah, in the tomb. The spirit of the bones alone remains buried with it, constituting, as we have said, the Habal de Garmin. In the tomb this spirit exists in an obscure state of lethargy which, for the just, is a gentle sleep; several passages in the books of Daniel, the Psalms and Isaiah allude to this. And since the Habal de Garmin retains a vague sensory capacity in the tomb, the rest of those who sleep this last sleep can be disturbed in all sorts of ways. This is why it was prohibited for Jews to bury persons near each other who during their lifetime had been enemies, or to inter a holy man near a wrongdoer. On the contrary, care was taken to bury together those persons between whom there had been affection, for this

[1] See page 156.

attachment was known to continue in death. The greatest disturbance for those who sleep in the tomb is evocation; for although Nephesh has quitted the sepulchre, the 'spirit of the bones' still remains attached to the cadaver and can be called forth; and this evocation can also reach Nephesh, Ruah and Neshamah. These have already taken up residence in their distinct abodes, but they remain united to one another in certain respects, and what one feels the others experience also. This is why Holy Scripture (5 Moses, 18:11) prohibited the evocation of the dead[1].

As our material senses can perceive only the lowest circle, the most inferior sphere of the world Assiah, so there is only the body of man which is visible to our material eyes, that which even after death remains in the domain of the sensory world. The upper spheres of Assiah are not perceptible for us, and likewise the Habal de Garmin escapes our perception. Thus the Zohar says: 'If such were permitted our eyes, at the coming of Sabbath or at the new moon or on feast days, we could see the Diuknim (spectres) in the night, standing up from their tombs to praise and glorify the Lord.'

The upper spheres of the world Assiah are the abode of Nephesh. The *Ez-ha-Chaiim* depicts this abode as the lower *Gan-Eden*[2], 'which in the world Assiah extends toward the south in the Holy country, above the Equator.'

The second principle of man, Ruah, finds an abode appropriate to its degree of spirituality in the world Yetzirah. And as Ruah, constituting the individual personality of man, is the support and the seat of the Will, residence of man's productive and creative forces, so the world Yetzirah, as its Hebrew name indicates, is the *mundus formationis*, the world of formation.

Finally Neshamah corresponds to the world Briah which the Zohar names 'the world of the divine throne', containing the highest degree of spirituality.

As Nephesh, Ruah and Neshamah are not entirely distinct forms of existence, but rather grow progressively out of one another while taking on greater and greater spirituality, so the

---

[1] And this, among other reasons, is why the practice of spiritism is to be condemned. (N. du Tr.)

[2] Gan-Eden means garden of delights. In the Talmud and in the Qabalah, according to the *Song of Songs* 4:13, it is also called *Pardes*, or garden of pleasure; whence our word Paradise.

spheres of the various worlds are linked each one to the next, rising from the deepest, most material world of Assiah, perceptible to our senses, to the most elevated, immaterial powers of the world Briah. From this it can clearly be seen that although Nephesh, Ruah and Neshamah each take up residence in the world which befits them, they nonetheless remain united in a single whole. It is particularly through the *Zelem* that these intimate relations of the separate parts are made possible.

By the name 'Zelem' the Qabalah means the figure, the envelope, the garment in which the divers principles of man subsist, through which they operate. Nephesh, Ruah and Neshamah, even after death has destroyed their outer corporeal shell, still conserve a certain form which corresponds to the bodily appearance of the original man. This form, by means of which each part continues and operates within its world, is only possible through the Zelem. Thus it is said in Psalm 39:7: 'They are like the Zelem (phantom) ...'

According to Loriah, the Zelem, by analogy with all of human nature, is divided into three parts: an interior spiritual light and two *Makifim* or enveloping lights. Each Zelem and its Makifim correspond in their nature to the character and degree of spirituality of the principles to which they belong. It is only through their Zelem that it is possible for Nephesh, Ruah and Neshamah to manifest themselves externally. It is upon them that rests all the corporeal existence of man on earth, for the entire flow from on high acting on the sentiments and internal senses of man is accomplished through the intermediary of the Zelem, susceptible moreover to weakening or reinforcement.

The process of death takes place uniquely in the divers Zelem, for Nephesh, Ruah and Neshamah are not modified by it. Thus the Qabalah teaches that thirty days prior to the death of a man, the Makifim withdraw first from Neshamah, then successively from Ruah and Nephesh. We must take this to mean that they cease to operate in any effective way. However, at the very instant when Ruah flies away, they clutch at the process of life, as the *Mishnath Chasidim* says, 'to taste the taste of death.' The Zelem must be regarded as purely magical beings; this is why the Zelem even of Nephesh cannot act directly in the world of our external sensory perception.

What presents itself to us in the apparition of the dead is either their Habal de Garmin or the subtle serial or etheric matter of the world Assiah with which the Zelem of Nephesh clothe themselves in order to become perceptible to our bodily senses.

This applies to any kind of apparition, whether it be that of an angel or the soul of a dead person or a lower being. It is not the Zelem itself which we can see and perceive with our eyes; it is only an image, made of the subtle 'vapour' of our exterior world, capable of dissolving in an instant.

Just as the life of man on earth offers so much variety, so their fate in other worlds is varied. For the more infractions of divine law one has committed here below, the more punishments and purifications one must undergo in the other world.

On this subject the Zohar says:

'The beauty of the Zelem of the pious man depends on the good works he has accomplished here below.' And further: 'Sin tarnishes the Zelem of Nephesh.' Lorish has this to say: 'In a pious man these Zelem are pure and clear; in the sinner they are troubled and dark.' This is why each world has for each of the principles of man its *Gan-Eden* (Paradise), its *Nahar Dinur* (river of fire for the purification of the soul) and its *Gei-Hinam*[1] (place of torture for punishment). Whence we have the Christian doctrine of heaven, purgatory and hell.

Our intention here is not to expose the theory of the Qabalah on the state of the soul after death, notably in regard to the punishments to which it is submitted. The reader will find an exposition of the utmost clarity in the celebrated work of Dante, *la Divine Comédie*.

---

[1] Gei-Hinam was actually the name of a place situated near Jerusalem where children were once sacrificed to the pagan god Moloch. The Qabalah uses this name to signify *place of damnation*.

Part Three

The Texts

All the 'scientific, philosophical and religious principles of the Qabalah are drawn from two fundamental books, *The Zohar* and *The Sepher Yetzirah*.

The first of these books is extremely long. It has been translated into Latin in the *Qabalah denudata* and into English in the *Qabalah Unveiled* of M.A. Matthers.

We give here a translation of the second of these works as we published it in 1887, with commentaries and notes. In several places, the reader will find repetitions of what we have touched on in the preceding pages; but these very repetitions will show the reader which points merit his special attention.

This translation of the *Sepher Yetzirah* is followed by that of two Qabalistic works of a much later composition: *The 32 paths of wisdom* and *The 50 gates of understanding*. The character of these works is shown in the remarks which introduce them.

Foreword to the Sepher Yetzirah

At the basis of all religions and all philosophies, one finds an obscure doctrine, known only to a few and whose origin, despite the work of scholars, escapes all analysis. This doctrine is designated under different names according to the religion which has preserved its keys; but even a superficial study is sufficient to identify it as the same, whatever name it bears. At first criticism rejoices to find the origins of the doctrine in the Apocalypse, that summary of Christian esoterism; but soon it stops short, for behind the Vision of

Saint John there appears that of Daniel, and the esoteric tradition of the two religions, Christian and Jewish, is discovered to be the same in the Qabalah. This secret doctrine has its origin in the religion of Moses, says the historian, and congratulating himself, he prepares to make his conclusions, when the four animals of the vision of the Jew melt into a single one, and the Egyptian Sphinx silently raises the head of man above the disciples of Moses. Moses was an Egyptian priest, thus Egypt is the source of symbolic esoterism, those mysteries which all of Greek philosophy following Plato and Pythagoras came to absorb in its teachings. But the four mysterious personifications separate again, and Adda Nari, the Hindu goddess, rises up, showing us the head of an angel equalizing the struggle between the wild Beast and the peaceful Bull, before the birth of Egypt and its sacred mysteries.

Continue your research, and always this mysterious origin will flee before you. You will make your way through all the ancient civilizations, so arduously reconstructed, and when at last, tired of the course, you rest your mind in the primeval antiquity of the red race, on the first civilization produced by the first continent, you will hear the inspired prophet singing of the divine inhabitants of the upper sphere who revealed the symbolic secrets of the sanctuary.

Let us leave this elusive Proteus, the origin of Esoterism, and consider the Qabalah in which with a little effort we can rediscover the common vein, the Unique Religion from which all cults have issued. To know what the Qabalah is, let us listen to a profoundly learned man, as scholarly as he is modest, one who never speaks until he is certain of the truth of what he advances, Fabre d'Olivet:

> It seems, according to the most famous rabbis, that Moses himself, foreseeing the fate which would befall his book and the false interpretations it would be given in later times, resorted to an oral law which he proclaimed aloud to certain trustworthy men whose loyalty he had tested, and whom he charged to transmit in the secrecy of the sanctuary to other men who in their turn passed it on from age to age, handing it down thus to a time incredibly distant from its origin. This oral law, which modern Jews claim still to possess, is called the Qabalah, from a Hebrew word signyfying that which is received, that which comes from elsewhere, that which is passed from hand to hand[1].

[1] FABRE D'OLIVET, *La langue hébraïque restituée*, p.29.

Two books can be considered as the basis for Qabalistic study: The Zohar and the Sepher Yetzirah. So far as I know, neither of them has been entirely translated into French. I am going to attempt to fill this gap partially by translating the Sepher Yetzirah to the best of my ability. I beg the reader to pardon at the outset whatever errors may have made their way into my work, to which incidentally I append a bibliography permitting the serious student to consult the originals, and to look favourably on the remarks which are intended to elucidate in so far as possible the obscure passages of the text.

THE SEPHER YETZIRAH

RECONSTRUCTION OF THE TEXT

by PAPUS

We were the first in France to give a translation, which commentary, of the *Sepher Yetzirah* or Qabalistic book of the creation.

That translation was based on texts in our possession at the time and which were incomplete.

Later Mr Mayer-Lambert, professor at the Israelite seminary, made a new translation, working from more complete Arabic and Hebrew manuscripts.

But a careful examination of the two translations makes it evident that both present certain gaps and repetitions.

It is thanks to these repetitions that we have been able to *approximately* reconstruct the text of the Sepher Yetzirah in accordance with the following remarks:

Ancient authors composed treatises such as the one under discussion by first giving a summary exposition of the subject to be treated, then developing each of its particular sections following the same method.

Thus the *Sepher Yetzirah* must begin with a summary of the subjects under consideration, and these are: the Ten Numerations or Sephiroth, the twenty-two letters and their use by the Creator for the constitution of the Universe on three planes: the Universe, the Year, Man.

Next each subject must be treated by first repeating the general exposition, then extending it into its various adaptations. Finally a series of repetitions has led us to believe that each chapter's end concludes with an exposition of the

Qabalistic combinations of letters or numbers two by two, three by three, etc.

Thus we offer the new text of the *Sepher Yetzirah* reconstructed in this manner:

1. As Chapter I, the general exposition regarding the Ten Numerations and the twenty-two letters divided into three principals, seven doubles and twelve singles.

2. As Chapter II, the development of the Ten Sephiroth with, at the end, their combinations according to the permutations of the letters of the tetragram.

3. As Chapter III, a general exposition of the twenty-two letters in their major divisions.

4. Chapter IV is devoted to a detailed development of the analogical correspondences between the three principal letters and the Trinity. It closes with a paragraph on their combinations.

Chapter V is a detailed study of the seven doubles and their correspondences with the septenary. It also concludes with a table of combinations: 'Two letters build two houses, three build six, etc.'

Chapter VI ends these particular developments with an exposition of the correspondences of the duodenary with the twelve singles.

From this moment the development ceases. We have proceeded from unity to the maximum of multiplicity, we stop and return by successive resumés to the unity of our departure point.

Chapter VII is entirely devoted to this progressive resumé and is divided into three sections: 1. list of correspondences 2. derivations of letters 3. general summary.

Thus constituted, the *Sepher Yetzirah* forms a homogenous whole, departing from one point and returning to it, having proceeded through the various levels of correspondence of the ternary, the septenary and the duodenary in the Universe, in the Year and in Man.

The author or interpolators may have established certain of these correspondences in an original manner. Thus the seven days of the week relate to the planets according to the order of these latter in the astrological heavens (Saturn, Jupiter, Mars, the Sun, Venus, Mercury, the Moon) and not according to their exact linear connections.

If one places the planets in a circle with the Sun on top, one

will find that the correspondence given by the *Sepher Yetzirah*
for the days of the week simply places these days together with
the planets beginning with Sabbath, Saturday, attributed to
Saturn. And so Sunday falls with Jupiter, Monday with Mars,
Tuesday with the Sun, Wednesday with Venus, Thursday
with Mercury and Friday with the Moon.

Certainly the author was acquainted with the true key to
the correspondences between the days and the planets which
is obtained by drawing straight lines among the planets so as
to form a star with seven points. But he no doubt wished to
train the minds of his readers according to that oft-repeated
expression: '*Seek, think, combine, imagine and restore the creature to
the place assigned it by the Creator.*'

Let the attentive reader also bear in mind that the
foundation of the system, the three principals, A Me Sh, read
in Sanskrit fashion given SHEMA, Sh-Me-A, indicating that
here again the learned Qabalist, author of the *Sepher Yetzirah*,
has furnished us with the schema and not the reality of the
exact correspondences to which the word AZOTH is the only
true key, as is demonstrated by the admirable archeometer of
Saint-Yves d'Alveydre. Armed with this preliminary
information, the reader may now fruitfully take up the reading
and contemplation of the *Sepher Yetzirah*, sum of the living
science of the Patriarchs.

CHAPTER ONE

GENERAL EXPOSITION

THE QABALISTIC BOOK OF THE CREATION, IN HEBREW SEPHER YETZIRAH, BY ABRAHAM

Transmitted orally to his sons, then, given the state of affairs in Israel, committed by the wisemen of Jerusalem to arcana and writings of the most secret order.

It is with the thirty-two paths of Wisdom, admirably hidden paths, that YOAH (יהוה) GOD of Israel, LIVING GOD and King of the Centuries, GOD of mercy and grace, sublime and most high GOD, GOD dwelling in Eternity, holy GOD inscribed his name. through three numerations: SEPHER, SEPHAR and SIPUR, that is, NUMBER, NUMBERING and NUMBERED[1], contained in ten Sephiroth, that is, ten properties, excepting the ineffable, and twenty-two letters.

The letters are made up of three principals, seven doubles and twelve singles. The ten Sephiroth, excepting the ineffable, are formed of the number X, that of the fingers of the hand, five against five; but in their midst is the ring of unity. In the interpretation of the language and of the ritual of circumcision, the ten Sephiroth excepting the ineffable are to be found.

Ten and not nine, ten and not eleven, understand this in your wisdom and in your understanding you will know it. Exercise your mind upon them, search, note, think, imagine, restore things to their place and seat the Creator on his throne.

Ten Sephiroth, excepting the ineffable, whose ten

---

[1] Abendana translates these three terms as Scripture, Numbers and Word.

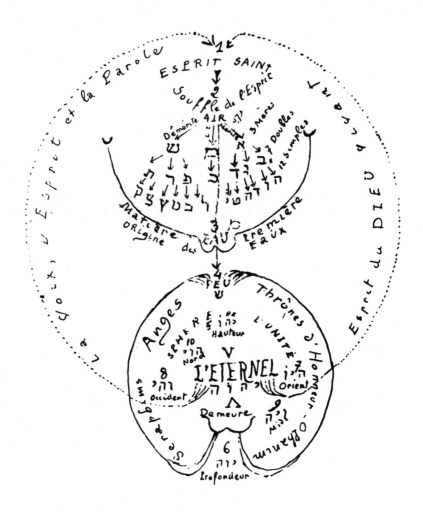

The Ring of Unity

properties are infinite: the infinity of beginning, the infinity of the end, the infinity of goodness, the infinity of evil, the infinity of height, the infinity of depth, the infinity extending to the East, the infinity extending to the West, the infinity extending to the North, the infinity extending to the South, and the Lord alone is above them. Faithful King, he governs them from on high, enthroned in the centuries of centuries.

Twenty-two fundamental letters, three principals: *aleph, mem, shin*. They correspond to the weight of worthiness, the weight of unworthiness and the scale of the law which establishes a balance between them. Seven doubles: *beth, gimel, daleth, kaph, pe, resh, tau*, which correspond to life, peace, wisdom, wealth, posterity, favour, domination. Twelve singles: *he, vau, zayin, cheth, teth, yod, lamed, nun, samekh, ayin, tzaddi, qoph*, which correspond to sight, hearing, smell, the word, nutrition, cohabitation, action, gait, anger, laughter, thought and sleep.

By which Yah, Eternal Sabaoth, God of Israel, ever-living God, omnipotent God, elevated and sublime, inhabiting Eternity and whose name is holy, has drawn three fathers and their posterity[1], seven conquerors and their legions[2], twelve edges of the cube[3]. The proof of the thing is given by witnesses worthy of faith, the world, the year and man, all with the rule of ten, three, seven and twelve. Their guardians are the dragon, the sphere and the heart.

---

[1] Air, water, fire and all that derives therefrom.
[2] The planets and the stars.
[3] The word   here does not seem to signify *diagonal*.

CHAPTER TWO

THE SEPHIROTH OR THE TEN NUMERATIONS

Ten Sephiroth, excepting the ineffable; their aspect is like that of sparkling flames, their end is lost in infinity. The word of God moves in them; leaving and returning ceaselessly like a whirlwind, they execute the divine word in an instant and bow down before the throne of the External.

Ten Sephiroth, excepting the ineffable; know that their end is united to the principle as the flame is united to the ember, for the Lord alone is above them and there is no second unto him. What number can you give before the number One?

Ten Sephiroth, excepting the ineffable. Close your lips and cease your meditation, and if your heart fails, return to the beginning. This is why it is written: Leave and return, for it is for this that the covenant was made: Ten Sephiroth, excepting the ineffable.

The first of the Sephiroth, one, is the Spirit of the living God, it is the blessed and again blessed name of the eternally living God. Voice, Spirit and Word, this is the Holy Spirit.

Two is the breath of the Spirit, and with it are engraved and inscribed the twenty-two letters, the three principals, the seven doubles and the twelve singles, and each of them is spirit.

Three is the water which comes from the breath, and with it He formed and sculpted primary matter, inanimate and empty. He set up TOHU, the line which winds about the world, and BOHU, the occult stones buried in the abyss and from which issue the Waters[1].

---

[1] This is the variant of this passage given by Mr Mayer-Lambert:
Thirdly, he created the water and the air. He traced and sculpted the *tohu* and the *bohu*, the mud and the clay. From them he made a kind of floor, he shaped them into a kind of wall, covered them with a kind of roof; and he made water to flow over them, and this became the earth, as it is written: *For he said to the snow, be of the earth.* (*Tohu* is the green line which surrounds the entire world; *bohu*, the stones, pierced and buried in the Ocean from which the waters come, as it is said: *He will set forth the line of tohu and the stones of bohu.*)
This last explanation is probably an interpolation. The author of the Sepher Yetzirah seems to have explained תהו ובהו by רפש וטיט.

Four is the Fire which comes from the Water, and with it He sculpted the throne of honour, the Ophanim (celestial wheels), the Seraphim, the Holy Animals and the Serving Angels, and He made their dominion his dwelling-place, as it is said: It is He who made his angels and ministering spirits by awakening fire.

Five is the seal with which He sealed the height when he contemplated it above him. He sealed it with the name IEV (יהו).

Six is the seal with which he sealed the depth when he contemplated it below him. He sealed it with the name IVE (יוה).

Seven is the seal with which he sealed the East when he contemplated it before him. He sealed it with the name EIV (היו).

Eight is the seal with which he sealed the West when he contemplated it behind him. He sealed it with the name VEI (והי).

Nine is the seal with which he sealed the South when he contemplated it on his right hand. He sealed it with the name VIE (ויה).

Ten is the seal with which he sealed the North when he contemplated it on his left hand. He sealed it with the name EVI (הוי).

Such are the ten ineffable Spirits of the living God: Spirit, Breath or Air, Water, Fire, Height, Depth, the East, the West, the North and the South.

CHAPTER THREE

THE TWENTY-TWO LETTERS

(*General Summary*)

The twenty-two letters are constituted of three principals,
seven doubles and twelve singles.

The three principals are: E M S (אמש), that is, Air,
Water and Fire. The Water, M (מ), mute, the Fire, S (ש),
sibilant, the Air, A (א), between the two, like the scales of the
law OCH (חק) which occupies the mid-point between
worthiness and guilt. To these twenty-two letters He gave
form and weight; by mingling them and transforming them in
divers ways, he created the soul of all that is created and all
that shall be.

The twenty-two letters are engraved in the voice, inscribed
in the Air, assigned in pronunciation to five places: the throat,
the palate, the tongue, the teeth and the lips[1].

The twenty-two letters, the foundations, are places on the
sphere, numbering 231. The circle which contains them can
turn directly forward, signifying happiness, or backward,
signifying the reverse. This is why He gave them weight and
made them permutable, Aleph (א) with all of them and all of
them with Aleph, Beth (ב) with all of them and all of them
with Beth, etc.

It is by this means that the 231 gates were born, that all
idioms and all creatures derive from the same formation, and
that all creation issues from a single name. Thus he made (את),
that is, Alpha and Omega, that which will never change nor
age[2].

The sign of all this is twenty-two totals and a single body.

Twenty-two fundamental letters: three principals, seven

---

[1] Variant of Mr Mayer-Lambert: The gutturals are pronounced with the
end of the tongue; the linguals toward the middle of the tongue; the
sibilants between the teeth; and the vowels with the tongue inactive.

[2] The author no doubt wishes to say that although numbers are infinite
for us, they are not so for God.

doubles, twelve singles. Three principals, *shin, aleph, mem*; fire, air and water. The origin of the sky is fire, the origin of the atmosphere is air, the origin of the earth is water. Fire rises, water descends, and air is the regulatory medium equilibrating the two. *Mem* is grave, *shin* is accute, *aleph* is intermediate between them. *Aleph-mem-shin* is sealed with six seals and enveloped in the male and the female[1]. Know, think and imagine that fire supports water.

Seven doubles: *b, g, d, k, p, r, t*, used with two pronunciations: *beth, bheth; gimel, ghimel, daleth, dhaleth; kaph, khaph; pe, pheh; resh, rhesh; tau, thau*; one soft, the other hard, in imitation of the weak and the strong. The doubles represent opposites. The opposite of life is death. The opposite of peace is unhappiness. The opposite of wisdom is foolishness. The opposite of wealth is poverty. The opposite of cultivation is desert. The opposite of grace is ugliness. The opposite of power is servitude.

Twelve single letters: *he, vau, zayin, cheth, teth, yod, lamed, nun, samekh, ayin, tzaddi, qoph*. He traced them, hewed them, multiplied them, weighed them and exchanged them; how did he multiply them? Two stones build two houses, three build six houses, four build twenty-four houses, five build one hundred and twenty houses, six build seven hundred and twenty houses, seven build five thousand and forty houses. From then on, go and count what your mouth cannot express, what you ear cannot hear.

With them Yah, the Eternal Sabaoth, God of Israel, living God, all-powerful Lord, most-high and sublime, inhabiting eternity and whose name is holy, laid out the world. YaH is composed of two letters, YHVH of four letters. *Sabaoth*: it is like a sign in His army. *God of Israel* is a prince before God. *Living God*: three things are called living, living God, living water and the tree of life. *El*: strong. *Shaddai*: sufficient to the day. *Most-high*: for He resides in the heights of the world and is above all elevated beings. *Sublime*: for He carries and sustains the high and the low; and whereas the carriers are below and their burden above, HE is on high and He bears what is below him; He carries and sustains eternity. *Inhabiting Eternity*: for His reign is cruel and uninterrupted. *His name is holy*: for He

---

[1] For there are six combinations, three strong and three weak.

and His servants are holy and they say to Him each time: holy, holy, holy.

The proof of the thing is given by witnesses worthy of faith: the world, the year, the soul. The twelve are the lowest, the seven are above them, and the three are above the seven. He made his sanctuary of the three, and all are attached to the One; Sign of the One which has no second, unique King in his world, which is one and whose name is one.

CHAPTER FOUR

THE THREE PRINCIPALS

Three principals E M S (אמש) are the foundations. They represent the side of merit, the side of guilt and the scale of the law OCH (הכ) which is in the middle.

Three principals, E M S. Untellable secret, most wonderful and hidden, graven by six rings from which issue fire, water and air, divided into male and female. Three principals, E M S, three mothers and with them three fathers. It is with them that all things are created.

Three principals, E M S, in the world, Air, Water and Fire. In the beginning, the Heavens were created from Fire, the Earth from Water and the Air from the Spirit which is between them.

Three principals, E M S, in the year, Warm, Cold and Moderate. The Warm was created from Fire, the Cold from Water and the Moderate from the Spirit between them.

Three principals, E M S, in Man, the Head, the Stomach and the Breast. The Head was created from Fire, the Stomach from Water and the Breast, between them, from the Spirit.

Three principals, E M S. He sculpted, engraved and formed them, and from them were created three principals in the world, three in the year, three in man, male and female.

He made Aleph (א) reign over the Spirit, uniting them by a bond and composing them one of the other, and with them He sealed the air in the world, the temperate in the year and the breast in man, male and female. Males in E M S (אמש), that is, in Air, Water and Fire; females in A S M[1], that is, in Air, Fire and Water.

He made Mem (מ) reign over the Water, He united and combined them in such a way that with them He sealed the earth in the world, the cold in the year and the fruit of the womb in man, males and females.

[1] For an explanation of this passage see the section headed REMARKS.

He made Shin (‫ש‬) reign over the Fire, and united and combined them in such a way that with them He sealed the heavens in the earth, the warm in the year and the head in man, males and females.

How did He mingle them together? *Aleph, mem, shin; aleph, shin, mem; mem, shin, aleph; mem, aleph, shin; shin, aleph, mem; shin, mem, aleph.* The sky is of fire, the atmosphere is of air, the.earth is of water. The head of man is of fire, his heart is of air, his stomach is of water.

CHAPTER FIVE

THE SEVEN DOUBLES

Seven doubles {	T	R	P	K	D	G	B
	ת	ר	פ	כ	ד	ג	ב

constitute the syllables of: Life, Peace, Knowledge, Wealth, Grace, Seed, Dominion.

Double because they can be exchange with their opposites. Instead of Life there is Death. Instead of Peace, War. Instead of Knowledge, Ignorance. Instead of Wealth, Poverty. Instead of Grace, Abomination. Instead of Seed, sterility. Instead of Dominion, Slavery. The seven doubles are set up against seven terms: the East, the West, the Height, the Depth, the North, the South, and the Holy Palace, fixed in the middle and sustaining everything.

He sculpted these seven doubles, engraved them, combined them, and with them created the Stars in the World, the Days in the Year, and the Openings in Man, and with them He sculpted seven heavens, seven elements, seven animal kingdoms. And this is why He chose the septenary under heaven.

1. Seven double letters, *b, g, d, k, p, r, t*; He traced them, formed them, mixed them, equilibrated them and exchanged them; with them He created the planets, the days and the openings. 2. He made *beth* to reign and gave it a crown, and combined them with one another, and from this He created Saturn in the world, Sabbath in the year, and the mouth in man. 3. He made *gimel* to reign, gave it a crown and mingled them together; with this He created Jupiter in the world, Sunday in the year, the right eye in man. 4. He made *daleth* to reign, gave it a crown, mingled them together, and from this He created Mars in the world, Monday in the year and the left eye in man. He made *kaph* to reign, gave it a crown, mingled them

together, and from this created the Sun in the world, Tuesday in the year, and the right nostril in man. 6. He made *pe* to reign, gave it a crown, mingled them together, and from this created Venus in the world, Wednesday in the year, and the left nostril in man. 7. He made *resh* to reign, gave it a crown, multiplied one by the other and so created Mercury in the world, Thursday in the year, and the right ear in man. 8. He made *tau* to reign, gave it a crown, multiplied them together and so created the Moon in the world, Friday in the year and the left ear in man. 9. He separated the witness and placed each one apart, the world apart, the year apart and man apart.

Two letters build two houses, three build six; four, twenty-four; five, one hundred and twenty; six, seven hundred and twenty; and from there numbers progress towards the indescribable and unknowable[1]. The planets in the world are the Sun, Venus, Mercury, the Moon, Saturn, Jupiter and Mars. The days of the year are the seven days of creation, and the seven gates of man are the two eyes, the two ears, the two nostrils and the mouth.

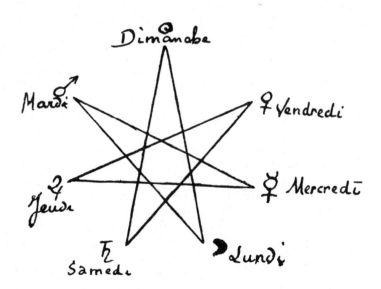

Sepher Yetzirah. – Days of the week and planetary correspondences.

[1] See REMARKS.

CHAPTER SIX

THE TWELVE SINGLES

Twelve singles	Q	Tz	Gh	S	N	L	I	T	Ch	Z	V	E
	ק	צ	ע	ס	נ	ל	י	ט	ח	ז	ו	ה

These are the foundations of the following: Sight, Hearing, Smell, Word, Nutrition, Coitus, Action, Movement, Anger, Laughter, Meditation, Sleep. Their measure is bounded by the twelve limits of the world:

The North-East, the South-East, the East-height, the East-depth.

The North-West, the South-West, the West-height, the West-depth.

The South-height, the South-depth, the North-height, the North-depth.

The limits increase and advance through centuries of centuries and these are the arms of the Universe.

These twelve singles He sculpted, engraved, assembled, weighed and changed, and with them He created twelve signs in the Universe, Aries, Taurus, etc.

Twelve months in the year.

And these letters are the twelve directors of man, as follows:

Right hand and left hand, the two feet, the two kidneys, the liver, the bladder, the spleen, the colon, the gall-bladder and the arteries.

He made *he* to reign, gave it a crown, mingled them together and from this intermingling created Aries in the world, *nisan* (March) in the year and the liver in man.

He made *vau* to reign, gave it a crown, mingled them together and with this created Taurus in the world, *iyyar* (April) in the year, gall in man.

He made *zayin* to reign, gave it a crown, mingled them together and from this created Gemini in the world, *sivan* (May) in the year and the spleen in man.

He made *cheth* to reign, gave it a crown, mingled them together and with this created Cancer in the world, *tammuz* (June) in the world and the stomach (colon) in man.

He made *teth* to reign, gave it a crown and multiplied them together and so created Leo in the world, *ab* (July) in the year and the right kidney in man.

CHAPTER SEVEN

1.–LIST OF CORRESPONDENCES

1. Air, temperate, breast. – Earth, cold, abdomen. – Sky, warm, head, and these are *aleph, mem, shin.* – 2. Saturn, Saturday, mouth. – Jupiter, Sunday, right eye. – Mars, Monday, left eye. – Sun, Tuesday, right nostril. – Venus, Wednesday, left nostril. – Mercury, Thursday, right ear. – Moon, Friday, left ear; these are *beth, gimel, daleth, kaph, pe, resh, tau.* – 3. Aries, *nisan,* liver. – Taurus, *iyyar,* gall. – Gemini, *sivan,* spleen. – Cancer, *tammus,* stomach. – Leo, *ab,* right kidney. – Virgo, *elul,* left kidney. – Libra, *tishri,* great intestine. – Scorpio, *marheshvan,* small intestine. – Sagittarius, *kislev,* right hand. – Capricorn, *tebet,* left hand. – Aquarius, *shebat,* right foot. – Pisces, *adar,* left foot. And these are *he, vau, zayin, cheth, teth, yod, lamed, nun, samekh, ayin, tzaddi, qoph.*

2.–DERIVATIVES OF THE LETTERS

From *aleph* were formed: the air, the atmosphere, the temperate, the breast and the rule of equilibrium (scourge). From *mem* were formed: water, earth, winter, the abdomen, the side of unworthiness. From *shin* were formed: fire, the heavens, summer, the head and the side of worthiness. From *beth* were formed: Saturn, the Sabbath, the mouth, life and death. From *gimel* were formed: Jupiter, Sunday, the right eye, peace and misfortune. From *daleth* were formed: Mars, Monday, the left eye, wisdom and foolishness. From *kaph* were formed: the sun, Tuesday, the right nostril, wealth and poverty. From *pe* were formed: Venus, Wednesday, the left nostril, growth and desert. From *resh* were formed: Mercury, Thursday, the right ear, grace and ugliness. From *tau* were formed: The Moon, Friday, the left ear, dominion and servitude. From *he* were formed: Aries, *nisan,* the liver, vision and blindness. From *vau* were formed: Taurus, *iyyar,* gall, hearing and deafness. From *zayin* were formed: Gemini, *sivan,* the spleen, the sense of smell and the absence of same. From *cheth* were formed: Cancer, *tammuz*, the stomach, speech and muteness. From *teth* were formed: Leo, *ab*, the right kidney, nutrition and hunger. From *yod* were formed: Virgo, *elul*, the left kidney, sexual commerce and castration. From *lamed* were formed: Libra, *tishri*, the great intestine, activity and powerlessness. From *nun* were formed: Scorpio, *marheshvan*, the small intestine, normal gait and lameness. From *samekh* were formed: Sagittarius, *kislev*, the right hand, anger and the removal of the liver. From *ayin* were formed: Capricorn, *tebet*, the left hand, laughter and the removal of the spleen. From *tzaddi* were formed: Aquarius, *sehebat*, the right foot, thought and the removal of the heart. From *qoph* were formed: Pisces, *adar*, the left foot, sleep and langour. And all are attached to the Dragon, the sphere and the heart.

Three[1] things are in man's power (the hands, the feet, the lips). Three things are not within man's power (the eyes, the ears, the nostrils). Three things are painful to hear: a curse, blasphemy and bad news. Three things are agreeable to hear: a blessing, praise and good news. Three looks are bad: the look of the adulterer, the look of the thief and the look of the miser. Three things are agreeable to see: the look of modesty, the look of candour and the look of generosity. Three odours are bad: the odour of corrupt air, the odour of sultry wind and the odour of poisons. Three odours are good: the odour of spices, the odour of feasts and the odour of aromatic substances. Three things are bad for the tongue: gossip, prattle and falsehood. Three things are good for the tongue: silence, reserve and sincerity.

3.–GENERAL RÉSUMÉ

Three principals, seven doubles and twelve singles. Such are the twenty-two letters which make the tetragram IEVE והיה, that is, Our God Sabaoth, the sublime God of Israel, the Most-High enthroned in the centuries; and his holy name created three fathers and their descendants and seven heavens with their celestial cohorts and twelve limits to the Universe.

[1] Added following Sabbatai Donolo.

The proof of all this, the faithful testimony, is the Universe, the year and man. He set them up as witness and formed them of three, seven and twelve. Twelve chiefs and signs in the heavenly Dragon, the Zodiac and the Heart. Three, fire, water and air. Fire above, water below and air in between. This means that air partakes of the other two.

The heavenly Dragon, that is, Intelligence in the world, the Zodiac in the year and the Heart in man. Three, fire, water and air. The fire above, the water below, the air between for it partakes of the other two.

In the universe the heavenly dragon is like a king on his throne. The Zodiac in the year is like a king in his city. The Heart in man is like a king in battle.

And God made Good and Evil opposites. He made the Good of Good and the Evil of Evil. Good proves Evil and Evil, Good. Good seethes in the just and Evil in the impious. And each is constituted from the ternary.

Seven parts are made up of two ternaries and unity fixed in the middle.

The duodenary is composed of opposite parts: three friends, three enemies, three givers of life, three givers of death, and God, faithful king, governs all from the threshold of His holiness.

Unity holds sway over the ternary, the ternary over the septenary, the septenary over the duodenary, but each part is inseparable from all the others, as our father Abraham understood it. And he considered it, examined it, fathomed it, understood it, ordered it and set it down, thereby joining creature to creator. Then the master of the Universe made Himself manifest to Abraham, called him His friend and committed Himself to an eternal covenant with him and his posterity, as it is written: HE believed in IOAH (יהוה) and this was credited to him as a work of Justice. HE made with Abraham a pact between his ten toes, this is the pact of circumcision, and another among the ten fingers of his hand, this is the pact of the language. HE attached the twenty-two letters to the language and showed him their mystery. HE made them go down into the water, made them rise into the fire, threw them into the air, lit them in the seven planets and made them flow into the twelve heavenly signs.

4.–REMARKS

In these short observations it is not our intention to make an extensive commentary on the *Sepher Yetzirah*. In order to have some value, such a commentary must be based on the Hebrew text, the Hebrew language having preserved its triple significance[1], and this alone would do justice to the complete thought of the author. Moreover, two of the most eminent masters of occultism, Guillaume de Postel and the Alchemist Abraham, have given excellent commentaries in Latin. We can do no better than to refer to them the reader desirous of extending his examination of such questions.

We will limit ourselves to clarifying, hopefully, the obscure passages with notes and the translation of two little-known Qabalistic works: The Fifty Gates of Understanding and the Thirty-two Paths of Wisdom.

Generally speaking, one might call the Sepher Yetzirah the book of Qabalistic creation rather than the Qabalistic book of creation. For the entire book reposes on the mysterious name IOAH (יהֹה) and the creation of the world by HE-THE-GODS[2] is limited to the entirely Qabalistic creation of the numbers and letters. By this means the author of the Sepher sets forth from the beginning the characteristic method of Occult Science: Analogy.

The form which the artist has given his work exactly expresses the grandeur of the germinal idea. There exists a mathematical relationship between the visible form and the invisible idea responsible for its coming into being, between the assemblage of letters forming a word and the idea that this word represents. Thus to create words is to create ideas, and it is understandable why the Sepher Yetzirah, in telling of the

---

[1] 'In this Moses followed the method of the Egyptian priests; for I must say before anything else that these Priests had three ways of expressing their thought. The first was simple and clear, the second was symbolic and figurative, the third holy and hieroglyphic ... The same word could take on at will the proper, figurative or hieroglyphic sense. Such was the genius of their language. Heraclitus expressed this difference perfectly by assigning the epithets *speaking, meaning and hiding*.' (FABRE D'OLIVET)

[2] An exact translation of the word אֱלֹהִים (Elohim). Moreover, at the beginning of the Sepher Yetzirah one can see God designated as plural.

creation of the world, limits itself to a development of the creation of the Hebrew letters, which represent ideas and laws.

The Zohar is a kind of Light, the Sepher Yetzirah, a ladder of truths. Here are explained the thirty-two absolute signs of the word, the letters and numbers. Each letter reproduces a number, an idea and a form, so that mathematics is as rigorously applicable to ideas and forms as to numbers, the proportions being exact and the correspondences perfect.

Through the knowledge of the Sepher Yetzirah the human mind is fixed in truth and reason and can realize the possible progress of understanding by the evolutions of numbers. The Zohar represents then absolute Truth and the Sepher Yetzirah gives the means of grasping it, of making it one's own and using it.

(Eliphas LEVI, *History of Magic*)

The general law which gives birth to the world once created under the name of IOAH[1] will be seen to develop in the Universe through the ten Sephiroth or Numerations.

What then do these ten Sephiroth express? Few terms have given rise to so many commentaries. In accordance with the Hebrew roots of this word, I believe one can express the idea it contains by the following definition: *stopping point of a cyclical movement.* Thus the ten Sephiroth are only ten concepts at different degrees of a single and self-same thing which Qabalists designate under the name of En-Soph, the ineffable, representing the divine essence in its greatest abstraction and occurring in the name (IEVE) in the first and right hand letter I י (יהוה).

[1] I believe it will be a help to my readers to include part of a commentary by Fabre d'Olivet on this mysterious name whose study is purposely neglected by occult writers:

'First, this name offers the indicative sign of life, doubled and forming the essentially living root EE (הה). This root is never used as a noun and it is the only such one. From its formation, it is not only a verb, but a unique one from which all others are derived: in word, the verb הוה (EVE), to be-being. As can be seen and as I took care to make clear in my grammar, the sign of intelligible light ו (vau) stands in the middle of the root of life. Moses, taking this ultimate verb in order to form the name of the Being of Beings, adds the sign of potential manifestation and of eternity (I) and obtains יהוה (IEVE) in which being finds itself placed between a past without origin and a future without end. Thus this admirable name signifies exactly the Being-who-is-who-was-and-who-will-be.

The Sepher shows us the application of these ideas by using this same word (EVE) (הוה) combined in various ways, indicative of the last six Sephiroth (Chap. 1).

M. Franck, interpreting the Qabalists, says: 'Although all are equally necessary, the attributes and distinctions which the Sephiroth express cannot make us understand the divine nature always from the same point of elevation. But they do show it to us in various aspects which in the language of the Qabalists are called faces or persons.[1]'

But it is Kircher who will clarify this for us by showing us in a single sentence the origin of modern work on the unity of the force which fills the Universe, work undertaken so fruitfully by Louis Lucas[2]. Let us listen to our author:

This is why all the Sephiroth or numbers are a single and identical force differently modified according to the medium through which they pass.[3]

Then through new modifications the divine substance gives rise to further unknown concepts manifested in the divine letters. Here the great laws which govern nature appear one by one in the analogical applications which the Sepher's author employs when speaking of the Universe, the year and man.

The first distinction appears in the ternary division of the letters into principals, doubles (expressing two sounds, one positive and strong, the other negative and weak) and singles (expressing only one sound).

This idea of the Trinity is to be found again and again in the Sepher. Its development is especially extensive in Chapter III where its constitution is given: a positive (שׁ) S, Fire; a negative (מ) M, Water; and a neuter (א) A, Air, intermediary between the two and resulting from their reciprocal action.

If we consider each Trinity as a single person, we see a positive Trinity, a negative Trinity and Unity which brings them together in the Septenary, as the text says:

[1] FRANCK, *La Kabbale.*

[2] See *l'Occultisme contemporain* by PAPUS (ed. Carré).

[3] KIRCHER, *Oedipus Aegyptiacus (Cabala Hebraeorum,* 11).

Seven parts are made up of two Ternaries between which stands Unity.

In similar fashion, the duodenary is formed of four ternaries standing in opposition two by two.

In these few numbers are contained all the laws which Occult Science considers to be primordial laws, the *why* of Nature.

And this is so true that the author closes his book by synthesizing in a single sentence all the laws he has earlier analysed.

Alongside this evolution, issued from Divinity to spread through all creation, the idea of which is at bottom rather clear, there appear from time to time certain obscure passages referring to divinatory, hence occult, practices of the sanctuary.

A few letters suffice to express an incalculable number of ideas, and this through a simple combining of them. Here for example are four of our letters, N, M. E, A, which will express entirely different ideas according to whether they are written NAME or MEAN or AMEN. The 231 gates at the end of Chapter II and the houses of Chapter IV refer to these combinations of letters, and consequently of numbers and ideas.

The 231 gates are connected with the use of a table called Ziruph by the Qabalah and indicating all the world which can be formed from the twenty-two letters, substituted one for another. But in the present case, here is the explanation of Guillaume Postel:

Multiply the twenty-two letters by eleven (the ten Sephiroth + the ineffable) and this gives two hundred and forty-two. Now subtract this same eleven, giving $242 - 11 = 231$ gates.

The table of substitutions is obtained by replacing the first letter of the alphabet by the last, the second by the next-to-the-last, and so forth.

Using our alphabet as an example,
ABCDEFGHIJKLMNOPQRSTUVWXYZ becomes
ZYXWVUTSRQPONMLKJIHGFEDCBA

Thus the word ART will be written using the lower alphater ZIG. This method combined with the following is extremely helpful for the practical use of the Rota of Guillaume Postel[1].

The second passage (end of Chapter IV) refers to the number of combinations possible for a certain quantity of letters; thus two letters can form only two combinations, three can form six, etc. Example:

1. A B C
2. A C B
3. B A C
4. B C A
5. C A B
6. C B A

The number of combinations increases according to mathematical law. As can be seen, the Sepher Yetzirah is deductive, beginning with the idea of God and descending from this into the domain of natural phenomena. Of the two books which I wish to speak of now, one follows the system of the Sepher. This is *The Thirty-two Paths of Wisdom*. The other is inductive, beginning with Nature and building toward the idea of God, presenting a remarkable system of evolution which it is interesting to compare to modern ideas on the subject and to the basic principles of Theosophy[2]. This is the *Fifty Gates of Understanding*.

According to the Qabalists each of these two systems issues from one of the primary Sephiroth. The thirty-two paths of Wisdom derives from Chokmah and the fifty gates of Understanding from Binah, as Kircher teaches:

As the thirty-two paths of Wisdom, issued from Chokmah, spread throughout the circle of created things, so from Binah, which we have seen to be the Holy Spirit, issue the fifty gates leading to these paths; their function is to lead to a practical use of the thirty-two paths of Wisdom and Power.

They are called Gates because, according to the Cabalists, no one can arrive at a perfect notion of the aforementioned paths, unless he first enters by them.

---

[1] See ELIPHAS LEVI, *Ritual de la Haute Magie*, Ch. XXI.
[2] See the second part of *Traité élémentaire de Science occulte*.

5.–THE 50 GATES OF UNDERSTANDING

1st CLASSIFICATION
PRINCIPLES OF THE ELEMENTS

Gate 1 – (the lowest) Primary matter, Hyle, Chaos.
Gate 2 – Empty and inanimate: that which is without form.
Gate 3 – Natural attraction, the abyss.
Gate 4 – Separation and rudiments of the Elements.
Gate 5 – Element Earth from which all seed is as yet absent.
Gate 6 – Element Water acting on the World.
Gate 7 – Element Air issuing from the abyss of waters.
Gate 8 – Element Fire warming and giving life.
Gate 9 – Representation of Qualities.
Gate 10 – Their attraction toward a mixture of all.

2nd CLASSIFICATION
DECADE OF MIXED CREATIONS

Gate 11 – Appearance of metals by the sundering of the earth.
Gate 12 – Flowers and saps ordered for the generation of metals.
Gate 13 – Seas, Lakes, Secret Flowers among the cavities of the Earth.
Gate 14 – Production of Grasses, of Trees, of vegetable nature.
Gate 15 – Strength and seed given to each of them.
Gate 16 – Production of sensitive Nature.
Gate 17 – Of Insects and Reptiles.
Gate 18 – Of Fish }
Gate 19 – Of Birds } each with its special properties
Gate 20 – Procreation of the Quadrupeds.

3rd CLASSIFICATION
DECADE OF HUMAN NATURE

Gate 21 – Production of man.
Gate 22 – Clay of the Earth of Damas, Matter.
Gate 23 – Breath of Life, Soul.
Gate 24 – Mystery of Adam and Eve.
Gate 25 – Man-All, Microcosm.
Gate 26 – Five external powers.
Gate 27 – Five internal powers.
Gate 28 – Man Heaven.
Gate 29 – Man Angel.
Gate 30 – Man image and likeness of God.

4th CLASSIFICATION
ORDERS OF HEAVENS, WORLD OF THE SPHERES

Gate 31 –		Of the Moon.
Gate 32 –		Of Mercury.
Gate 33 –		Of Venus.
Gate 34 –		Of the Sun.
Gate 35 –	Heavens	Of Mars.
Gate 36 –		Of Jupiter.
Gate 37 –		Of Saturn.
Gate 38 –		Of the Firmament.
Gate 39 –		Of the *primum mobile*.
Gate 40 –		Empyrean.

5th CLASSIFICATION
ORDERS OF ANGELS, ANGELIC WORLD

Gate 41 – Holy Animals   Seraphim.
Gate 42 – Ophanim, that is, Wheels   Cherubim.
Gate 43 – Angels great and strong   Thrones.
Gate 44 – Hashmalim   Dominions.
Gate 45 – Seraphim   Virtues.
Gate 46 – Malachim   Powers.
Gate 47 – Elohim   Principalities.
Gate 48 – Beni-Elohim   Archangels.
Gate 49 – Cherubim   Angels.

6th CLASSIFICATION
EN-SOPH, IMMENSE GOD
SUPER-WORLDLY AND ARCHETYPAL WORLD

Gate 50 – God, Sovereign Good, He whom mortal man has not seen, nor which even the most searching mind can reach. This is the 50th gate which Moses did not succeed in opening.

And such are the fifty gates by which Intelligence or the Holy Spirit has prepared the way to the 32 paths of Wisdom for him who is serious in his investigation and obedient to the law.

'The 32 paths of Wisdom are the luminous roads by which holy men of God, through long usage, long experience of divine things and long meditation upon them, can attain the hidden centres.'

KIRCHER

6.–THE 32 PATHS OF WISDOM

The first path is called the Admirable Intelligence, the Supreme Crown. It is the light which imparts understanding of the beginning which is without beginning, and this is also the First Glory. No created being can attain to its essence.

The second path is called the Illuminating Intelligence. It is the Crown of Creation and the splendour of the Supreme Unity, to which it is most in proximity. It is exalted above every head and called by the Qabalists: the Second Glory.

The third path is called the Sanctifying Intelligence and is the foundation of Primordial Wisdom, named the creation of Faith. Its roots are אמן . It is the mother of Faith, which issues therefrom.

The fourth path is called the Arresting or Receptive Intelligence for it arises like a boundary to receive the emanations of the higher intelligences which are sent down to it. From it emanate all spiritual virtues by way of subtlety, which itself emanates from the Supreme Crown.

The fifth path is called the Radical Intelligence, because it is more similar than any other to the Supreme Unity and emanates from the depths of the Primordial Wisdom.

The sixth path is called the Intelligence of Median Influence, for the flow of emanations is multiplied within it. It communicates this affluence to those blessed men who are united with it.

The seventh path is called the Hidden Intelligence, for it pours out a brilliant splendour onto all intellectual virtues which are looked upon with the eyes of the spirit and by the ecstasy of faith.

The eighth path is called the Perfect and Absolute Intelligence. From it emanates the preparation of principles. The only roots to which it adheres are in the depths of the Sphere of Magnificence, from the very substance of which it issues.

The ninth path is called the Purified Intelligence. It purifies the numerations, prevents and stops the breaking of their images, for it establishes their unity, to preserve them from destruction and division by their union with it.

The tenth path is called the Resplendent Intelligence, for it is exalted above all heads and has its seat in BINAH. It enlightens the fire of all lights and brings about the emanation of the power of the principle of forms.

The eleventh path is called the Fiery Intelligence. It is the veil placed before the dispositions and order of the superior and inferior causes. Whoever possesses this path is certain to enjoy great dignity, for to possess it is to be face-to-face with the Cause-of-Causes.

The twelfth path is called the Intelligence of Light, for it is the image of magnificence. It is said to be the source of vision in those who behold apparitions.

The thirteenth path is called the Inductive Intelligence of Unity. It is the substance of glory and makes known the truth to every spirit.

The fourteenth path is called the Illuminating Intelligence. It is the institutor of arcana, the foundation of Holiness.

The fifteenth path is called the Constituting Intelligence, for it constitutes creation in the warm darkness of the world. According to Philosophers, it is itself that darkness mentioned by Scripture (Job 38), the cloud and its envelope.

The sixteenth path is called the Triumphant and Eternal

Intelligence, the delight of glory, the paradise of pleasure made ready for the just.

The seventeenth path is called the Disposing Intelligence. It disposes the devout to faithfulness and thus prepares them to receive the Holy Spirit.

The eighteenth path is called the Intelligence or House of Affluence, and from it are drawn the arcana and hidden meanings which repose in its shadow.

The nineteenth path is called the Intelligence of the Secret or of all spiritual activities. The fullness which it receives derives from the highest benediction and the supreme glory.

The twentieth path is called the Intelligence of Will. It prepares all created beings individually for the demonstration of the existence of Primordial Wisdom.

The twenty-first path is called the Intelligence which rewards all those who seek. It receives the divine influence, and by its benediction influences all things that exist.

The twenty-second path is called the Faithful Intelligence, for spiritual virtues are deposited and augment within it until they pass to those who dwell under its shadow.

The twenty-third path is called the Stable Intelligence. It is the cause of consistency in all the numerations.

The twenty-fourth path is called the Imaginative Intelligence. It gives similarity to the likeness of beings created to its agreement and according to its aspects.

The twenty-fifth path is called the Intelligence of Temptation or Trial, for it is the first temptation by which God tests the devout.

The twenty-sixth path is called the Renewing Intelligence, for through it GOD (blessed be He!) renews all that can be renewed in the creation of the world.

The twenty-seventh path is called the Active Intelligence, for from it is created the spirit of every creature of the supreme Orb, and the activity, that is, the motion to which they are subject.

The twenty-eighth path is called the Natural Intelligence. Through it the nature of everything found in the orb of the sun is completed and perfected.

The twenty-ninth path is called the Corporeal Intelligence. It forms every body which is incorporated under all orbs, and it is the growth thereof.

The thirtieth path is called the Collective Intelligence, for from it the Astrologers, by the judgement of the stars and heavenly signs, derive their speculations and the perfection of their science according to the movement of the stars.

The thirty-first path is called the Perpetual Intelligence. Why? Because it rules the movement of the sun and the moon according to their constitution and causes each to gravitate in its respective orb.

The thirty-second path is called the Assisting Intelligence, for it governs and concurs with all the operations of the seven planets, with their divisions.

There follows the practical usage to be made of these 32 paths.

Qabalists, wishing to consult God by any one of the pathways of natural things, go about it thus:

First as a preliminary they examine the 32 aspects of the first chapter of Genesis, that is, the pathways of created things, and give them their fullest study and attention[1].

Then by means of certain prayers derived from the name ELOIM (אלהים) they beg God to generously accord them the light necessary to the pathway which they seek, and by appropriate ceremonies, constitute themselves adept to the Light of Wisdom, ultimately finding themselves, through their unshakable faith and their ardent charity, at the centre of the world, and it is from this central point that they make their consultation. So that their prayer will have greater power, they make use of the name of 42 letters[2], and by this means believe they will obtain what they ask.

*

* *

Readers in quest of further details on the Qabalah will find them in the writings of all contemporary Qabalists, Eliphas Lévi, Stanislas de Guaita, Joséphin Peladan, Albert Jhouney. Those who desire to penetrate to the heart of the Qabalistic system outlined in the *Sepher Yetzirah* will find extensive developments in my study, *The Tarot of the Bohemians*, a large volume of nearly 400 pages, based on the third divine name.

[1] In the first chapter of Genesis the divine name Elohim is mentioned 32 times.

[2] This name derives from the combinations of the Tetragram. See KIRCHER, op. cit.

7.–THE DATE OF THE 'SEPHER YETZIRAH'

> Search, think, ponder, imagine
> and re-establish the creature in
> the place assigned it by the
> Creator.
>
> (*Sepher Yetzirah*)

It is not without apprehension that we undertook this work, perhaps a presumptuous one for the humble student we are. But should this apprehension prevent us from revealing the fragment of truth which we believe to possess? We do not think so. 'Do not hide your light under a bushel,' said the Master, and the slightest gleam in the darkness is perhaps sufficient to indicate the hidden road which flaming torches and greater lights will fully illuminate at some later time. Moreover, our work is a practical confirmation of that counsel which the *Sepher Yetzirah* itself gives to the student of the occult and which we have taken for our epigraph: 'Search, think, ponder, imagine and re-establish the creature in the place assigned it by the Creator.'

To establish a date for a work such as the *Sepher Yetzirah* is no easy task for the rationalistic critic. This needs no other testimony than the considerable differences of opinion separating various critics in this regard. Nearly all of them begin with the preconceived notion that any mystical or Qabalistic work is nothing more than a more or less heterogeneous jumble of puerile ramblings. Others, like Dr Karppe, while attempting to keep an open mind, as proved by the latter's learned and extremely conscientious *Etude sur les origines et la nature du Zohar*, finish all the same by arriving at an almost identical conclusion.

The reason for this is that all of them, despite their knowledge, despite the power of their reasoning, can comprehend nothing – and understandably so – in these writings, being unable even to distinguish what the least student of Occultism can clearly see. Thus they are inevitably given to considering any mystical work either the simple derivation of a philosophical or religious system wrapped in extravagant and incomprehensible obscurities, or the product of a desire to incorporate, more or less adroitly, the philosophy of a certain school into a given religious system.

An attempt to make them admit that underneath these veils there, may be hidden (there are hidden in reality) the most powerful scientific and moral doctrines, doctrines reaching back to the most ancient times, will only produce the disdainful smile which he who *believes* he knows indulgently gives to the poor ignorant who *wishes* to know.

Are the proofs on which they base their judgements so irrefutable? Are they so invulnerable to criticism that they must be accepted blindly? Certainly not, and we will attempt to demonstrate this.

Such proofs are of two kinds:

1. Proofs drawn from the general philosophical ideas contained in the book under study. We will call these philosophical or moral proofs.

2. Proofs drawn from the language in which the book was written. These we will call grammatical proofs or proofs of written signs.

We find these proofs masterfully applied in the new work of which we have already spoken, that of S. Karppe. Let us see how the author, supporting himself on such proofs, attempts to assign the *Sepher Yetzirah* a relatively recent origin.

After having lengthily discussed the philosophical ideas of the *Sepher Yetzirah* – a discussion we will not take up, since such is not our aim – the author concludes as follows, warning the reader that it is a question here of personal opinion, given without reservation, but also without any scientific basis:

> The *Sepher Yetzirah* is perhaps not the initial point but rather the final one in a long series of ideas, and it is possibly the work of a teacher devoted to the summarization in a short manual, a kind of Mishnah, of all elementary scientific knowledge:
>
> Knowledge relative to reading and grammar: the twenty-two letters of the alphabet with all their combinations, such as figure on tables aimed at teaching children to read, such as were to be found, according to Sadyah, in the cities of Palestine and Egypt at the time; then the division of the letters according to the organs of pronunciation, the nature of letters capable of a double pronunciation, etc.
>
> Cosmological and physical knowledge, such as the names and

nature of the elements, the relationships and differences existing among them, their density, etc.

Knowledge relative to the division of time, the days of the week, the months of the year, linked to the Zodiac and to the planets.

Knowledge relative to space, the cardinal points, the directions of the compass-card, including geometrical notions concerning the square, the cube, etc.

Knowledge relative to anatomy, such as the division of organs, their names and functions, the all-important role of the heart.

Finally, knowledge relative to Jewish doctrine, monotheism, the cosmogony of Genesis, circumcision and the concepts concerning the Mercavah.

So the *Sepher Yetzirah* can be considered in no wise a mystical work, but rather an elementary 'primer' designed to bring together, by means of letters and numbers, all the notions which generally form the object of primary teaching[1].

Such is not our opinion of course, assured as we are that a most elevated doctrine lies hidden in the terminology of the *Sepher Yetzirah*. In any case our author's conclusion cannot seemingly be supported. When men of our critic's quality admit to the difficulties experienced with such a work, what could a child possibly understand of it? And none of this serves to date the *Sepher Yetzirah* as a relatively recent phenomenon, since the themes treated in the book, and so clearly summarized by our critic, go back to the beginning of time. But let us take care not to confuse the examination of the foregoing proofs with an examination of the grammatical ones, the proofs of written signs, with which there is a certain overlapping; for these latter are far more important.

So as not to prolong this study unduly, we will give only the conclusions of the discussion at the close of which Karppe fixes what he feels to be the probable date of the *Sepher Yetzirah*. Readers desirous of following the total discussion can of course consult the book itself.

Certainly it (the *Sepher Yetzirah*) exists at the moment when Agobard writes his letter to King Louis the Devout, for the letter quite clearly alludes to it. This takes us back to the year 829. In addition, the author of the *Sepher Yetzirah* is acquainted with the grammatical distinctions concerning the double pronunciation of the letters *b, g, d, k, p, r, t,* as well as the division of letters by

[1] S. KARPPE, *Etude sur les origines et la nature du Zohar*, p.162 *et. seq.*

organ; but he seems to be ignorant of the vowel markings. The
vowel markings are the work of the Massorites. Had the author
known of them, surely he would have been struck by their
number 7 and would not have failed to include them in his work.
These considerations lead us to believe that the *Sepher Yetzirah*
appeared at the beginning of the grammatical age, that is,
between the eighth and ninth centuries[1].

The proofs which Karppe advances, although they appear
convincing, do not have, it seems to us, all the weight which
might be superficially attributed to them. We willingly agree
with him that the drawing up of the document which he
translated dates back to the time at which he places it. His
remarks on the grammatical knowledge of the document's
scribe seem securely founded. However, because a book whose
author's name and precise date are unknown appears to
belong to a given era, must one necessarily conclude that this
book is the original, dating from the selfsame period of time?
If, for example, the Hebrew copies of the *Sepher Yetzirah* were
to disappear without trace, would one be correct in
concluding some several thousand years hence, from a French
translation of our time, preserved by chance, that the book
was written by a French mystic of the twentieth century? I am
aware that such a question might be countered with the
objection that the ideas contained in the book bear no relation
to other works of the same period; but when have mystics ever
busied themselves with the ideas of *reasonable people*?

Thus these grammatical remarks prove only one thing: that
the *Sepher Yetzirah* was set down in writing for the first time in
approximately the eighth century. They in no way prove that
it did not exist, orally transmitted, before this time.

Our critic makes a summary of acquired knowledge of that
time. Now is it not true that most of the knowledge given by
the *Sepher* goes back to a far far earlier period? And do not still
other notions seem, on the contrary, singularly modern?

For example, it seems to be admitted that the *Sepher
Yetzirah*'s author was acquainted with the 'the capital role of
the heart'; in which case it is not to the ninth but to the
seventeenth century that he would have to belong. How in
reality could the author of the *Sepher Yetzirah*, writing in the
eighth or ninth century, be aware of the all-important role of

[1] S. KARPPE, *Loc. cit.*, p. 167.

the heart? Was this physiological truth a part of official science of the time? No. Thus one must logically conclude that either the *Sepher Yetzirah* is subsequent to Harvey (*William Harvey – discoverer of the circulation of the blood 1628*), or that the unknown Qabalist who composed the book was far ahead of the science of his age.

The first conclusion is of course absurd. The second, however, is tenable for us, students of the Occult, who know that science and truth are veiled in the *Sepher Yetzirah* as in the *Sepher Bereschith* and in many other ancient books. But let us not over-emphasize this point.

Whatever the truth of the matter, the *Sepher Yetzirah* existed before the era assigned it by our critic. Indeed it had existed for many centuries, but had never been written down. A simple oral tradition, it was secretly transmitted from initiate to initiate. This explains why the Talmudists living before the ninth century never speak of it; for the non-Qabalistic Talmudists were ignorant of it, and initiate Talmudists would have considered it unwise to make such matters public.

This also explains the words 'of a fourteenth century Qabalist, Isaac Delatès, who in his preface to the Cremona edition of the *Zohar*, is the first to ask who might have authorized R. Akiba to write the *Sepher Yetzirah*, calling it Mishna, since it is a book which has been transmitted orally since Abraham?'[1]

And finally this explains in part the discrepancies existing among various copies of the *Sepher Yetzirah*, discrepancies especially notable in the correspondences of the letters, as can be seen by comparing the translation of Papus with that of S. Karppe.

Although we have shown that modern criticism has in no way proved the recency of the *Sepher Yetzirah*, we have not ourselves demonstrated the antiquity of the work. Now it is our belief that it dates back at least to the patriarchal age, if not further, and that if it is not the work of Abraham himself, as the Qabalistic tradition would have it, it belongs to an earlier rather than a later time.

The proof is based not on the occult tradition which is without value for rationalistic criticism, but on a purely scientific detail furnished by the very text of the work.

---

[1] S. KARPPE, *Loc. cit.*, p.166.

Let us begin by comparing the two translations given by Papus and Karppe of the passage of the *Sepher Yetzirah* now under consideration.

PAPUS

CHAPTER VII

S. KARPPE

CHAPTER VI

3. Three principals, 7 doubles and 12 singles. Such are the 22 letters with which the tetragram IEVE   , that is, Our God Sabaoth, the Sublime God of Israel, the Most-High enthroned in the centuries, is made. And his holy name created 3 fathers and their descendants and 7 heavens with their celestial· bands and 12 limits to the Universe.

The proof of all this, the faithful witness, is the universe, the year and man. He set them up as witnesses, and sculpted them by 3, 7 and 12. Twelve signs and authorities in the *Celestial* Dragon, the zodiac and the heart. Three, fire, water and air. Fire above, water below, and air between the two.

In the universe the Dragon is like a king on his throne; in the zodiac the year is like a king in his city; in man the heart is like a king in battle.

These are the 3 principals: *Aleph, mem, shin,* and from them issued 3 fathers, *air, water* and *fire.* From the fathers issued the generations, 7 constellations and their hosts and 12 intersecting diagonals. The proof of the thing, the faithful witnesses are: the world, the year, the person, and the law is: 12, 7, 3. He *suspended them from the Dragon,* from the sphere and from the heart. Three principals, *Aleph, Mem, Shin,* corresponding to *air, water, fire.* Fire above, water below, and air, a breath occupying the space between.

In the universe the Dragon is like a king on his throne; in the year the sphere is like a king in his city; in the person the heart is like a king in his provinces.

First we note that while the two texts are not identical, they do bear a striking similarity. Except for a few words, the last sentence is particularly alike in both translations.

Now the passage which we have just quoted was a most troublesome one for the author of *l'Etude sur le Zohar.* He feels that here there is something important, an interesting problem to work out, but no clear solution appears.

We can do no better than to quote his own words. Concerning the words 'he suspended them from the Dragon', he writes: 'This word has been diversely interpreted. Apparently the author intends that the Dragon is to the universe what the sphere is to the year, what the heart is to the person, that is, the centre or motivating force of everything. The Dragon may then be something like the constellation of the Serpent, the intersecting points of the Sun's orbit and the equator. Thus the two points of intersection would be the head and tail of the Dragon.'[1] And further on, concerning the final sentence which we gave above, he says: 'That is, the Dragon does not leave the palace of the sky, the sphere remains in proximity to the sky, and the heart is a purely terrestrial centre. All three are manifestations of God, but each is farther from him than the preceding. Or else the Dragon is a motionless centre, the sphere revolves without changing orbit, and the heart is like a king in battle, that is, presiding over the order of the many organs deployed around it. I offer these explanations with all reservation, having not been able to arrive with any certain clarity at the intentions of the author.'[2]

As we can see, Karppe frankly admits not having been able to elucidate this passage; and this inability, we are certain, is due to his absolute conviction, based on previous work, that the *Sepher Yetzirah* cannot date back further than the eighth century. Without question, before desperately latching onto the constellation of the Serpent which has nothing to do with the matter, he ought to have thought of the constellation of Draco, the Dragon, spelled out plainly in the text, and which, depending on the season in which it is observed, 'sometimes hunts from one end of the sky to the other ... and sometimes introduces its tail into its mouth like a coiled serpent.'[3]

We can only account for this oversight by a realization that no more in the ninth century than today was this constellation thought to occupy a position in the sky 'like a king on his

---

[1] S. KARPPE, *Loc. cit.*, p.157, note 1.
[2] S. KARPPE, *Loc. cit.*, p.157, note 3.
[3] This is the description given by the *Sepher Raziel*, quoted by KARPPE, *Loc. cit.*, p.157, note 1.

throne'. That is, it was not considered to be a fixed point around which all the universe seemed to turn, in a word, the pole. He did understand perfectly, however, that the *Sepher Yetzirah* thus designates the centre of the world, and we are most surprised that he should have sought to make of this centre the point of intersection of the equator and the ecliptic.

It is impossible, though it requires a short digression, for us to remain silent in regard to the serious error of placing the intersecting points of the equator and the ecliptic in the constellation of the Serpent. In spring the equinoctial point is in Pisces; in autumn, in Virgo, and in the 25,000 years which constitute the duration of revolution of these points, they can never be in the Serpent, which is not a zodiacal constellation.

There can be no doubt that the king on his throne in the universe, the king around which gravitates the entire court of stars, is the Polar Star. Still at the present day, although we know the contrary to be true, we still take the Polar Star to be, practically speaking, the centre of the sidereal universe. If the author of the *Sepher Yetzirah* was as well acquainted as we with the system of the earth – and of this fact we are firmly persuaded – he could not have otherwise, nor more clearly have designated the centre. Therefore, if he gives the Dragon as pole, this must mean that at the time of the *Sepher Yetzirah*'s formulation, the Polar Star was a part of this constellation.

If on a star map we follow the circle described by the pole in the long period of 25,000 years, we find that this pole, at the present time near the star *Alpha* of Ursa Minor, during the entire stretch of time extending from the year 2000 B.C. to about the year A.D. 1000, has gravitated through a space almost entirely devoid of bright stars. The star to which it drew closest during this time, and the distance was great, was *Beta* of Ursa Minor. About a thousand years before the Christian era, this star was an approximate indication of the pole, which then withdrew gradually from it, arriving in the year A.D. 850 in the neighbourhood of its present position.

Going back still further, from 3,500 and 2,000 years before Christ, we find that the pole, not yet having reached the constellation of Ursa Minor where it is today, cut obliquely across the constellation of the Dragon. Towards the year 2800 B.C. the pole was the closest to the brilliant alpha, *Thuban*, of the Dragon – nearly as close as it now is to the alpha of Ursa Minor – but during the entire fifteen century period which separates the year 3500 B.C. from the year 2000 B.C. it was certainly this star which was taken as an indication of the pole, since during this time, Thuban was the brightest and closest star in its proximity.

At this period of history the Dragon was then most assuredly 'the King on his throne', the centre of the Universe; and if the *Sepher Yetzirah* gives it this title, the work itself must necessarily date from the same epoch.

It remains for us to find out to what period belongs the existence of the Hebrew patriarch who, according to Qabalistic tradition, put together the *Sepher Yetzirah*, and if this period falls within the fifteen centuries during which the Dragon was indicative of the pole. If we open *l'Histoire ancienne des peuples de l'Orient* by Maspéro – a name towards which modern science certainly bears no ill will – we read:

'A fragment of an old chronicle inserted into the sacred Book of the Hebrews speaks discreetly of another Elamite who waged war in person almost to the boundaries of Egypt. This was Kuturlagamar who supported Rimsin against Hammurabi and could not prevent his fall. He had reigned for thirteen years over the Orient when the cities of the Dead Sea, Sodom, Gomorrha, Adamah, Zeboim and Belah, revolted against him. He called together his greatest vassals, Amraphel of Chaldea, Ariok of Elassar, Tideal of Guti, and departed with them to the edge of his domain ... In the meantime, however, the kings of the five rebel cities has assembled their troops and awaited him resolutely on the plain of Siddim. They were conquered; of those who fled, some perished in the bitumen pits which scored the area, others escaped, not without difficulty, to the mountains. Kuturlagamar sacked Sodom and Gomorrha and re-established his hegemony everywhere, then he returned loaded with bounty. Hebrew tradition has it that near the headwaters of the Jordan he was attacked by the patriarch Abraham.'[1]

And so, thanks to historical criticism itself, the epoch during which Abraham lived is established. He was a contemporary and adversary of Kuturlagamar, the Chodorlahomor of the Bible, who unsuccessfully went to the aid of his vassal Rimsin against Hammurabi. Now Hammurabi is the sixth king of the first Babylonian dynasty and his reign in Chaldea began

[1] MASPERO, *Histoire ancienne des peuples de l'Orient classique*, vol. II, p.47 et. seq.

towards the end of the twenty-fifth century before our era. Although scholars of Assyrian history are far from being in agreement as to the exact date of his reign – Oppert, for example, dates this from 2394 to 2339 B.C. and Carl Niebuhr from 2081 to 2026 B.C. – none of them places it any later than the year 2000 B.C. G. Smith and Pinches give dates midway between these two extremes, and we ascribe to their view, placing the reign of Hammurabi from 2287 to 2232 B.C.

Moreover, the Bible tells us that Abraham was eighty-six years old at the time of the birth of Ishmael, which no doubt came about a few years after his attack against Kuturlagamar. If then the patriarch was about eighty when Rimsin waged war against Hammurabi, we can consider im to have lived between 2300 and 2200 B.C. Historically and astronomically speakingn nothing opposes the tradition that Abraham was in fact the author of the *Sepher Yetzirah*, since at this time the Polar Star was in the constellation of the Dragon.

And if the objection were raised that this is all merely a matter of wishful thinking, 'supported' by a few simple coincidences, might we not ask if it is also a matter of pure coincidence that the reign of Hoang-Ti has been fixed in the year 2700 B.C. precisely because of a reference in his royal annals to the self-same alpha of the Dragon? And is it also a coincidence that the pyramids of Giseh were built so as to open facing the Polar Star of the time: the Alpha of the Dragon? All the other dates attributed to ancient works from astronomical concordances furnished by the works themselves, are these all simply a matter of chance?

Let us then summarize what we have said and so conclude. The *Sepher Yetzirah* is ancient in origin. It cannot belong to the eighth century A.D., nor even to the Essenians, as Jellinek would have it, a fact mentioned by Karppe who refuses to accord the work even this relative antiquity. Nothing opposes the view that the *Sepher* dates from the time of Abraham; and although the work cannot have been much after him, the pole having moved away from the Dragon a few centuries later, it is possible that the book originated at an even earlier time, since twelve centuries separate the probable dates of the patriarch from the original entry of the pole into this constellation.

If the Qabalist who later set down the *Sepher Yetzirah* in writing left the Dragon in the Universe like a king on his throne, this signifies only that he did not in any way modify the oral tradition he had received, simply thickening the veil of obscurity which for so many centuries had covered works of an occult nature, the veil which can alone be lifted by him who seeks, thinks, combines, imagines and re-establishes the creature in the place assigned by the Creator.

Dr SAIR A.C.

8.–EXTRACTS FROM THE ZOHAR

Notes on the Origin of the Qabalah

שלשלתהקבלה

R. Gedalyah ihn Yachnir hen Don Yosef d'Imola (1523-1588) called in the Shelsheleth ha quabalah, Ravenna, 1549.

At the end of the year 5050 of creation (1290 A.D.) there were several persons who declared that all the parts of the Zohar written in the dialect of Jerusalem (the Talmudic dialect) were composed by R.S.B.I., and that all the parts in sacred language (Hebrew gur) should not be attributed to him.

Others affirm that R. Moses Ben Nachman discovered the book on holy ground, sent it to Catalonia, from whence it passed into Aragon and the hands of R. M. de L.

Still others say that R. M. de L. was a most learned man who drew the whole thing from his imagination, attributing it to R.S.B.I. This he did because of poverty and a great accumulation of debts.

For my part I hold that none of these opinions is well founded and that R.S.B.I. and his holy society composed it all, as well as many others; but they did not judge the time appropriate for an over-all assembling of these works, which were copied and later put in order. This should not surprise us, for it is the way in which the master Ishuda the Holy composed the Mishna, compiling it from various scattered manuscripts; and R. Ashi did likewise for the Gemara.

A long discussion as to the ancientness of the Zohar has taken place in the Qabalah. One of its most remarkable defenders, David Luriah, has summarized his conclusions in the 5 points which follow (Kadmooth ha Zohar).

1. R.M.D.L. did not compile the Zohar.
2. The Geonim (657-1036) referred to certain citations from the Zohar under the name of Midrash Yerushalmi. In particular, Sherirah Gaon (969-1038) used the expression הסמתהקבלה. Groetz, an adversary of the antiquity of the

Zohar, himself recognizes that the Geonim were acquainted with the Book Nistaroth ha R.S.B.I. which was the Zohar. Lastly Saadya Gaon, of whom there exists in Oxford a manuscript, Commentaries on the Sepher Yetzirah, quotes the Midrash of R.S.B.I. (900).

3. The Zohar was completed before the Talmud.

4. A large part of the Zohar was composed at the time of R.S.B.I. and his disciples.

5. The Aramaic dialect of the Zohar proves its contemporaneity with the midrashim of the Talmudic period.

Let us join to this the testimony of St Agobard (800) who quotes from the mysterious books of the Hebrews; references scattered through the writings of Philon and of Strach; the Book of Wisdom, a work contemporary with the birth of Christ; the testimonies of Menahem de Recanati (1280) and R. Jose ben Abr. Eba Wakkar of Toledo (1290) who refer to several midrashim, the Zohar among them, as works of mystical philosophy, copies of which began to circulate in 1200.

1st edition
{
1558, Cremona. Vincenczo Conti. 400 pp. (Zohar ha Gadol).

1558, Mantua. J. Winkel, 3 vol., 700 pp. (Zohar ha Keton).
}

Since that time there have been a great many editions, both in the east and the west.

For works before the Zohar, Cf. Molitor, pp. 36, 37. I have found nothing better. Everything to be found in Molitor conforms to tradition, save p.38 where the two treatises, Haminchad and Higgereth Trasodoth, are judged to be of a much more recent date.

THE IDRA SUTA OR THE GREAT SYNOD

Commentary on the Siphra Dzeniuta by Simeon Ben-Jochai

I

Jerusalem had just been destroyed by the Romans. It was forbidden to the Jews, on pain of death, to return to mourn the ruins of their homeland. The entire nation had been dispersed, the holy traditions lost. The true Qabalah had given way to puerile and superstitious subtleties. Those who claimed to preserve the heritage of hidden doctrine were nothing more than sorcerers and fortune-tellers, justly proscribed by the laws of nations. It was then that a venerable rabbi named Simeon Ben-Jochai gathered round him the last initiates of primitive science, having resolved to explain to them the book of high theogony called the Book of Mystery. Each of them know the text by heart, but only the rabbi Simeon was acquainted with the profound meaning of this book which had, up to this time, been transmitted from mouth to mouth, from memory to memory, without explanation or even benefit of the written word.

In order to assemble them round him, here are the words he sent them:

Why, in these days of great torment, should we remain as a house supported by a single column, or as a man who stands on only one foot? It is time to take action for the Lord, for men have lost the true sense of the law.

Our days grow short, the master calls; the harvest has been abandoned, the reapers have strayed far from the ripened vine.

Come together in this same countryside where so much has so lately gone undone. Come, as if for combat, armed with wisdom, counsel, intelligence, knowledge and attention; let your feet be as unencumbered as your hands.

Acknowledge as your only master he who holds sway over life and death, and together we shall utter the words of truth which heaven's saints are wont to hear, and they will come down among us to hear us.

On the appointed day, the rabbis assembled in the fields, in a circular space enclosed by a high wall.

They arrived in silence. Rabbi Simeon sat down in the midst of them, and seeing them all together, he wept.

'I am lost,' he cried, 'if I reveal the great mysteries! I am lost if I leave them unexplained!'

The rabbis remained silent.

At last one of them, named Rabbi Abba, spoke, saying:

'With the master's permission. Is it not written: "The secrets of the Lord belong to those who fear him?" And all we who are here, do we not fear the Lord, and are we not already privy to the secrets of the Temple?'

Now here are the names of those who were present: Rabbi Eleazar, son of Rabbi Simeon, Rabbi Abba, Rabbi Jehuda, Rabbi José, son of Jacob, Rabbi Issac, Rabbi Thiskia, son of Raf, Rabbi José and Rabbi Jesa.

All, binding themselves to secrecy, put their hand in that of Rabbi Simeon and with him pointed towards heaven. Then they took their seats in the circumscribed area, where they were well hidden by large trees.

Rabbi Simeon stood and prayed; then he sat down again and said to them: 'Come, all of you, and place your right hand on my breast.'

They did so; and he, taking all these hands in his own, said solemnly, 'Cursed be he who makes for himself an idol and hides it! Woe unto him who covers falsehood with the veils of mystery!'

The eight rabbis answered: 'Amen.'

Rabbi Simeon went on: 'There is only one true God, before whom no other gods exist, and there is only one true people, the body of those who worship the one true God.'

Then he called his son Eleazar and had him seat himself before him. Near him, he placed Rabbi Abba and said: 'We now form a triangle, the primordial figure of all that exists; we represent the door of the temple and its two columns.'

Rabbi Simeon then refrained from speaking, and his disciples likewise. An obscure murmur made itself heard, like that of a large gathering. It was the spirits of heaven who had come down to listen.

The disciples trembled, but Rabbi Simeon said to them: 'Fear nothing and rejoice. For it is written: "Lord, I have heard the sound of your presence and I trembled."'

'Formerly God ruled over man through fear, but now his reign is that of love. Has it not been said: "You shall love your God"? Ahd did not he himself say: "I have loved you"?'

Then he added: 'The secret doctrine is for reflective souls; the troubled and restless soul cannot understand it. Can one have confidence in a nail fixed to a moving wall, ready as it is to crumble at the slightest shock?

'The whole world is founded on mystery, and if discretion is necessary in worldly affairs, how much greater should be our reserve when dealing with the mysterious dogmas which God does not even reveal to the highest of his angels?

'Heaven bends down to listen to us, but my words must remain veiled. The earth moves in order to hear, but what I say will be in symbols.

'We are, at this very moment, the gate and the columns of the universe.'

At last Rabbi Simeon spoke, and tradition preserved in the mystery of mysteries assures us that when he opened his mouth, the earth trembled beneath his feet and that his disciples felt its trembling.

II

He spoke first of the kings who ruled over Edom before the coming of the king Israel, symbols of the unbalanced powers which manifested themselves at the beginning of the universe, before the triumph of harmony.

'God,' said he, 'when he wished to create, threw over his radiance a veil and in its folds he cast his shadow. From this shadow there arose giants who said: "We are kings"; but they were nothing more than phantoms. They appeared because God had hidden himself by creating night within chaos; they disappeared when there was brought forth in the east that luminous head, that glowing head that humanity gives itself by proclaiming the existence of God, the sun, governor of our aspirations and our thoughts.

'The gods are mirages made of shadow, and God is the synthesis of splendours. Usurpers fall away when the king mounts his throne, and when God appears, the gods are banished.'

III

'Thus, when God had permitted the night to exist, in order that the stars might appear, he turned towards the shadow he had made and considered it, to give it a face.

'He formed an image on the veil with which he had covered his glory, and this image smiled at him, and he regarded this image as his own, so that he might create man in accordance with it.

'In a manner of speaking, he tried out this prison reserved for created spirits. He looked at this face that was to become one day the face of man, and his heart was moved, for already he seemed to hear the lamentations of his creations.

'You who wish to subject me to the law, it seemed to say, give me proof that this law is just, by subjecting yourself to it as well.

'And so God became man in order that he might be loved and understood by men.

'Now, of him we know only this image, formed on the veil which hides his splendour. This image is our own, and he wishes that we recognize it to be also his.

'Thus we know him without knowing him; he shows us a form and possesses none. We have given him the image of an old man, he who has no age.

'He is seated on a throne from which escape eternally sparks of light by the millions, and he commands them to become worlds. His hair radiates and stirs the stars. Universes revolve around his head, and suns bathe themselves in his light.'

IV

'The divine image is a double one. There are the heads of light and shadow, the white ideal and the black ideal, the upper head and the lower. One is the dream of the Man-God, the other is the invention of the God-Man. One represents the God of the wise, and the other, the idol of the lowly.

'All light, in truth, implies shadow and possesses its
brilliance only in opposition to that shadow.

'The luminous head pours out upon the dark one a constant
dew of splendour. "Let me in, my beloved," says God to
intelligence, "for my head is filled with dew, and among the
curls of my hair wander the tears of the night."

'This dew is the manna by which the souls of the just are
nourished. The elect are hungry for it and gather it
abundantly in the fields of heaven.

'These drops are round pearls, brilliant as diamonds and
clear as crystal. They are white and glow with all colours, for
there is one simple truth alone: the splendour of all things.'

V

'The divine image has thirteen rays: four on each side of the
triangle in which we enclose it and one at its uppermost point.

'Draw it in the sky with your thought, trace its lines from
star to star, it will contain three hundred and sixty multitudes
of worlds.

'For the high old one called the Macroprosopus or the great
creative hypothesis is also called Arich-Anphin, the immense
countenance. The other, the human god, the face of shadow,
the Microprosopus, the limiting hypothesis, is called Seir-
Anphin or the contracted countenance.

'When this countenance beholds the face of light, it grows
and becomes harmonious. Order is thus restored; but this
cannot last, for the thoughts of man are as changeable as man
himself.

'But there is always a luminous thread which attaches
shadow to light. This thread runs through the innumerable
conceptions of human thought, linking them all to divine
splendour.

'The head of light sends out its whiteness to all thinking
heads or entities, when they follow the path of law and
reason.'

VI

'The head of the supreme old one is a closed receptacle, where infinite wisdom lies at rest like a fine wine whose lees cannot be disturbed.

'This wisdom is impenetrable, possessor of itself in silence within eternity, inaccessible to the vicissitudes of time.

'It is the light, but it is the dark head which is the lamp. The oil of intelligence is melted out, and its brilliance, by thirty-two ways, is made manifest.

'God revealed is God hidden. This human shadow of God is like the mysterious Eden from which there issued a spring that divided itself into four rivers.

'Nothing pours forth from God himself. His substance is without issue. Nothing departs from him and nothing enters in, for he is impenetrable and immutable. All that begins, all that appears, all that is divided, all that flows and passes, begins, appears, is divided, flows and passes in his shadow. He is, unto himself, immovable in his light, and he remains thus, like an old wine laid to rest.'

VII

'Do not seek to penetrate the thoughts of the mysterious head. Its intimate thoughts are hidden, but its exterior creative thoughts shine forth like a head of hair. White hair without shadow and whose strands are never tangled.

'Each strand is a thread of light attached to millions of worlds. The hairs are divided at the forehead and descend on either side; but each side is the right side. For in the divine image which constitutes this head of light, the left side has no place.

'The left side of the head of light is the dark head, for in traditional symbolism, the lower reaches are the equivalent of the left.

'Now, between the heights and the depths of the image of God there must be no more antagonism than between the left hand and the right hand of man, since harmony results from the analogy of opposites.

'Israel in the desert grew discouraged and asked: "Is God with us or against us?"

'Thus they spoke of him whom one knows and of him who is not known.

'Thus they separated the white head from the dark head.

'The god of shadow became, then, an exterminating phantom.

'They were punished because they had doubted through lack of confidence and love.

'One does not understand God, but one loves him; and it is love that produces faith.

'God hides from the mind of man, but reveals himself to the heart.

'When man says: "I do not believe in God," it is as if he were to say: "I do not love."

'And the voice of shadow answers: "You will die because your heart renounces life."

'The Microprosopus is the great night of faith, and it is in faith that the just live and breathe. They stretch forth their hands and take hold of the hair of the father, and from these splendid strands fall drops of light which come to illuminate their night.

'Between the two sides of these divided strands is the pathway of initiation, the middle path, the path of opposites in harmony.

'There, all is reconciled and understood. There, only good triumphs and evil is no longer.

'This pathway is that of supreme balance and is called the last judgement of God.

'The hairs of the white head spread out in perfect order on all sides, but do not cover the ears.

'For the ears of the Lord are always open to prayer. And nothing can prevent them from hearing the orphan's cry or the wail of the oppressed.'

THE CLASSICS OF THE QABALAH
THE TALMUDISTS AND THE TALMUD

The importance of the Talmud, derisively denied by the ignorance of Christians, and blindly maintained by the common superstition of the Jews, rests entirely on the great and changeless truths of the holy Qabalah.

The Talmud, the name of which is composed of the sacred Tau and a Hebrew word meaning teaching, contains seven distinct parts which the scholar must take care not to confuse: the MISHNA or the Talmud of Jerusalem, the two GEMARA or the Talmud of Babylon, the TOSEPH-THOTH or additions, the BERICHTA or appendices, the MARSHIN or allegorical commentaires, and the HAGGADA or traditional tales.

The Talmudists, compilers of this variegated work, belonged to three classes of rabbins whose successive authority preserved, interpreted and commented upon these primitive texts. These were the Thenaim or initiates, the Amoraim or more popular disciples of the Thenaim; then came the Massorites and the Shashamin, blind preservers of the texts, systematic calculators of written signs whose absolute value was not known to them, doctors who glimpsed the Qabalah only in the mathematical games of a poorly understood GEMATRIA and an insufficient THEMURAH.

With Christians and Jews alike, the tendency of the official church or synagogue has always been towards the materialization of signs in order to substitute a hierarchy of temporal influence for the hierarchy of knowledge and virtue. Thus it was that before the coming of Christ, prophecy, representing initiation and progress, had always maintained an open struggle or at least a mute state of hostility with the priesthood. Thus also the Pharisaism of Jesus's time persecuted the new Essenian school, of which he was founder, and later opposed the teachings of the disciples of Hillel and Chamai. Later the Kohanin were antagonistic to Israelite initiates of the school of Alexandria, and the synagogue of the

Shashamin and the Massorites harried the Koanim, or excellent teachers, leaving them in relative peace only due to an occultism which was no doubt one of the secret roots of the Masonic institutions during the shadows of the Middle Ages. And so it is not to the official synagogue to which we must turn for the keys of the high Qabalah and the hidden meaning of the Talmud. Present-day representatives of ancient biblical theology will tell you that Maimonides, that great light of Israel, not only was never a Qabalist, but considered the study of the Qabalah to be useless and even dangerous. Disciples of Maimonides, however, venerated the Talmud, rather resembling the mystical-minded idealists who reject Christianity but revere the Gospels. Never at any time has contradiction given the human spirit cause for fear.

If the Talmud had not originally been the great Qabalistic key to Judaism, its very existence and the traditional veneration it receives would be incomprehensible. We have in fact quoted from the Israelite catechism which asserts that all devout Jews must consider the Talmud as the authentic classical anthology of the secret laws of Jehovah, preserved by the wisdom of Moses for the traditional teaching of the priestly tribe. Moreover, we know that the body of this occult theology is definitely what all serious initiates have taken to be the totality of the Qabalah. Thus the key to this science, which alone opens all the secret doors, allowing one to penetrate the profundities of the Bible, must also be applicable to all the mysteries of the Talmud, another conventional bible, assembled above all as a test of the Biblical keys. This is why the Talmudists, wishing to underscore the allegorical sense of certain patently absurd passages of the sacred texts, augment this very absurdity by 'explaining' an improbable passage with a perfectly impossible commentary. Here is an example of this method:

The author of the allegorical book of Job symbolizes brute force in two monsters, one terrestrial, the other marine, which he names Behemoth and Leviathan. Certainly it is with Qabalistic intention that he employs the number two, the binary, for brute force always exists in opposition to itself, in accordance with the fatal or providential laws of equilibrium. And as in the eternal generation of things, harmony results from the analogy of opposites, in titanic excesses of force, harmony is preserved or re-established by the antagonism of equalities. This is the meaning of the author of the book of Job. Here are the comments of the Talmudist in this regard.

'Elohim permitted the sea to give itself a visible master and the earth, a king.'

– This reminds us of the fable of the frogs and the crane.

'The sea gave birth to Leviathan and the earth brought forth Behemoth from its agitated womb.

'Leviathan was the great serpent of the sea.

'Behemoth was the cherub with immense horns.'

– This is the origin of our devil.

'But presently Leviathan so filled the sea that the waters cried out to Elohim, not knowing where to take refuge.

'The earth, in her turn, bemoaned her fate, crushed beneath the feet of Behemoth and robbed by him of all her greenery.

Elohim took pity and removed Leviathan from the sea and Behemoth from the earth.

'And he salted them in order to preserve them for the banquet on the last day.

'Then the elect will eat of the flesh of Leviathan and Behemoth, and they will find it delectable, for it is the Lord who has preserved and prepared it.'

– Who is Voltaire to laught at this monstrous salting, this God-chef, and a banquet consisting of the frightful flesh of mummies! We admit that the rabbinical allegories are often somewhat shocking to the taste and finesse which later literature derived. But what will our amused audience have to say if shown that the fable of Leviathan and Behemoth portrays the solution to the enigma of evil? What would they answer, for example, if told: Christianity's devil represents the blind excesses of the vital force, but nature preserves and maintains equilibrium. Even monstrosities have their place and will serve sooner or later to nourish universal harmony. Do not be afraid of phantoms. Everything above man must be more beautiful and better than man; below, there is the beast, and the beast, however wild and immoderate, must be the auxiliary of man, his pasture! Frightened children, fear no more lest the devil eat you! Be men, and it is you who will eat the devil, for the devil, that is, the spirit of absurdity and lack of intelligence, cannot rise higher than the beast. This is what must be understood in the Qabalistic final feast of the Behemoth and the Leviathan!

Now imagine a commentator, Kohanim or Massorite,

taking the Talmudic allegory face value, seriously discussing its literal reality, proving the real existence of Leviathan and Behemoth, establishing for example that the Moon is the saltvat of the Eternal Father, that having emptied it out and filled it with salt, he transported the monsters there, etc., etc., and you have an idea of the entire composition of the Talmud, of its veiled lights and naive errors.

The first Talmud, the only truly Qabalistic one, the Mishna, was composed during the first century of the Christian era by the last leader of the Thenaim, Rabbi Yehuda-Hakadosh-Hanassi, that is, Yuda the most holy and the prince. The names Kadosh and prince were given to great initiates of the Qabalah, and have been maintained among the adepts of occult Masonry and the Rosy-Cross. Rabbi Yehuda composed his book in accordance with all the rules of high initiation, wrote it from within and from without, in the words of Ezekiel and Saint John, indicating its transcendental sense by the sacred letters and numbers corresponding to the Bereschith of the first six Sephiroth. The Mishna comprises six books called *Sederim*, whose order and subjects correspond to the absolute signs of Qabalistic philosophy, as we will show.

We have already stated that the Qabalists do not define God, but worship him in his manifestations which are idea and form, intelligence and love. They posit a supreme power founded on two laws, fixed wisdom and active intelligence, or in other terms, necessity and freedom. Thus a first triangle is formed:

KETHER the crown
BINAH intelligence   CHOKMAH wisdom

Then, like a reflection of this supreme concept of the ideal plane, they establish a second triangle in reverse. Absolute justice, corresponding to supreme wisdom or necessity, absolute love, corresponding to active intelligence or freedom, and supreme beauty which results from the harmonization of justice and love, corresponding to divine power.

GEDULAH love   GEBURAH justice
TIPHERETH beauty

By combining and overlapping these two triangles, one obtains the flaming star or seal of Solomon, that is, the complete expression of the theological philosophy of Bereschith or universal genesis.

It was on this base that Rabbi Yehuda established the divisions of his work. The first book or Sederim, corresponding to the idea Kether, is entitled ZERAIM, sowing of seeds, for in the notion of the supreme crown there is contained the concepts of the fecundating principle and of universal production.

The second book corresponds to the Sephira Chokmah. It is called MOED and is concerned with sacred things which must not be changed since they stand for eternal order.

The third book, relative to Binah, freedom or the creative power, treats of women and the family and bears the name NASHIM.

The fourth book, inspired by the idea of Geburah or justice, treats of iniquities and their punishments. It is entitled NAZCHIM.

The fifth book, corresponding to Gedulah, that is, mercy and love, bears the title KADOSHIM, and speaks of consoling beliefs and holy things.

Lastly the sixth book, relative to the Sephira Tiphereth, contains the most hidden secrets of life and related morality. Its subject is purification, that is, the medicine of the soul, and it bears the mysterious name of THAROTH or TAROT, expressing in a word all the hidden meanings of the symbolical wheels of Ezekiel and also the name Thorah, which rabbis still in our day give to the entire Scripture.

At the beginning of the Mishna, Rabbi Yehuda-Hakadosh-Hanassi placed the inherited tradition of the sages of Judaism. These are the proverbs and sayings of the successor of Solomon, in the extent of sovereign wisdom.

The earth, said Simon the Just, subsists through three things:

'Through the teaching of the law,

'The duties and services of worship,

'And works of charity.'

Here again we find the Qabalistic triangle, stable law, progressive religion and charity, which is the life and common reason of worship and law.

Antigonus said: 'Do not be like the servant who obeys in

order to receive payment. Let your recompense be in your obedience itself, and let the respect for higher things be inherent in you.'

There is nothing superstititious in this and might advantageously be pondered upon by a great number of Catholics.

'The day is short,' said Rabbi Tarphon, 'the task is great and the workers are slothful; and still they will receive most generously their day's payment, for the master answers for them and compensates for their indolence with his activity.'

'A promise of salvation for all; a daring denial of sin and evil, giving responsibility to providence and excluding the idea of punishment in the temporary necessity of suffering, considered only as a spur to the idleness of men.'

Akabiah said: 'Know three things and you will never sin:

'Where you come from,

'Where you are going,

'And to whom you are responsible.'

– These are three things which one must know in order to no longer do deliberate evil.

He who knows these three things can no longer sin, unless he is a fool.

He who does not yet know them cannot yet sin; how indeed can one fail at duties of which one is ignorant?

Such are the maxims gathered by master Yudah, the saint and the prince, and given at the start of the book concerning seeds or universal principles. Next it moves from the figurative to the practical and speaks of agriculture. Here Volney and Dupuis find the calendar to be fundamental to the supreme mysteries of the Jewish religion. And why not? Does not the crown of Kether correspond to the crown of the year? And are not the religious festivals the visible points of this diadem of supreme beliefs? But the transcendental philosophy of the Talmud is far removed from all the superstitions of materialistic beliefs.

'He who says: I wish to sin and the day of pardon will come in which I will be absolved, he makes the day of pardon useless and will not be absolved of his voluntary iniquities.'

'Sins,' said the Talmudists again, 'when they are between man and God, can be absolved by God on the day of pardon; but when they are between man and man, that is, when they are the property of justice within the brotherhood of mankind, they can only be set right by man, declaring before the law that reparation has been made.'

This is magnificent and needs no commentary.

Such is the wisdom which presides over the feasts of Israel as described in the second book of the Talmud of Jerusalem, so closely aligned to the first, since the one deals with the culture of fields and souls, and the other with the worship of God and the symbolic calendar.

The third book or *Sederim* is consecrated especially to the subject of women and the unit of the family. Talmudic jurisprudence does not separate woman from man, avoiding the irritating questions of equality or superiority which seek to establish an antagonism in love, thereby destroying and negating love itself. For the Qabalists, woman is neither the equal, nor the servant, nor the mistress, nor the associate of man; she is man himself, conceived from the affectionate, maternal rib. Woman possesses all the rights of man in man, and man respects himself in woman.

'Let human folly never separate what divine wisdom has united! And woe to those who live alone!!!'

Questions of the emancipation of women and of civil equality are in fact the fancies of celibrate women; and before natural law, celibacy is an outrage.

'Oh, soul of my soul, heart of my heart, flesh of my flesh,' an initiate into the mysteries of the Mishna might say, 'you speak of becoming my equal? And so you wish to become something other than myself?! You wish to tear your heart away from mine, to make two of what was one; and as god formed you from the flesh and bone of my breast, so you desire to take from yourself without me some monstrous thing with which to complete yourself and replace me in your being! But when you have become my rival in love, can you ever become my equal in sorrow and regret?'

Said a Talmudic rabbi: 'The altar weeps when a husband is separated from his wife.'

The fourth book of the Mishna, discussing injustices and damages, is a collection of civil laws far superior to the codes of the Middle Ages. It is to the source of this secret legislation that must be ascribed the preservation of Israel through so many persecutions, and its deliverance through industry, the final material term of civilization and the safeguard of all the political rights which have been so painfully and completely regained by the rehabilitated children of the ancient pariahs of Israel.

The books entitled *Kadoshim* and *Tharoth* complete the body of supreme Jewish tradition and bring to a magnificent close the cycle of revelations of Rabbi Yehuda. It is a long way from this beautiful initiatory work to the commentaries of the two Gemara and to the aristotelian exegesis of Moses Maimonides.

This Maimonides, however, was a learned doctor and even a great man. But he was prejudiced against the Qabalistic keys of the Talmud by a horror of superstition and a reaction against mysticism. In his *Noreh Nevushin* (the guide of the wanderers), he traces the traditions of the Thalmud to the vulgar laws of nature and reason, then in *Jad Haksaka* (the strong Hand) he reassembles the Jewish beliefs into a symbol of thirteen articles, a masterpiece of simplicity and reason, but which, unbeknown to him, is so in keeping with the purest Qabalah, that the first keys of the Tarot, that great Qabalistic wheel, correspond exactly in their hieroglyphic signs to the thirteen fundamental articles of Maimonides' symbol.

(From *La Clef des Grands Mystères*, by ELIPHAS LEVI)

9.–THE PRACTICAL QABALAH

The 72 Spirits corresponding to the 72 names according to
LENAIN.

FIRST SPIRIT

Name: Vehuiah (יהויה).
Attribute: **God raised and exalted above all things.**
Corresponding Divine Name: *Jehova* יהוה.
Dwelling place: Region of fire.
Sign: Aries.
To be illuminated by the spirit of God.
Biblical reference: Ps. 3:5.
Et tu Domine susceptor meus et gloria mea et exultans
caput meum.
Subtle spirit. Endowed with great wisdom, enthusiastic for
science and the arts, capable of undertaking and accom-
plishing the most difficult things.
Feature: *Energy.*
Negative influence: Unquiet man. Anger.

2nd Spirit   יליאל   (Jeliel)
Helpful God

DN   *Aydy*

To quell popular uprisings. To obtain victory over those
who attack unjustly.
Ps. 21:20.
Tu autem Domine ne elongareris auxilium tuum a me ad
defensionem meam conspice.

*Sprightly spirit, agreeable and courteous manners, passionate for sex.

Negative influence: All that is harmful for animate beings.

3rd Spirit   סיטאל   (Sitael)
God, hope of all creatures

11th to 15th degrees of the Sphere

Against adversities.
Ps. 90:2
Dixit Domino susceptor meus es tu et refugium meum:
Deus meus sperabo in eum.
Protects against weapons and wild beasts.
* Loves truth, will keep his word, will oblige those in need of
his services.
Negative influence: Hypocrisy, ingratitude, falsehood.

4th Spirit   עלמיה   (Elemiah)
Hidden God

Alla
16th to 20th degrees

Against mental troubles and for the identification of
traitors.
Ps. 6:4
Convertere Domine et eripe animam meam: salvum me fac
propter misericordium tuam.
Governs voyages, sea travels.
* Industrious, successful, keen for travel.
Negative influence: Poor upbringing, dangerous discoveries, hampers all undertakings.

5th Spirit   מחשיה   (Mahasiah)
God the Saviour

21st to 25th.   *Toth, Teut, Theuth*

To live in peace with everyone.
Pronounce the divine names and Ps. 33:4.
Exquisivi Dominum et exaudivit me et ex omnibus tribu-
lationibus meis eripuit me.

Governs: High Science, Occult Philosophy, Theology, the Liberal Arts.

* Learns easily, keen for honest pleasures.

Negative influence: Ignorance, licentiousness, bad qualities of body and mind.

6th Spirit   ללהאר   (Lelahel)

Praiseworthy God

Abgd

26th to 30th.

To acquire knowledge and cure disease.

Ps. 9:11.

Psalite Domino qui habitat in Sion: annuntiata inter gentes studia ejus.

Governs: Love, Renown, Science, Arts and Fortune.

* Features: Ambition, Fame.

Negative influence: Evil ambition. Fortune by illicit means.

7th Spirit   אכאיח   (Achaiah)

Good and patient God

31 to 35°

Ps. 102:8.

Miserator et Misericors Dominus, longanimis et multum misericors.

Governs: Patience, Secrets of nature.

* Loves learning, proud to accomplish the most difficult tasks.

Negative influence: Enemy of knowledge.

8th Spirit   כהתאל   (Cahetel)

Adorable God

Moti

36 to 40°

Ps. 94:6.

Venite adoremus et procidamus et ploremus ante Dominum qui fecit nos.

To obtain the benediction of God and to drive away evil spirits.

Governs: Agricultural production. Inspires man to rise towards God.

* Loves work, agriculture, countryside, hunting.

Negative influence: All that is harmful to crops, blasphemy against God.

9th Spirit   הזיאל   (Aziel)

God of Mercy

Agzi

41 to 45°

Ps. 24:6.

Reminiscere miserationum tuarum, Domine, et misericordiarum tuarum quae a saeculo sunt.

Mercy of God, friendship and favour of the great, execution of a promise made.

Governs: Good faith and reconciliation.

* Sincere in promises, will easily extend pardon.

Negative influence: Hate, hypocrisy.

10th Spirit   אלדיה   (Aladiah)

Propitious God

Sire and Eipi

46 to 50°

Ps. 32:22.

Fiat misericordia tua, Domine super nos, quemadmodum speravimus in te.

Good for those guilty of hidden crimes and fearing discovery.

Governs: Rage and pestilence, cure of disease.

* Good health, successful in his undertakings.

Negative influence: Ill health, failure.

11th Spirit   לאויה   (Lauviah)

God exalted and praised

Deus

51 to 55°

Ps. 17:50.

Vivit Dominus et benedictus Deus meus et exsultatur Deus salutis meae.

Against lightning and for the obtainment of victory.
Governs: Renown.
* Great personage, learned, celebrated for personal talents.
Negative influence: Excessive pride, jealousy, calumny.

12th Spirit   חהעיה   (Hahaiah)
God the refuge

56 to 60°

Against adversity.
Ps. 9:22.
Ut quid Domine recessisti longe despicis in oppor-
tunitatibus in tribulatione.
Governs: Dreams. Mysteries hidden from mortals.
* Gentle, witty, discreet manners.
Negative influence: Indiscretion, lies, abuse of trust.

13th Spirit   יזלאל   (Iezalel)
God glorified above all things

Boog

61 to 65°

Ps. 97:6.
Jubilate Deo omnis terra, cantate et exultate et psallite.
Governs: Friendship, reconciliation, conjugal fidelity.
* Learns easily. Adroit.
Negative influence: Ignorance, falsehood, error.

14th Spirit   מבהאל   (Mebahel)
Preserving God

Dios

66 to 70°

Against those who seek to usurp the fortunes of others.
Ps. 9:9.
Et factus est Dominus refugium pauperis: adjutor in
opportunitatibus in tribulatione.
Governs: Justice, Truth, Liberty. Delivers the oppressed
and protects prisoners.
* Loves jurisprudence, affinity for law courts.
Negative influence: Calumny, false witness, law suits.

15th Spirit   חריאל   (Hariel)

God the creator

Idio

71 to 75°

Against the impious.

Their names should be pronounced along with the divine names.

Ps. 93:22.

Et factus est mihi Dominus in refugium et Deus meus in adjutorium spei meae.

Governs: Sciences and Arts.

* Religious sentiments, morally pure.

Negative influences: Schisms, religious wars, impiety, heretical sects.

16th Spirit   חקמיה   (Hakamiah)

God who erects the Universe

God

76 to 80°

Against traitors and for deliverance from those who seek to oppress us.

Pronounce their names along with the following:

O all-powerful God of the armies, you who construct the Universe and protect our nation, I invoke you, I am unknown, in the name of Hakamiah, that you may deliver the nation from its enemies.

Ps. 87:1.

Domine Deus salutis meae in die clamavi et nocte coram te.

Governs: Crowned heads, great captains. Gives victory.

* Frank, loyal, brave character, sensitive to points of honour, an affinity for Venus.

Negative influence: Treachery.

17th Spirit   לאויה   (Lauviah)

Admirable God

Goth

81 to 85°

To be invoked while *fasting*.

Ps. 8:1.

Domine Dominus noster quam admirabile est nomen in universa terra.

Against mental anguish, sadness.

Governs: High Sciences. Marvellous discoveries. Gives revelations in dreams.

* Loves music, poetry, literature and philosophy.

Negative influence: Atheism.

18th Spirit   כליאל   (Caliel)

God prompt to fulfil

Boog

86 to 90°

To obtain prompt aid.

Ps. 9:9.

Judica me Domine secundum justitiam meam et secundum innocentiam meam super me.

Makes truth known in law suits, causes innocence to triumph.

* Just, honest, loves truth, judiciary.

Negative influence: Scandalous trials, base men.

19th Spirit   לוייה   (Leuviah)

God who hears sinners

Bogy

91 to 95°

To be invoked while facing south.

Ps. 39:1.

Expectans, expectavi Dominum et intendit mihi.

To obtain the grace of God.

Governs: Memory, human intelligence.

* Amiable, lively, modest, bearing of adversity with resignation.

Negative influence: Losses, debauchery, despair.

20th Spirit   פהליה   (Pahaliah)

God the redeemer

Tios

96 to 100°

Ps. 119:2.

Domine libera animam meam a lablis iniquis et a lingua dolosa.

Against enemies of religion, for the conversion of nations to Christianity.

Governs: Religion, theology, morality, chastity, purity.

* Ecclesiastical vocation.

Negative influence: The irreligious, apostates, libertines, renegades.

21st Spirit   נלבאל   (Nelebael)

God unique and alone

Beug

101 to 105°

Ps. 30:18.

Ego autem in te speravi, Domine, dixi deus Meus es tu, in manibus tuis sortes meae.

Against calumniators and spells and for the destruction of evil spirits.

Governs: Astronomy, Mathematics, Geography and all abstract sciences.

* Loves poetry, literature, avid for study.

Negative influence: Ignorance, errors, prejudice.

22nd Spirit   ייאל   (Ieiael)

The right hand of God

Good

106 to 110°

Ps. 120:5.

Dominus custodit te: Dominus protectio tua super manum dexteram tuam.

Governs: Fortune, renown, diplomacy, commerce, influence on voyages, discoveries, protection against storms and shipwreck.

* Loves business, industriousness, liberal and philanthropic ideas.

Negative influence: Pirates, slaves.

23rd Spirit   מלהאל   (Melahel)

God who delivers from evil

Dieh

111 to 115°

Ps. 120:8.

Dominus custodiat introïtum tuum et exitum tuum et ex hoc nunc et in saeculum.

Against weapons and for safety in travel.

Governs: Water, produce of the earth, and especially plants necessary for the cure of disease.

* Courageous, accomplishes honourable actions.

Negative influence: All that is harmful to vegetation, causes sickness and plagues.

24th Spirit   חחויח   (Hahuiah)

God good in himself

116 to 120°

Divine name in Ps. 32:18.

Ecce oculi Domini super metuentes eum et in eis qui sperant in misericordia ejus.

To obtain the grace and mercy of God.

Governs: Exiles, fugitives, defaulters.

Protects against harmful animals.

Preserves from thieves and assassins.

* Loves truth, the exact sciences, sincere in word and deed.

Negative influence: Governs harmful beings.

25th Spirit   נתהיח   (Nith-Haiah)

God who gives Wisdom

Orsy

121 to 125°

Divine name in Ps. 9:1.

Confitebor tibi Domine in toto corde neo: narrabo omnia mirabilia tua.

For the acquisition of wisdom and the discovery of the truth of hidden mysteries.

Governs: Occult Sciences. Gives revelations in dreams,

particularly to those born on the day over which he presides.
Influences those who practice the magic of the sages.
Negative influence: Black magic.

26th Spirit   הׂאאיה   (Haaiah)
Hidden God
Agdu and Abdi

126 to 130°

Divine name: Ps. 118:145.
Clamavi in toto corde meo exaudi me Domine: justifications
tuas requiram.
For the winning of a law suit.
* Protects those who search after truth. Influences politics.
Diplomats, secret expeditions and agents.
Negative influence: Traitors, conspirators.

27th Spirit   ירתאל   (Jerathel)
God who punishes the wicked
Teos

131 to 135°

Divine name: Ps. 139:1.
Eripe me Domine ab homine malo; a viro iniquo eripe me.
To confound wrong-doers and liars and for deliverance
from one's enemies.
Governs: Propagation of light, civilization.
* Love peace, justice, sciences and arts; special affinity for
literature.
Negative influence: Ignorance, slavery, intolerance.

28th Spirit   שאהיה   (Seeiah)
God who heals the sick
Adad

136 to 140°

Divine name: Ps. 70:15.
Deus ne elongeris a me: Deus meus in auxilium meum
respice.
Against infirmities and thunder, protects against fire, the
ruin of buildings, falls and *illnesses*.
Governs: Health, simplicity.

* Has much judgment.
Negative influence: Catastrophes, causes apoplexy.

29th Spirit   רייאל   (Reiiel)

God prompt to aid

Zimi

141 to 145°

Divine name calls for Ps. 53:4.
Ecce enim Deus adjuvat me et Dominus sesceptor est animae meae.
Against the impious and enemies of religion; for deliverance from all enemies both visible and invisible.
* Virtue and Zeal for the propagation of truth, will do his utmost to destroy impiety.
Negative influence: Fanaticism, hypocrisy.

30th Spirit   אורנאל   (Ornael)

Patient God

Tura

Divine name: Ps. 70:6.
Quoniam tu es patientia mea Domine; Domine spes mea a juventute mea.
Against sorrow, despair and for the acquisition of patience.
Governs: Animal kingdom, watches over the generation of beings. Chemists, doctors, surgeons.
* Affinity for anatomy and medicine.
Negative influence: Unnatural phenomena.

31st Spirit   לכבאל   (Lecabel)

God who inspires

Teldi

151 to 155°

For the acquisition of knowledge.
Calls for the divine name: Ps. 70:16.
Quoniam non cognovi litteraturam; introibo in potentias Domini; Domine memorabor justitiae tuae solius.
Governs vegetation and agriculture.
* Loves astronomy, mathematics and geometry.
Negative influence: Avarice, usury.

32nd Spirit   וישריה   (Vasariah)

God the just
                                                    Anot

156 to 160°

Against those who attack us in court.
Name the person, give the motive.
Pronounce the divine names in Ps. 32:4.
Quia rectum est verbus Domini et opera ejus in fide.
Governs: Justice.
* Good memory, articulate.
Negative influence: Bad qualities of body and soul.

33rd Spirit   יחויה   (Iehuiah)

God who knows all things
                                                    Agad

161 to 165°

Ps. 33:11.
Dominus scit cogitationes hominum quoniam vanae sunt.
For the identification of traitors.
Negative influence: Encourages rebels.

34th Spirit   להחיה   (Lehahiah)

God the clement
                                                    Aneb

166 to 170°

Ps. 130:5.
Speret Israel in Domino ex hoc nunc et usque in saeculum.
Against anger.
* Known for his talents and acts, the confidence and fervour
of his prayers.
Negative influence: Discord, war, treason.

35th Spirit   כוקיה   (Chevakiah)

God who gives joy
                                                    Anup

171 to 175°

To regain the favour of those one has offended.

Pronounce the request, the divine names and the name of the person.

Ps. 114:1.

Dilexi quoniam exaudiet Dominus vocem orationis meae.

Recite daily until reconciliation occurs.

Governs: Testaments, successions and all private financial agreements.

* Loves to live in peace with everyone. Loves rewarding the loyalty of those in his service.

36th Spirit	מנדאל	(Menadel)
	Divine God	

Alla

176 to 180°

To retain one's employment and to preserve one's means of livelihood.

Recite the divine names and Ps. 25:8.

Domine dilexi decorem domus tuae et locum habitationis gloriae tuae.

Against calumny and for the deliverance of prisoners.

Negative influence: Protection for fugitives from justice.

37th Spirit	אניאל	(Aniel)
	God of virtues	

Abada

181 to 185°

Divine names and Ps. 79:8.

Deus virtutem converte nos et ostende faciem tuam et salvi erimus.

To obtain victory and stop the siege of a city.

Governs: Sciences and arts. Reveals the secrets of nature, inspires philosophers, sages.

* Distinguished savant.

Negative influence: Spirit of perversity, charlatans.

38th Spirit   העמיה   (Haamiah)
God the hope of all children of the earth
Agla (God triune and one)
186 to 190°

For the acquisition of all the treasures of heaven and earth.
Ps. 90:9.
Quoniam tu es Domine spes mea altissimum posuisti refugium tuum.
Against fraud, weapons, wild beasts and infernal spirits.
Governs all that relates to God.
Negative influence: Falsehood.

39th Spirit   רהעאל   (Rehael)
God who receives sinners

Goot

191 to 195°

Ps. 29:13.
Audivit Dominus et misertus est mei: Dominus factus est meus adjutor.
For the healing of the sick.
Governs: Health and longevity.
Influences paternal and filial affection.
Negative influence: Dead or condemned land.
The cruelest known: infanticide and patricide.

40th Spirit   ייזאל   (Ieiazel)
God who rejoices

Goed

196 to 200°

Divine names and Ps. 87:15.
Ut quid Domine repellis orationem meam avertis faciem tuam a me.
This psalm has marvellous properties.
For the deliverance of prisoners, for consolation, for deliverance from one's enemies.
Governs: Printing and books.
* Men of letters and artists.
Evil influence: on lugubrious spirits and those who flee society.

41st Spirit   ההאל   (Hahahel)
God in three persons

Gudi

201 to 205°

Ps. 119:2.
Domine libera animam meam a labiis iniquis et a lingua dolosa.
Against the impious, slanderers.
Governs Christianity.
* Greatness of soul, energy. Consecrated to the service of God.
Negative influence: Apostates, renegades.

42nd Spirit   מיכאל   (Mikael)
Virtue of God, House of God, Like unto God

Biud

206 to 210°

Address the divine name: Ps. 120:7.
Dominus custodit te ab omni malo: custodiat animam tuam Dominus.
For safety in travel.
For the discovery of conspiracies.
* Concerned with political affairs, diplomatic.
Negative influence: Treacheries, false news, malevolence.

43rd Spirit   וההיה   (Veuahiah)
Ruling king

Solu

211 to 215°

Ps. 87:14.
Et ego ad te Domine clamavi et mane oratio mea præveniet te.
For the destruction of the enemy and deliverance from bondage.
* Love glory and the military.
Evil influence: Discord among princes.

44th Spirit   יְלָהִיה   (Ielahiah)
                         Eternal God
                                                        Bosa
                         216 to 220°

Success of a useful undertaking.
Recite the divine names and Ps. 118:108.
Voluntaria oris mei bene placita fac Domine et judicia tua
doce me.
Protection of magistrates. Trials.
Protects against armies, gives victory.
* Fond of travel and learning. All his undertakings are
crowned with success; distinguished for military capabilities
and courage.
Negative influence: Wars.

45th Spirit   סאליה   (Sealiah)
                      Mover of all things
                                                        Hobo
                         221 to 225°

Ps. 93:18.
Si dicebam motus est pes meus misericordia tua Domine
adjuvebat me.
To confound the wicked and the proud, to exalt the
humiliated and the fallen.
Governs: Vegetation.
* Loves learning, much aptitude.
Negative influence: Governs the atmosphere.

46th Spirit   אריאל   (Ariel)
                       Revelatory God
                                                        Pino
                         226 to 231°

To procure revelations.
Address the request to the divine names of Ps. 144:9.
Suavit Dominus universus et miserationes ejus super omnia
opera ejus.
To thank God for the good he sends us.
Discovers hidden treasure, reveals the greatest secrets of
nature, causes the objects of one's desire to be seen in dreams.

* Strong, subtle mind, new and sublime thoughts, discreet, circumspect.

Negative influence: Tribulations of mind.

47th Spirit   עשליה   (Asaliah)
God, the just, who shows the truth
                                                            Hana
231 to 235°

Ps. 103:25.

Quam magnificata suti opera tua Domine! omnia in sapientia fecisti impleta est terra possessione tua.

For the praising of God and the growing toward him when he enlightens us.

Governs justice, makes the truth known in legal proceedings.

* Agreeable character, avid for the acquisition of secret knowledge.

Negative influence: Immoral and scandalous acts.

48th Spirit   מיכאל   (Michael)
God, helpful father
                                                            Zaca
236 to 240°

Ps. 97:3.

Notum fecit Dominus salutare suum in conspectu gentium revelavit justitiam suam.

For the preservation of peace and the union of man and wife.

Protects those who address themselves to him, gives premonitions and secret inspirations.

Governs: Generation of beings.

* Avid for love, fond of walks and pleasures in general.

Negative influence: Luxury, sterility, inconstancy.

49th Spirit   וזואל   (Vehuel)
God, great and exalted
                                                            Mara
241 to 245°

Divine name; Ps. 144:3.

Magnus Dominus et laudabilis nimis et magnitudinis ejus non est finis.

Sorrow, contrariness.

For the exaltation of oneself for the benediction and glory of God.

* Sensitive and generous soul. Literature, jurisprudence, diplomacy.

Negative influence: Egoism, hate, hypocrisy.

50th Spirit   דניאל   (Daniel)

The Sign of Mercy. The Angel of confession

Pola

246 to 250°

Ps. 102:8.

Miserator et misericors Dominus, longanimis et misericors.

To obtain the mercy of God and consolation.

Governs: Justice, lawyers, solicitors.

Furnishes conclusions to those who hesitate.

* Industrious and active in business, loves literature and is distinguished for eloquence.

Negative influence: Swindlers.

51st Spirit   ההשיה   (Hahasiah)

Hidden God

Bila

251 to 255°

Ps. 103:32.

Sit gloria Domini in saeculum laetabitur Dominus in operibus suis.

For the elevation of the soul and the discovery of the mysteries of wisdom.

Governs: Chemistry and Physics.

Reveals the secret of the philosopher's stone and universal medicine.

* Loves abstract science.

Devoted to the discovery of the properties and virtues of animals, plants and minerals.

Distinguished in medicine.

Negative influence: Charlatans.

52nd Spirit   עממיה   (Imamiah)

God elevated above all things

Abag

256 to 260°

Ps. 7:18.

Confitebor, Domine Secundum justitiam ejus et psallam nomini Domini altissim.

Destroys the power of enemies and humbles them.

Governs voyages in general, protects prisoners who turn to him and gives them the means of obtaining their freedom.

* Forceful, vigorous temperament, bears adversity with patience and courage, fond of work.

Negative influence: Pride, blasphemy, wickedness.

53rd Spirit   ננאאל   (Nanael)

God who humbles the proud

Obra

261 to 265°

Divine name and Ps. 118:75.

Cognovi Domine quia æquitas judicia tua et in virtute tua humiliasti me.

(This psalm is divided into 22 equal parts corresponding to the 22 Hebrew letters and to the 22 sacred names of God relating to them.

Qabalists claim that the Holy Virgin recited them daily.)

Governs the high sciences.

* Melancholy humour, avoids rest, meditation, well-versed in the abstract sciences.

Negative influence: Ignorance.

54th Spirit   ניתאל   (Nithael)

King of the heavens

Bora

266 to 270°

Ps. 102:19.

Dominus in cœlo paravit sedem suam: et regnum ipsius omnibus dominabitur.

To obtain the mercy of God and to live long.

Emperor, king and prince.

* Renowned for writings and eloquence, of great reputation among the learned.

Negative influence: Ruin of empires.

55th Spirit   מבהיה   (Mabaiah)
                    Eternal God

                                              Alay
                      271 to 275°

Address the divine name and recite.

Ps. 101:13.

Tu autem Domine in aeternum permanes et memoriale tuum in generationem.

Beneficial for obtaining consolation and compensations, and for those who desire children.

Governs: Morality and religion.

* Distinguished by good deeds and piety.

Negative influence: Enemies of virtue.

56th Spirit   פויאל   (Poiel)
              God who supports the Universe

                                              Illi
                      276 to 280°

Ps. 144:15.

Allevat Dominus omnes qui corruunt et erigit omnes elisos.

For the fulfilment of one's request.

Governs: Renown, fortune and philosophy.

* Well esteemed by everyone for his modesty and agreeable humour.

Negative influence: Ambition, pride.

57th Spirit   נממיה   (Nemmamiah)
                  Praiseworthy God

                                              Popa
                      281 to 285°

Ps. 113:19.

Qui timent Dominum speraverunt in Domino; adjutor eorum et protector eorum est.

For general prosperity and the deliverance of prisoners.

Governs: Great captain.

* Drawn to the military, distinguished for activity and courageous bearing of fatigue.

Negative influence: Treason.

58th Spirit   יילאל   (Ieialel)
God who hears the generations
Para

286 to 290°

Divine name and Ps. 6:3.

Et anima turbata est valde; sed tu Domine esque quo?

Protects against sorrow and care and heals the sick, especially afflictions of the eyes.

Influences *iron* and those involved in commerce.

* Brave, frank, affinity for Venus.

Negative influence: Anger, evil, murder.

59th Spirit   הרהאל   (Harahel)
God who knows all things
Ella

291 to 295°

Pronounce the name of the spirit with his attributes and Ps. 112:3.

A solis ortu usque ad occasum, laudabile nomen Domini.

Against the sterility of women and to make children obedient to their parents.

Governs: Treasure and Banks. Printings, books.

* Love of learning, successful in business (especially money market).

Negative influence: Fraudulent bankruptcy. Financial ruin.

60th Spirit   מצראל   (Mizrael)
God who comforts the oppressed
Gena

296 to 300°

Ps. 144:18.

Justus Dominus in omnibus viis suis, et sanctus in omnibus operibus suis.

For the cure of mental illness and deliverance from those who persecute us.

* Virtuous, longevity.
Negative influence: Insubordinate beings.

61st Spirit   **ומבאל**   (Umabel)
                  God above all things
                                              Sila
                      301 to 205°

Divine name and Ps. 112:2.
Sit nomen Domini benedictum ex hoc nunc et usque in saeculum.
To obtain the friendship of a given person.
* Fond of travel and honest pleasures, sensitive heart.
Negative influence: Libertines, vices contrary to nature.

62nd Spirit   **יההאל**   (Iah-hel)
                    Supreme Being
                                              Suna
                      306 to 310°

Ps. 118:159.
Vide quoniam mandata tua delixi domine, in misericordia tua vevifica me.
For the acquisition of wisdom.
Governs: Philosophers, illuminati.
* Loves tranquillity and solitude, modest, virtuous.
Negative influences: Scandal, luxury, inconstancy, divorce.

63rd Spirit   **אניאל**   (Anianuel)
                  God, infinitely good
                                              Miri
                      311 to 315°

Divine name and Ps. 2:11.
Servite Domino in timore; et exaltate ei cum tremore.
For the conversion of nations to Christianity. Protects against accidents, heals the sick.
Governs: Commerce, banking.
* Subtle and ingenious, industrious and active.

Negative influence: Folly, prodigality.

64th Spirit   מהיאל   (Mehiel)

God who gives life to all things

Alli

316 to 320°

Divine name and Ps. 32:18.

Ecce Domini super metuentes eum; et in eis qui sperant super misericordia ejus.

Against adversities.

Protects against rabies and wild beasts.

Governs: Savants, professors, orators and others.

*Distinguished in literature.

Negative influence: False scholars. Critics.

65th Spirit   דמביה   (Damabiah)

God, fountain of wisdom

Tara

321 to 325°

Ps. 89:15.

Convertere Domine et usque qua? et deprecibilis esto super servos tuos.

Against magic spells and for the obtainment of wisdom and the undertaking of successful ventures.

Governs: Seas, rivers, springs. Sailors.

* Sailor. Amasses a considerable fortune.

Negative influence: Tempests. Shipwrecks.

66th Spirit   מנקאל   (Manakel)

God who supports and maintains all things

Pora

326 to 330°

Ps. 37:22.

Ne derelinquas me Domine, Deus meus; ne discesseris a me.

For the appeasement of the anger of God and for the healing of epilepsy.

Governs: Vegetation, aquatic animals. Influences dreams.

* Gentleness of character.

Negative influence: Bad physical and moral qualities.

67th Spirit   איהאל   (Itaiel)
God, delight of the children of men
Bogo

331 to 335°

Divine name and Ps. 36:4.

Delectare in Domino et dabit tibi petitiones cordis tui.

To obtain consolation in adversity and for the acquisition of wisdom.

Influences occult science.

Makes *the truth* known to those who call on him in their work.

* Enlightened requirements of the spirit of God. Fond of solitude, distinguished in Higher Sciences.

Negative influence: Error, prejudice.

68th Spirit   חבויה   (Xabuiah)
God who gives liberally
Depos

336 to 340°

Ps. 105:1.

Confitemini Domini quoniam bonus quoniam in sæculum misericordia ejus.

For the preservation of health and the healing of the sick.

Governs: Agriculture and Fecundity.

* Fond of the countryside, hunting, gardens and all that is related to agriculture.

Negative influence: Sterility, famine, plague, harmful insects.

69th Spirit   ראחאל   (Rochel)
God who sees all
Deos

341 to 345°

Ps. 15:5.

Dominus pars hæreditatis meæ et calicis mei; tu es qui restitues hæreditatem meam mihi.

To find lost or stolen objects and discover the person responsible.

* Distinguished in the judiciary, morals and customs of all peoples.

Negative influence: Law, testament, inheritance.

70th Spirit　　　　　יבמיה　　　　　(Jabamiah)
Word which produces all things
Aris

346 to 350°

Divine name and 1st verse of Genesis. In the beginning God created the Heavens and the Earth.

Governs the generation of beings and phenomena of nature.

Protects those who wish to progress spiritually.

* Distinguished by genius. One of the great lights of philosophy.

Negative influence: Atheism.

71st Spirit　　　　　הייאל　　　　　(Haiel)
God, master of the Universe
Zeur

351 to 355°

Ps. 108:29.

Confitebor Domino nimis in ore meo et in medio multorum laudabo eum.

To confound the wicked and for deliverance from those who seek to oppress us.

Protects those who call upon him.

Influences fire.

* Brave.

Negative influence: Discord, traitors, infamy.

72nd Spirit　　　　　מומיה　　　　　(Mumiah)

356 to 360°

Pronounce the divine names, alpha and omega, with the name and attributes of the spirit, together with the request and Ps. 114:7.

Convertere anima mea in requiem tuam: quia Dominus benefecit tibi.

A divine talisman should be prepared under favourable

influences with the name of the spirit on the reverse side.

Protects in mysterious operations, brings success in all things.

Governs chemistry, physics and medicine. Influences health and longevity.

* Doctor.

Negative influence: Despair and suicide.

Evocations of the spirits should be done in the season corresponding to their element and, most important, while facing the part of the world over which they preside.

Fire	East	Spring
Water	West	Autumn

Sunday

Day							
1	☉	4	☾	7	♂	10	☿
2	♀	5	♄	8	☉	11	☾
3	☿	6	♃	9	♀	12	♄

Night							
1	♃	4	♀	7	♄	10	☉
2	♂	5	☿	8	♃	11	♀
3	☉	6	☾	9	♂	12	☿

Monday

Day							
1	☾	4	♂	7	☿	10	♃
2	♄	5	☉	8	☾	11	♂
3	♃	6	♀	9	♄	12	☉

Night							
1	♀	4	♄	7	☉	10	☽
2	☿	5	♃	8	♀	11	♄
3	☾	6	♂	9	☿	12	♃

Tuesday

Day							
1	♂	4	☿	7	♃	10	♀
2	☉	5	☽	8	♂	11	☿
3	♀	6	♄	9	☉	12	☾

Night							
1	♄	4	☉	7	☽	10	♂
2	♃	5	♀	8	♄	11	☉
3	♂	6	☿	9	♃	12	♀

Wednesday

Day							
1	☿	4	♃	7	♀	10	♄
2	☽	5	♂	8	☿	11	♃
3	♄	6	☉	9	☽	12	♂

Night							
1	☉	4	☾	7	♂	10	☿
2	♀	5	♄	8	☉	11	☾
3	☿	6	♃	9	♀	12	♄

Thursday

	1 ♃	4 ♀	7 ♄	10 ☉
Day	2 ♂	5 ☿	8 ♃	11 ♀
	3 ☉	6 ☾	9 ♂	12 ☿
	1 ☾	4 ♂	7 ☿	10 ♃
Night	2 ♄	5 ☉	8 ☾	11 ♂
	3 ♃	6 ♀	9 ♄	12 ☉

Friday

	1 ♀	4 ♄	7 ☉	10 ☽
Day	2 ☿	5 ♃	8 ♀	11 ♄
	3 ☽	6 ♂	9 ☿	12 ♃
	1 ♂	4 ☿	7 ♃	10 ♀
Night	2 ☉	5 ☽	8 ♂	11 ☿
	3 ♀	6 ♄	9 ☉	12 ☽

Saturday

	1 ♄	4 ☉	7 ☾	10 ♂
Day	2 ♃	5 ♀	8 ♄	11 ☉
	3 ♂	6 ☿	9 ♃	12 ♀
	1 ☿	4 ♃	7 ♀	10 ♄
Night	2 ☽	5 ♂	8 ☿	11 ♃
	3 ♄	6 ☉	9 ☽	12 ♂

PLANETS

Good	♃	♀
Evil	♄	♂
Indifferent	☉	☽

☿ good with good, evil with evil.

ZODIAC

Day		
	♈	midnight to 1 o'clock
	♉	1 o'clock to
	♊	2 o'clock to
	♋	3 o'clock to
	♌	4 o'clock to
	♍	5 o'clock to
	♎	6 o'clock to
	♏	7 o'clock to
	♐	8 o'clock to
	♑	9 o'clock to
	♒	10 o'clock to
	♓	11 o'clock to 12

ZODIAC

Night   Same as for day.

For a special study of the Spirits, and the construction of tables, see *l'esquisse hérmétique du Tout Universel d'apres la Théosophie chrétienne*, by Jacob (Paris 1902).

Part Four

Summary Bibliography of the Qabalah

CHAPTER ONE

INTRODUCTION TO THE BIBLIOGRAPHY OF THE QABALAH

1.–PREFACE

To our knowledge, there does not yet exist a special bibliography of the Qabalah in French. Certainly, in current manuals lists of works classified under this heading are to be found; but these have been compiled without order or method and are far from complete. These same remarks apply to articles in dictionaries devoted to the Qabalah and to the few volumes given as references, save for the study of the subject in the *Dictionnaire des Sciences Philosophiques*.

Thus for serious scholars there has existed a most detrimental lack which we have tried to fill to the best of our ability. Our aim then is less to present an interminable list of works gathered right and left (an operation not without a certain usefulness) than is it to establish certain divisions in this list, thereby sparing a great deal of effort for philosophers and historians who, following in the footsteps of A. Franck and other eminent critics involved in studies on the Qabalah, the Alexandrian School and neo-Platonic doctrines, seek more and more to deepen their knowledge of these subjects.

First we will have to examine the principal foreign bibliographies on the Qabalah. We will establish the particular character of these works, their usefulness or their failings.

In this connection, we will give the various sources from which we have borrowed, for the first duty of a writer is to 'render ... to Caesar the things that are Caesar's', thereby losing a little prestige but gaining a great deal of moral satisfaction.

Next we will be able to begin the actual bibliography itself, dividing the books according to the languages in which they are written, then according to the subjects treated, and finally establishing a short list of the most indispensable works. We will also take care within the larger divisions to point out secondary categories, such as the distinction between purely scientific studies on the Qabalah as against works inspired by the Qabalah and produced by mystical writers. We hope thus to attain our goal which is above all to prove useful and to facilitate the task of those more competent than ourselves who wish to take the results of our efforts into consideration.

2.–PRINCIPAL QABALISTIC BIBLIOGRAPHIES

A detailed study on each of the writers who has concerned himself with the bibliography of the Qabalah would require an entire volume. Thus one must not expect a complete analysis of each of these works. We will find it sufficient to quickly indicate the general character of these principal bibliographies, referring the reader desirous of further details to the Bibliothèque Nationale whose catalogue numbers we give.

JEAN BUXTORF

Jean Buxtorf is the head of a family which for two centuries grew to a position of eminence in Hebrew literature.[1] He was born on 25 December 1564, at Camen in Westphalia, and died at Basel on 13 September 1629. He taught Hebrew in this latter city for a period of thirty-eight years.

JOHAN BUXTORFI. – *De Abreviationis hebraicis liber novus*

[1] *Biographie universelle*, Vol. VI.

et copiosus cui assesserunt operis talmudici brevis recencio, cum ejusdem librorum et capitum Indici item 'Bibliotheca rabbinica' novo ordine alphabetico disposita Basilea, typis Conradi Waldkirchi impensis Ludovici Konig, 1613, in-8o. (Bib. Nat. A. 7505).

This small volume of 335 pages, although incomplete, is of great value, for it is the first work of this nature so seriously carried out. It was completed at a later date by the author and his sons.

It is printed, in contrast to ordinary works, from right to left. The following work is far more complete.

BARTOLOCCI

If not by order of date but at least by order of importance, the first great bibliography relative to the Qabalah is that of Bartolocci.

Bartolocci (Jules) was an Italian priest of the order of Saint Bernard. He spent the greater part of his life teaching Hebrew in the Collegio della Sapienza in Rome. He was born in Celano in 1613 and died of apoplexy on 1 November 1687.

BIBLIOTHECA MAGNA RABBINICA. – *De scriptoribus et scriptis rabbinicis, ordine alphabitico hebraice et latine digestis, auctore d. Iulio Bartoloccio de Celleno, Congreg. S. Bernardi Reform. Ord. Cistere et S. Sebastiani ad Catacumbes Abbato,* 4 vol. Rome, 1678-92. (Bib. Nat. A. 764).

This bibliography is alphabetically arranged. Its four folio volumes are printed in two columns; the beginning of the volume is located to the right as one opens the book as for books printed in the Hebrew language. All Hebrew passages quoted are translated into Latin, and numerous tables, established with minute care, allow one to proceed through the immense quantity of subjects treated without losing one's orientation.

With regard to each subject a bibliography is to be found, giving not only Hebrew works, but also all published treatises on the question. Thus for example, on page 166 of Volume I, one finds a study of *The Points* followed by bibliographical references to twenty-three Hebrew works and seven Latin works.

Most often these references give chapter and page numbers,

which is to indicate the conscientiousness with which this admirable treatise was composed.[1]

Bartolocci's work was continued and completed by the following.

IMBONATUS. – *Bibliotheca latina-hebraica sive de scriptoribus latinis qui ex diversis nationibus, contra Judæos, vel de re hebraica utcumque scripsere: additis observationibus criticis, et philologico-historicis, quibus quæ circa patriam, ætatem vitæ institutum, mortemque; auctorum consideranda veniunt, exponuntur, auctore et vindice* P. CAROLO IOSEPH IMBONATO MEDIOLANCASI, *Cong. S. Bernardi Ord. Cistere Monacho*, Rome, 1694, folio (Bib. Nat. A. 765).

Here are to be found the same qualities as in the *Rabbinical Library*.

*
* *

We now come, by order of date, to:

BASNAGE. – *Histoire des Juifs depuis Jésus-Christ jusqu'à présent*, Rotterdam, 1707, in-12mo, 5 vol. (Bib. Nat. H. 6947.52).

This tract contains a table of cited authors which can provide genuine biographical information.

*
* *

One of those who has greatly contributed to the spread of these studies is:

WOLF

Wolf (Jean-Christophe) was born on 21 February 1683 in Wernigerode in Upper Saxony. He died on 25 July 1739 at the age of fifty-six.

O. CHRISTOPH. WOLF. – *Bibliotheca hebræ, sive notitia tum*

[1] About 4,000 works written in the Hebrew tongue are quoted in this important work.

auctorum hebraicorum cujuscumque ætatis, tum scriptorum, quæ vol hebraice prinum exarata, vel ab aliis conversa sunt, ad nostram ætatem deducta, Hamburg and Leipzig, 1715, 4 vol., in-4to (Bib. Nat. Invent. A. 2967).

The first volume gives capsule accounts of Hebrew authors numbering 2,231; the second, bibliographical indications for all works, printed or in manuscript form relative to the Old Testament, the Massorah, the Talmud, and to Hebrew grammar and the Judaic and anti-Judaic libraries; plus accounts of the Chaldean paraphrases, books on the Qabalah and finally anonymous writings of Jews. The last two volumes contain corrections and supplements.[1]

Wolf's work is printed without columns from right to left. It contains the tract of *Gaffareli* on the manuscripts used by Picus da Mirandola: *Accedit in calce* JACOBI GAFFARELLI *index codicum cabbalistic, mss, quibus Jo. Picus Mirandulanus comes, usus est.*

Wolf's four volumes, condensed from the work of Bartolocci and containing numerous additions of publications more recent than the *Magna Bibliotheca rabbinica*, would form an almost perfect whole if it were not for a singular mania of the author which greatly depreciates the value of his work. This consists in the translating into Latin of all the titles and authors' names, except for the German authors, whose names are translated but whose works appear in the original language. The result is a regrettable confusion in the mind of the scholar and a promulgation of difficulties which never should be met with in a bibliographical work. Thus we recommend, except for modern authors, the use of Bartolocci. To gain an idea of Wolf's genre, the reader need only refer to the lists of his which we give further on.

*
* *

To conclude, let us give the two following works, both of them far more modern in date, and of which the second is unfortunately known to us only by name.

FURST. – *Bibliotheca Judaïca: Bibliographisches Handbuch umfassend die 'Druckwerke der Jüdischen Literatur' einschliesslich der über juden und Judenthum veroffentlichten Schriften nach alfabetischer*

[1] WEISS, *Biographie universelle*, Vol. XLV.

ordnung der Verfasser bearbeitet. Mit einer Geschichte der Judishen Bibliographie Sowie mit Indices versehen und herasugegeben, von D. JULIUS FURST, *Leherer an der Universitat zu Leipzig. Leipzig, Verlag von Wilhelm Engelmann,* 1863 (Bib Nat. Q. 5136, 5140, 5141).

Nothing in this work demands particular mention except the Hebrew dictionary at the end of the third volume, which is printed like one of our dictionaries, that is, from left to right.

Catalogue of hebraïca and judaïca in the library of the Corporation of the City of London, London, 1891, in-8o, 231 pp.

3.–OUR SOURCES

In addition to the preceding works, we have consulted the lists at the ends of studies on the Qabalah given in most encyclopedias.

Thus we must make particular mention of the *Grande Encyclopédie* (article by M. Isidore Loëb), the *Encyclopédie des Sciences religieuses* by Lichtenberger (article 'Kabbale' by M. Nicolas), the *Dictionnaire de la conversation*, the *Dictionnaire encyclopédique* of Larousse, Diderot's *Encyclopédie* (article 'Cabbale' by the abbot Pestré, followed by a note by d'Alembert, this article is one of the best ever published on the question), the *Biographie universelle* of Michaud (article by M. Tabaraud).

And from abroad, the *English Cyclopedia*, the *Encyclopedia Britannica* and the *Bibliotheca britannica* of Watt, a most remarkable bibliography from several points of view.

*
* *

Among the works which have proved extremely useful in the establishment of our bibliography, we must cite especially that of M. AD. FRANCK on *la Kabbale*, the only French publication in which a good bibliography of Qabalism is to be found.

We will not speak of *Basnage, Bartolocci, Buddeus, Buxtorf, Imbonatus, Isid. Loëb, Molitor, Wolf* and *Watt* from whom we have borrowed only slightly.

The *Collections de la Bibliothèque Nationale* have furnished some of the entries on our list.

Lastly, we cannot conclude without mentioning the usefulness of the *private library* of our friend Stanislas de Guaita, the esteemed Qabalist, for the catalogue of mystical works on the subject.

PLAN OF OUR BIBLIOGRAPHY

1. *Order*

We have classified the works on the one hand by language, on the other by subject matter.

The classification by languages was done according to the order of our investigations.

The classification by subject matter was done according to the order adopted by the catalogues of the Bibliothèque Nationale. We have added several headings drawn from our general classification of works relative to the Hebraic tradition.

2. – *Sources – Character of each work*

Each of the works given is preceded by a classification number.

Between the author's name and the title of the work or before this title when the work is anonymous, a letter is given which indicates *the source* from which the work has been taken.

The bibliographical notations conclude with the following abbreviations:

(SCT), if the character of the work is purely 'scientific'; if it is a question of a didactic or bibliographical study.

(MYS), if the work possesses 'mystical' or 'occult' tendencies or origin.

(PHIL), if the work is thoroughly 'philosophical'.

3. *Alphabetical tables*

Finally, to facilitate the work of the scholar as much as possible, we have added to our bibliography two alphabetical tables, one by authors' names, the other by titles.

It can be seen that we have sought above all to create a useful tool, to spare others the efforts of trial and error which we have personally undergone in carrying out our research.

Our greatest desire is to be 'pillaged' as often as possible for the benefit of study. We would especially like to see this incomplete and summary bibliography taken up and extended by an author more capable than ourselves. Thus France would become the possessor of a work barely sketched by our attempts here, a work which numerous occupations prevent us from undertaking. We have prepared the earth; now who will come to make it prosper?

CATALOGUE OF BIBLIOGRAPHICAL SOURCES

(B)   Basnage.
(BC)   Bartolocci.
(BD)   Buddeus.
(BN)   Bibliothèque Nationale.
(BX)   Buxtorf.
(DV)   Divers authors.
(F)   Ad. Franck.
(G)   Library of de Guaita.
(I)   Imbonatus.
(L)   Isidore Loëb.
(M)   Molitor.
(P)   Papus.
(W)   Wolf.
(Wt)   Watt.

CHARACTER OF EACH WORK

(SCT)   Scientific (Bibliographies, didactis studies, etc.)
(MYS)   Mystical (Inspired by Occult Science or portraying mystical tendencies.)
(PHIL)   Philosophical (Occupying an intermediate position between the two preceding.)

CHAPTER TWO

CLASSIFICATION BY LANGUAGES

1. – WORKS IN FRENCH

1. AD. FRANCK (P), La Kabbale, Paris, 1843, in-8vo (SCT).

2. RICHARD SIMON (F), Histoire critique de Vieux Testament (SCT).

3. BURNET (F), Archéologie philosophique, chap. IV (SCT).

4. HOTTINGER (F), Théorie philosophique (SCT).

5. BASNAGE (F), Histoire des Juifs (SCT).

6. E. AMELINEAU (F), Essai sur le gnosticisme égyptien, ses développements et son origine égyptienne, 1 vol. in-4to, pub. in 1887 (Bib. nat. o³ A 690) (SCT).

7. PAUL ADAM (P), Etre, novel (MYS).

8. AMARAVELLA (P), La Constitution de microcosme (Review: Le Lotus) (MYS).

9. F. CH. BARLET (P), Essai sur l'évolution de l'Idéee, 1891, in-18mv (SCT and PHIL).

10. BERTHELOT (P), Des Origines de l'Alchimie, Paris, 1887, in-8vo (SCT).

11. DE BRIERE (P), Essai sur le symbolisme antique des peuples de l'Orient. Paris. 1854, in-8vo (SCT).

12. RENE CAILLIE (P), L'Etoile, la Revue des Hautes Etudes (various articles). Avignon, 1889-92 (MYS).

13. AUGUSTIN CHABOSEAU (P), Essai sur la philosophie bouddhique, p. 156 and 157, Paris, 1891, in-8vo (PHIL).

14. P. CHRISTIAN (P), L'Homme rouge des Tuileries, Paris, 1854, in-8vo (MYS).

15. (VARIOUS) (P), Spirit congress of 1889, 1 vol. in-8vo, pp. 70, 89 et.seq. (MYS).

16. COURT DE GEBELIN (P), Œuvres (PHIL).

17. HENRY DELAAGE (P), La Science du vrai, Paris, 1884, in-8mo (PHIL).

18. LOUIS FIGUIER (P), L'Alchimie (PHIL and SCT).

19. PAUL GIBIER (P), Analyse des choses (MYS).

20. ELIPHAS LEVI (P), Dogme et rituel de la haute Magie, Paris, 1854, in-8vo; La clef des grands mystères; Histoire de la Magie; Fables et symboles (MYS and SCT).

21. FABRE D'OLIVET (P), La langue hébraïque restituée, Paris, 1825, 2 vol., in-4to (PHIL and SCT).

22. S. DE GUAITA (P), Au Seuil du Mystère, Paris, 1890, in-8vo (SCT and MYS); Le Temple de Satan, Paris, 1891, in-8vo (MYS).

22. S. DE GUAITA (P), Au Seuil du Mystère, Paris, 1890, in-8vo (SCT and MYS); Le Temple de Satan, Paris, 1891, in-8vo (MYS).

23. ALBERT JHOUNEY (P), Le Royaume de Dieu, Paris, 1888, in-8vo (MYS).

24. H.C. AGRIPPA (P), Philosophie occulte, 2 vol. The Hague, 1727, in-8vo (SCT and MYS).

25. LACOUR (P), Les Aeloim ou dieux de Moïse, Brodeaux, 1829, in-8vo (MYS).

26. LACURIA (P), Harmonies de l'Etre exprimées par les nombres, Paris, 1854, in-8vo (MYS).

27. LEONCE DE LARMANDIE (P), Eoraka, novel, Paris, 1891, in-8vo (MYS).

28. JULIEN LEJAY (P), La Science secrète, Paris, 1890, in-8vo (MYS and Phil).

29. LENAIN (P), La Science cabalistique. Amiens, 1823, in-8vo (MYS).

30. JULES LERMINA (P), A Brûler, novella, Paris, 1889, in-8vo (MYS).

31. EMILE MICHELET (P), L'Esotérisme dans l'art, Paris, 1891, in18mo (MYS).

32. MOLITOR (P), La Philosophie de la Tradition, Paris, 1834, in-8vo, (MYS).

33. GEORGE MONTIERE (P), La chute d'Adam, Paris, 1890 (Review: L'Initiation) (MYS).

34. PAPUS (P), Traité élémentaire de Science occulte, Paris, 1887, in-8vo (MYS); Le Tarot des Bohémiens, Paris, 1889, in-8vo (MYS and PHIL); Traité méthodique de Science occulte, Paris, 1891, in-8vo (PHIL and SCT).

35. JOSEPHIN PELADAN (P), La Décadence latine, 11 vol., Paris, 1884-91, in-18mo (MYS).

36. ALBERT POISSON (P), Théories et symboles des

Alchimistes, Paris, 1891, in-8vo (PHIL).

37. DUCHESSE DE POMAR (P), Théosophie sémitique, Paris, 1887, in-8vo (MYS).

38. ABBE ROCA (P), Nouveau Cieux, nouvelle Terre, Paris, 1889, in-8vo (MYS).

39. R.P. ESPRIT SABATHIER (P), Ombre idéale de la sagesse universelle, 1679 (MYS and PHIL).

40. L.-C. DE SAINT-MARTIN (P), Le Crocodile, Paris, in-8vo (Bib. Nat. Ye 10.272) (MYS).

41. ED. SCHURE (P), Les Grands Initiés, Paris, 1889, in-8vo (MYS and PHIL).

42. SAINT-YVES D'ALVEYDRE (P), Mission des Juifs, Paris, 1884, in-8vo (SCT and PHIL).

43. J.-A. VAILLANT (P), Les Rômes, histoire vraie des vrais Bohémiens, Paris, 1854 (MYS).

44. G. VITOUX (P), L'Occultisme scientifique, Paris, 1891, in-8vo (MYS and PHIL).

45. WRONSKI (HOENE) (P), Messianisme ou réforme absolue du savoir humain, Paris, 1854, folio (PHIL).

46. (P) De la Magie transcendante et des méthodes de guérison dans le Talmud (MYS).

47. (P), La Vierge de Jacob, Lyon, 1693, in-12mo (MYS).

48. LAGNEAU (P), Harmonie mystique, 1636, in-8vo (MYS).

49. ABRAHAM LE JUIF (G), La Sagesse divine, dédié à son fils Lamech, manuscript end of XVIIIth c., 2 vol., in-8vo (Translation of a German manuscript) (MYS).

50. GAFFAREL (G), Curiosités inouïes (MYS).

51. JEROME CARDAN (G), De la subtilité (MYS).

52. SIEUR DE SALERNE (G), La Géomancie et nomancie des anciens, la nomancie cabalistique, in-16mo, 1669 (MYS).

53. D'ECKHARTHAUSEN (G), La Nuée sur le Sanctuaire ou quelque chose dont la philosophie orgueilleuse de notre siècle ne se doute pas (MYS).

54. M.P.R.Q.D.G. (G), La Physique de l'Acriture, in-8vo (MYS).

55. KELEPH BEN NATHAN (G), La philosophie divine, appliquée aux lumières naturelles, magique, astrale, surnaturelle, céleste et divine, ou immuables vérités que Dieu a révélées de Lui-même et de ses ouvres dans le triple miroir analogique de l'Univers, de l'Homme et de la Révélation

écrite, 1793, in-8vo (MYS).

56. QUANTIUS AUCLERC (G), La Threicie, ou la seule voie des sciences divines et humaines du culte vrai et de la morale, Paris, year VII (MYS).

57. L. GRASSOT (d.m.m.) (G), La Philosophie céleste, Bordeaux, year IX (1803), in-8vo (MYS).

58. F. VIDAL COMINEM (G), L'Harmonie du monde où il est traité de Dieu et de la Nature-Essence, Paris, 1671, in-12mo (MYS).

59. PIERRE FOURNIE (tonsured cleric) (G), Ce que nous avons été, ce que nous sommes et ce que nous deviendrons, London, 1861, in-8vo (MYS).

60. DRACH (G), Le Chevalier Drach, former rabbi, De l'harmonie de l'Eglise et de la Synagogue, Paris, 1844, 2 vol., in-8vo (MYS).

61. ADOLPHE BERTET (G), (pure Qabalist, direct disciple of Eliphas Lévi), doctor in civil law and canonical law, barrister in the court of Chaméry, Apocalypse du Bienheureux Jean dévoilée (Qabalah and Tarot on every page), Paris, Arnauld de Vresse, 1861, in-8vo (MYS).

62. GOULIANOF (G) (chevalier of), Essai sur les hiéroglyphes d'Horapollon et quelques mots sur la CABALE, Paris, 1827, in-4to (MYS).

63. ANONYMOUS (G), Cabala Magica tripartita, that is, three Qabalistic tables with explanation and instructions for use, S.L., 1747, in-8vo (German and French translation) (PHIL and MYS).

64. ISAAC OROBIO (G), Israël vengé, ou Exposition naturelle des prophéties hébraïques que les chrétiens attribuent à Jésus, leur prétendu messie, London, 1770, in-8vo (PHIL and MYS).

65. ALEXANDRE WEILL (G), חוקימ ונסתרת אהבה (Laws and Mysteries of Love), after rabbis and the Qabalah, translated from a Hebrew missel, Paris, Dentu, 1880, in-8vo (PHIL and MYS).

66. LODOIK (count of Divonne, S   I) (G), La Voie de la Science divine (translation from the English of Law, disciple of Höhme), preceded by La Voix qui crie dans le désert, Paris, 1805, in-8vo (MYS).

67. LOPOUKINE (mystical Russian Qabalist) (G), Quelques traits de l'Eglise intérieure, Moscow, 1801 (illustrated, in-8vo (MYS).

68. MUNCK (L), Mélanges de Philosophie juive et arabe, Paris, 1859, pp. 275 and 490 (SCT(; (L) La Palestine, pp. 520 and 521 (SCT).

69. HERZOG (DV), Encyclopédie, vol. VII, pp. 203, 205 and 206 (SCT).

70a. MARQUIS LE GENDRE (WT), Traité de l'Opinion, ch. VII (SCT).

70b. MALFATTI DE MONTEREGGIO (D) (P), La Mathèse, translated by Ostrowski, Paris, 1839, in-8vo (MYS).[1]

70c. S. KARPPE, Le Sohar, Paris, Alcan, 1900, in-8vo.

2. – WORKS IN LATIN

71. RAYMOND LULLY (F), Works, 10 vol., Folio, Mayence, 1721 (PHIL).

72. PICUS DA MIRANDOLA (F), Conclusiones cabalisticae, Rome, 1486 (PHIL).

73. REUCHLIN (F), De Arte cabbalistica (PHIL).

74. De Verbo Mirifico (PHIL).

75. H.–C. AGRIPPA (F), De occulta philosophia (SCT and MYS).

76. POSTEL (F), Abscunditorum a constitutione mundi clavis, Basel, 1547, in-4to, and Amsterdam, 1646, in-12mo (MYS).

77. PISTORIUS (F), Artis cabalisticae scriptores, Basel, 1587, folio (PHIL and MYS).

78. KIRCHER (F), Oedipus Aegyptiacus, Rome, 1623, folio (SCT and PHIL).

79. KNOR DE ROSENROTH (F), Kabbala denudata (SCT and PHIL).

80. RICCI (F), De celesti agricultura (MYS and PHIL).

81. JOSEPH VOYSIN (F), Disputatio cabalistica (MYS(.

82. GEORGES WACHTER (F), Concordia rationis et fidei, sive Harmonia philosophiae moralis et religionis christianae, Amsterdam, 1692, in-8vo (MYS).

83. Elucidarius cabalisticus, Rome, 1706, in-8vo (PHIL).

---

[1] As we go to press, we receive word of a new work by EUGENE NUS, *A la recherche des destinées*, where an entire chapter is devoted to the Qabala, 1 vol., in-18mo, Paris, 1897. – 70b'.

84. THOLUK (F), De Ortu Cabbalae, Hamburg, 1837, (MYS).

85. BRUCKER (Jean-Jacques) (F), Institutiones philosophiae, Leipzig, 1747, in-8vo, re-edited and annotated by Fred. Born, Leipzig, 1790 (SCT and MYS).

86. PARACELSUS (F), Opera.

87. HENRY MORUS (F), Psycho-Zoïa or the Life of the Soul, 1640-1647, in-8vo, Latin translation, 3 vol., folio, 1679 (MYS).

88. ROBERT FLUDD (F), Works, 5 vol., folio, (MYS).

89. VAN HELMONT PERE (J.-B.) (F), Ortus medicinae, Amsterdam, 1647-52, in-4to, Venice, 1651, folio (PHIL).

90. MERCURE VAN HELMONT (F), Alphabete vere naturalis hebraice brevissima delineatio, Sulgbach, 1607, in-12mo (PHIL).

91. JACOB BOEHME (F), Aurora, 1612 (MYS).

92. De tribus principiis, 1619 (MYS).

93. BARTOLOCCI (F), Magna bibliotheca rabbinica, 4 vol., folio (SCT).

94. BUDDEUS (F), Introductio ad Historiam philisophiae Hebraeorum, 1702 and 1721, in-8vo (SCT).

95. ARIAS MONTANUS (B), Antiquitatum Judaïcarum (PHIL).

96. BARTENOVAE (B), Commentarii in Misnam (SCT).

97. BOOECIUS (B), De testid. templo Rabbinorum, vol. I, folio, Amsterdam (MYS).

98. CAPZIOVII (B), Introductio ad Theologiam Judaïcam (PHIL).

99. CHAIIM (B), Comment. in Siphra Zeunitha et Synodos Cabb. denudatae, in-4to (SCT).

100. COCH (B), or COCCEIUS (Johanne), Duo tituli Thalmudici, San hedrim et Maccoth (SCT).

101. DRUSII (B), Questiones Hebraïcae (PHIL).

102. FREY (Ludor) (B), Excepta Aharonis Plrush al Attorah explicationis Pentateuchum, in-4to, Amsterdam, 1705 (PHIL).

103. HOOGT (B), Prefatio in Biblia hebraïca in-8vo, 2 vol., Amsterdam, 1705 (SCT).

104. LEUSDEN (B), Prefatio ad Bibliothecam hebraticam, in-8vo, 2 vol. Amsterdam, 1680 (SCT).

105. LORIAE (Isacci) (B), Cabbala recentior (SCT and PHIL).

106. MAIMONIDES (B), Commentarii in Misnam, Amsterdam, 1760, folio (SCT).

107. MISNAH (B), sive totius Hebreorum Juris Rituum, Antiquitatum systema cum Maimonides et Bartenovae Commentariis integris, quibus accedunt variorum Auctorum Notae ac Versiones Latine donavit et notis illustravit GILLEMUS SURENHUSIUS, folio, 6 vol., Amsterdam, 1700 (SCT).

108. MORI (Henrici) (B), Fundamenta cabbalae Actopaedomelissae (PHIL).

109. MOSIS NACHMANIDIS (B), Disputatio apud Wageniseli Tela ignea Satanae (MYS).

110. NAPHTALI HIRTZ (B), Introductio pro meliori intellectu libri Zohar (Kabbala denudata, p.3) (PHIL).

111. OTHONIS (Johan Henrici) (B), Historia doctorum misnicorum (PHIL).

112. PERINGERI (B), Praefatio ad Tract. Arodah Zarah in Misnae, vol. V. (PHIL).

113. RELANDI (Hade) (B), Analecta Rabbinica, in-8vo, Ultraj, 1702 (SCT).

114. URSINI (Gorgio) (B), Antiquitates hebraicae Scholasticae Academiae, in-4to, Hasnia, 1702 (SCT).

115. WAGENSEILII (B), Tela ingea Satanae, 2 vol., 1681, in-4to, in Misna, p.911, editionis Amstel (MYS).

116. PARACELSUS (BD), Isagoge (PHIL).

117. PETI GASSENDUM (BD), MARC MERSENNUM, Works (PHIL).

118. KHUNRATH (BD), Amphitheatrum Sapientiae Aeternae (MYS).

119. GAFFAREL (BD), Codicum Kabbalisticorum manuscriptorum (MYS).

120. CHENTOPHORI STEBBII (BD), Coelum Sephiroticum Ebreorum per portas intelligentiae Moysi Revelatum, 1679, folio (MYS).

121. IUL. SPERBERUS (BD), Isagogue in veram Dei naturaeque cognitionem (PHIL).

122. MICHAELIS RITTHALERI (BD), Hermathena philosophica theologia, 1684 (PHIL and MYS).

123. FRANCISCUS MERCURIUS HELMONTIS (BD), Seder olam (PHIL).

124. IAC. BOHMIUS (BD), Opera (MYS).

125. IOACHIMUS HOPPERUS (BD), Seduardus sive de

vera jurisprudentia, 1656 (PHIL).

126. IONAS CONRADUS SCHRAMMIUS (BD), Introductio ad dialecticam Kabbalorum, 1703 (PHIL).

127, JORDANO BRUNO (P), De Specierum scrutneo; de lampade combinatoria lulliana; de progressu et lampade venatoria logicorum (PHIL and MYS).

128. VALERIUS DE VALERIIS (G), Aureum opus in arborem scientiarum et in artem generalem (MYS).

129. BURGONOVO (Archangelus de) (G), I. – Apologia pro defensione doctrinae Kabbalae (PHIL); II. – Conclusiones Cabalisticae, No. 71, secundum Mirandulam (PHIL) (These conclusions are different from those in Pistorius, although from the same author and with the same title – St. de Guaita), 1 vol. in-16mo, Bononiae, 1564.

130. GALATINI (G), De Arcanis catholicae veritatis, book XII, 1 vol., folio, 1612 (MYS).

131. JOHANNES FRANKIUS (G), Systema ethices divinae. And several other tracts. Brandeburgi-Mecklinburgi, 1724, in-4to (MYS).

132. VUOLFGANGUS SIDELIUS (G), De Templo Salomonis Mystico, prope Maguntiam, 1548, in-12 (MYS).

133. TRITHEME (G), De Septem secundeis, Coloniae, 1567, in-12mo (MYS).

134. (G), Veterum Sophorum Sigilla et Imagines Magicae, cui accessit catalogus Rariorum magico-cabbalisticorum (MYS and SCT).

135. (Anonymous) (G), Trinuum magicum, sive secretorum magicorum opus (MYS).

136. CHRISTOPHORUS WAGENSEILIUS (G), Tela ignea Satanae, Containing Hebrew works with Latin translation and commentaries (MYS and PHIL).

137. LIPMANN, Carmen memoriale.

(Anonymous), Liber nizzachon vetus.

138. RABBI JECHIEL, Acta disputationis cum quodam Nicolao.

139. RABBI MOSES NACHMANIDES, Acta disputationis cum fratre Paulo Christiani et fratre Raymundi Martini.

140. RABBI ISAACCI, Sepher Chissuck Emuna (Munimen fidei).

141. (Anonymous), Sepher Toladoth Jeschua (Liber Generationum Jesu).

142. RELANDI (Hadrian) (G), Antiquitates sacrae

veterum hebreorum breviter delineatæ, trajecti ad Rhenum, 1741, in-4to (SCT).

143. HEINIUS (J. Philip) (G), Dissertationum sacrorum libri duo, Amsterdam, 1736, in-4to (PHIL).

144. F. BURNETII (G). – I. Telluris Theoria sacra. – II. Doctrina Archeologiae philosophicæ (a large chapter on the Qabalah, Amstelodami, apud Ionnem Wolters, 1699, in-4to (Frontispiece and illustrations) (MYS).

145. ROBERT FLUDD (DV) – 1. Utriusque cosmi metaphysica, physica atque technica historia, Oppenheim, 1617, folio.

146. – 2. De supernaturali, naturali, præternaturali et contranaturali microcosmi historia, Oppenheim, 1619, 1621.

147. – 3. De natura sinia seu technica macrocosmi historia, Frankfurt, 1624.

148. – 4. Veritatis procenium seu demonstratio analytica, Frankfurt, 1621.

149. – 5. Monochordan mundi symphoniacum, Frankfurt, 1622, in-4to, 1623, folio (these last two tracts in response to Kepler).

150. – 6. Anatomia theatrum, triplici et effigiæ designatum, Frankfurt, 1623, folio.

151. – 7. Medicina catholica, seu mysticum artis medicandi sacrarium, Frankfurt, 1629.

152. – 8. Integrum morborum mysterium, Frankfurt, 1631.

153. – 9. Pulsus, seu nova et acarnas pulsurum historia.

154. – 10. Philosophia sacra et vere christiana, seu meteorologia cosmica, Frankfurt, 1629.

155. – 11. Sophiae cum Moria certamen, 1629.

156. – 12. Summum bonum, quod est verum magiae, cabalae et alchymiae veræ ac fratrum Roseae-Crusis subjectum, 1629.

157. – 13. Clavis philosophiæ et alchymiæ Fluddanæ, Frankfurt, 1633.

158. – 14. Philosophia Mosaïca, in quo sapientia et scientia créaturarum explicantur, Ghent, 1638; Amsterdam, 1640, folio, translated into English, London, 1659, folio.

159. – 15. De unguento armario (discourse in the) Theatrum sapientiæ, 1662, in-4to.

160. – 16. Responsum ad Hoplocrismaspongum Forsteri, London, 1631, in-4to.

161. – 17. Pathologia dæmoniaca, Ghent, 1640, folio.

162. – 18. Apologia compendiaria, fraternitatem de Rosea-Cruce suspicionis et infamiæ maculis aspersam abluens, Leyden, 1616, in-8vo.

163. – 19. Tractatus apologeticus integritatem societatis de Rosea-Cruce defendens, Leyden, 1647; translated into German, Leipzig, 1782.

164. – 20. Tractatus theologo-philosophicus de vita, morte et resurrectione, fratribus Rosea-Crucis dicatus, Oppenheim, 1617, in-4to.

165. BUXTORF (DV) (Works), Manualehebraicum et chaldaicum, Basel, 1658, in-12mo.

166. – Synagoga Judaice, Basel, 1603 (German); Hesse, 1604 and 1622, in-8vo (Latin); Amsterdam, 1650, in-8vo (Flemish); Basel, 1641, Latin (reviewed by his son); Basel, 1682, Latin (reviewed and corrected by Jacques Buxtorf, great-nephew of the author).

This work is concerned with Jewish ceremonies and dogmas.

167. Institutio epistolaris hebraica cum epistolarum hebraicarum centuria, Basel, 1603, 1616, 1629, in-8vo.

The author gives rules and models for a literary correspondence in Hebrew.

168. Epitome grammaticæ hebræ, Leyden, 1673, 1701, 1707, in-12mo.

169. Epitome radicum hebraicæ et chaldaicæ, Basel, 1607, in-8vo.

170. Thesaurus grammaticus linguæ hebreæ, Basel, 1609, 1613 and 1615, in-8vo.

171. Lexicon hebraicum et chaldaicum cum brevi lexico Rabbinico, Basel, 1607, in-8vo, and 1678, in-8vo.

172. Grammaticæ chaldaicæ et syriacæ libri tres, Basel, 1615, in-8vo.

173. Bibliotheca hebræa Rabbinica, Basel, 1618-19, 4 vol., folio.

174. Tiberias, Basel, 1620, in-4to.

Historical and critical treatise on the Massorah in which the author attributes the invention of the vowel points to Ezra. He also gives a history of the Jewish Academies after the Diaspora.

175. Concordantiæ Bibliorum hebraicæ, published by his sons with Chaldean concordances. Basel, 1632, folio; reprinted in 1636, Basel, and summarized separately by

'Chrétien Ravius' at Frankfurt-on-the-Oder, 1676; Berlin, 1677, in-8vo, with the title *Fons Sion*; this is the one of Buxtorf's best works.

176. Lexicon chaldaicum thalmudicum et rabbinicum, Basel, 1639, folio.

Buxtorf left this work incomplete after twenty years of preparation, and still it required ten more years of his son before it was ready for publication.

177. Disputatio Judæi cum Christiano, Hesse, 1604, 1622, in-8vo.

178. Epistolarum hebraic, decus (Hebrew and Latin), Basel, 1603, in-8vo.

179. KIRCHER (P), The complete outline of his study on the Qabalah of the Hebrews in the Edipus Egyptiacus:

THE QABALAH OF THE HEBREWS

Concerning the allegorical wisdom of the ancient Hebrews, parallel to the Egyptian, hieroglyphic cabala, showing new sources of the exposition of the hieroglyphic doctrine, and indicating the origins of this superstitious doctrine and its refutation.

Chap. I – Definition and division of the Qabalah.

1. Example of Gematria.
2. Example of Notaria.
3. Example of Themurah (or Ziruph).

Chap. II – On the origin of the Qabalah according to Qabalists.

Chap. III – Concerning the basis of the Qabalah: the alphabet and the mystical order of its characters.

Chap. IV – On the names and appellations of God.

1. The divine Tetragram or name of 4 letters, יהוה.
2. Mysteries of the name יהוה.
3. The Duodecagram or Divine Name of 12 letters.
4. The Divine Name of 22 letters, which, according to the

Rabbis, the priests once used to bless the people.
5. The Divine Name of 42 letters.

Chap. V – Concerning the Table Ziruph or the combinations of the Hebrew alphabet.

1. How the Divine Name of 42 letters is drawn from the table Ziruph.
2. Names of the 42 angels, deriving from the Divine Name of 42 letters and their interpretations.

Chap. VI – On the Divine Name of 72 letters and its use.

The 72 verses taken from various Psalms containing the words of God and the names of the angels, collected from divers rabbinical works.

Chap. VII – The Divine Name of 4 letters was not unknown to ancient pagans. The name IESU contains all that has been said of the Tetragram.

Chap. VIII – On the most secret mystical theology of the Hebrews: the Kabbala of the ten Sephiroth.

1. En-Soph, infinite, hidden, eternal essence.
2. Kether, the supreme crown, the first Sephira; the other Sephiroth.

Chap. IX – On the various representations of the 10 divine names of the Sephiroth, their influence and their channels, according to the Rabbis.

1. Representation of the 10 Sephiroth by the image of the human form.
2. On the channels and influences of the Sephiroth, according to Qabalists.
3. Derivation of the channels (see the figure).
4. On the 32 Paths of Wisdom and their interpretation.
5. On the 32 passages of the 1st chapter of Genesis where the divine name ELOHIM is mentioned. List of the 32 Paths of Wisdom.
6. On the 50 Gates of Understanding.

7. Concerning the 30 powers emanating from the right-hand in Gedulah and the 30 powers emanating from the left-hand in Geburah. On the name of 72 letters and the 32 Paths of Wisdom.

8. On the negative and affirmative precepts annexed to the sephirotic channels of Gedulah and Geburah to Netzach and Hod, according to the Rabbis.

9. Interpretation of the sephirotic paths.

10. On the ternary, septenary and duodenary constituting the 22 letters and sephirotic channels, and their mysteries, according to the Hebrews.

Chap. X – On the natural Qabalah called 'Bereschith'.

1. What this Qabalah consists of.

2. Astrological Qabalah.

3. On the Qabalah Bereschith, or of Nature, that is, on the knowledge of the character of the things of Nature through the true and legitimate Qabalah.

4. On Qabalistic Magic, compared with Egyptian and Pythagorian magic.

3. – WORKS IN GERMAN

180. EPSTEIN (E), Mikad minot haychondin, Beiträge zur jüdischen, Alterthumskunde, Vienna, 1887 (SCT).

181. KLEURER (F), On the Nature and Origin of the Doctrine of Incarnation among the Qabalists, Riga, 1786, in-8vo (German) (PHIL).

182. FREYSTAD (F), Kabbalismus und Pantheismus, Kœnigsberg, 1832, in-8vo (PHIL).

183. WACHTER (F), Spinozism in Judaism, Amsterdam, 1699, in-8vo (German) (PHIL).

184. ZUNZ (L), Gottesdienstliche Vorträge, Berlin, 1832, Ch. IX and XX (SCT).

185. LANDAUER (L), Literaturblatt de l'Orient de Furst, 1845, vol. VI, p. 178 (SCT).

186. GRAETZ (L), Geschichte der Juden, vol. V, pp. 201-208, vol. VII, word 'Kabbala' (SCT).

187. J. HAMBURGER (L), Real-Encylopædie f. Bibel u. Talmud, 2nd part, 1874-83, articles: Geheimlehre, Kabbala,

Mystik, Religions-philosophie, and in the supplement, articles: Kleinere Midraschim and Sohar (SCT).

188. STEINSCHENEIDER (L), Judische Literatur in the Encyclopedie Ersch and Grüber (SCT).

189. H. JOEL (L), Die Religions philosophie des Sohar, Leipzig, 1849 (PHIL).

190. AD. JELLINCK (L), Moses ben Schemtob de leon und sien Verhältniss zum Sohar, Leipzig, 1851 (PHIL).

191. ID. (L), Beiträge zur Geschichte der Kabbala, Leipzig, 1852 (SCT).

192. GRAETZ (L), Gnosticismus und Judenthum, Krotoschin, 1846 (PHIL).

193. M. JOEL (L), Blicke in die Religionsgeschichte, Breslau, 1880, vol. 1, pp. 103-170 (SCT.

194. GUDEMANN (L), Geschichte des Erziehungswesens der Juden, Leipzig, 1800, vol. 1, p. 153 (German mysticism), p. 67 (mysticism in France in the XVIIIth c.) (SCT).

195. D. KAUFMANN (L), in Jubelschrift zum 90 ten Geburtstag of Drs L. Zung, Berlin, 1884, p. 143 (SCT).

196. CARL du PREL (P), Philosophie der Mystik, Leipzig, 1887 (PHIL and MYS).

197. (G), Cabala, Spiegel der Kunst in Kupperstück (MYS).

4. PRINCIPAL TREATISES IN HEBREW

Massorah.

198. MAJER HALEIN (M), M'sorah siag l'Thorah (The Massorah, a curb to the Law) XIIIth c.

Mishna and Gemarah.

199. (M), M'sachta sophrim (One sees), a description of the exterior form of the Bible.

200. NASI JUDA HAKADOSH (M), Mishnah.

201. MAIMONIDES (M), The powerful hand.

202. JOSEPH Karo (M), The Covered Table, 4 vols., 1550. The most complete compendium of Hebrew doctrine.

Kabbala.

203. ABRAHAM AKIBAH (?) (M), Sepher Yetzirah (Book of Creation), Mantua, 1552.

204. MOSES (?) (M), M'eine Hachochinh (The Sources of Wisdom); Raja M'chimnah (The Faithful Shepherd).

205. RAB. JUDA BEN BETHEIRA (M), Sepher Habethachun (The Book of Trust).

206. RAB. N'CHUNIAH (M), 40 B.C., The book Ha-Bahir (Light in the Shadows), Amsterdam, 1651, Berlin, 1706.

207. – (M), Hamiuchad (The Mystery of the Name of God).

208. – (M), Iggered Hasovoth (The Letter on the Mysteries), the first centuries A.D.

209. RAB. SAMUEL, son of Elisha (M), Sepher Kanah (The Fragments of the Temple).

210. Paraphraste ONKOLOS (M), different Midrashim Mei Haschiluach (The Waters Flowing Slowly) (120 A.D.).

211. RAB. SIMON, son of Jochai, disciple of Akibah (M), Zohar (The Splendour of Light).

Fragments of the Zohar.

212. – Sithrei Thorah (The Mysteries of the Thorah).

213. – I'muka (The Child).

214. – P'Kuda (The Mystical Explanation of the Law).

215. – Midrash Hanelam (The Mysterious Search).

216. – Maimer tha chasi (Come and See).

217. – Idra Rabba (The Great Assembly).

218. – Idra Suta (The Small Assembly).

219. – Siphra d'Zeniutha (The Book of Secrets).

Editions of the 'Zohar': Mantua, 1560, in-4to. – Dublin, 1623, folio. – Constantinople, 1736. – Amsterdam, 1714 and 1805, the better being the earlier one.

Principal publications from the Zohar to the XIIth century.

220. RAB. IUDA HANASI, 215 A.D. (M): 1. The Book of Sweet Fruits.

221. – 2. The Book of Points.

222. – 3. A Diamond in Urim and Thumim.

223. – 4. The Book of Adornment.

224. – 5. The Book of Paradise.

225. – 6. The Book of Redemption.

226. – 7. The Book of Unity.

227. – 8. The Covenant of Rest.

228. – 9. The Book of Study.

229. – 10. The Voice of the Lord in His Power.

230. – 11. The Book of the Collection of Various Explanations of the Numbers 42 and 72, Law and Morality, etc.

231. – 12. The Magnificence.

232. – 13. The Book of Recreation.

233. – 14. The Book of Future Life.

234. – 15. The Mystery of the Tora.

235. – 16. The Book on the Holy Names.

236. – 17. The Treasure of Life.

237. – 18. Eden of the Garden of God.

238. – 19. The Book of Redemption.

Principal publications from 1240 to the XVIth century.

239. – 20. (M), The Order of Divinity.

240. – 21. Perfumed wine.

241. – 22. The Book of Souls.

242. – 23. The Mystery of Spirit.

243. – 24. The Book of Angels.

244. – 25. The Book of the Relation of Forms.

245. – 26. The Book of Crowns.

246. – 27. The Book of Holy Voices.

247. – 28. The Book of the Mysteries of Unity and Faith.

248. – 29. The Book of the Gates of Divine Understanding.

249. – 30. The Mystery of Darkness.

250. – 31. The Book of the Unity of Divinity.

251. – 32. The Interior Garden.

252. – 33. The Holy of Holies.

253. – 34. The Treasure of Glory.

254. – 35. The Gate of Mysteries.

255. – 36. The Book of Faith.

256. – 37. The Fountain of Living Water.

257. – 38. The House of the Lord.

258. – 39. Urim and Thumim.

259. – 40. The Habitation of Peace.

260. – 41. The Spring in the Garden.

262. – 43. The Juice of the Pomegranate.

263. – 44. That Which Lights the Eyes.

264. – 45. The Tabernacle.

265. – 46. The Book of Faith.

266. – 47. The Book of the Ten.

267. – 48. The Book of Intuition.
268. – 49. The Book of the Mysteries of the Lord.
269. – 50. The Meaning of the Commandment.
270. – 51. Treatise on the Ten Sephiroth.
271. – 52. Explanation of the Thorah.
272. – 53. Aromatic powder.
273. – 54. The Light of God.
274. – 55. The Altar of Gold.
275. – 56. The Tabernacle.
276. – 57. The Book of Measure.
277. – 58. The Light of Reason.
278. – 59. The Mystery of the Thorah.
279. – 60. The Book of Suffering.
280. – 61. The Gate of Light.
281. – 62. The Tree of Life.
282. – 63. The Branch of the Tree of Life.
283. – 64. The Path Leading to the Tree of Life.
284. – 65. The Treasures of Life.
285. – 66. The Book of Devotion.

5. – WORKS IN ENGLISH

286. H. P. BLAVATSKY (P), Isis Unveiled, New York, 1875, 3 vols., in-8vo (MYS).
Confused compilation of French writers on the Qabalah. – No orderly method.
287. (P), The Secret Doctrine, London, 1889, 2 vols. in-8vo (MYS). Same remarks as for the preceding.
288. Dr C. DU PREL (P), Philosophy of Mysticism, trans. C–C. Massey (PHIL and MYS).
289. A. E. Waite (P), Lives of Alchemystical Philosophers (MYS).
290. S. LIDDELL MACGREGOR MATHERS (P), The Key of Solomon the King (Clavicula Alomonis).
291. – The Qabalah Unveiled (SCT).
292. FRANZ HARTMANN (P), Magic, White and Black (MYS).
293. The Literature of Occultism and Archaeology (MYS).
294. A. E. WAITE (P), The Mysteries of Magic (MYS).
295. (DV), Supernatural Religion, an Inquiry into the Reality of Divine Revelation, 3 vols., London, 1875 (PHIL).

296. HENRY MORUS (WT), A Conjectural Essay of Interpreting the Mind of Moses, According to a Threefold Cabala, London, in-8vo, 1654 (PHIL and MYS).

297. SMITH (DV), Dictionary of Christian Biography (Article: Cabalah) (PHIL).

298. GINSBURG (DV), The Kabbalah, its Doctrines, Development and Literature (PHIL).

299. AZARIEL (DV), Commentary on the Doctrine of the Sephiroth, Warsaw, 1798, Berlin 1850 (PHIL).

300. – (DV), Commentary on the Song of Songs, Altonn.. 1763 (MYS).

301. MACKAY (P), Memory of Extraordinary Popular Delusions, London, 1842, in-8vo (Portraits of J. Dee, Parcelsus and Cagliostro) (PHIL).

302. BARRETT (P), Magus, a Celestial Intelligence, London, 1801, in-4to, illus. (MYS).

303. AINSWORTH, Henry (B), Annotations upon the Five Books of Moses, folio, London, 1639 (PHIL).

304. CUDWORTH (B), The True Intellectual System of the Universe, folio, London, 1678 (MYS).

304b. ANNA KINSFORT (D), The Perfect Way, London, in-8vo, 1887.

6. – WORKS IN SPANISH

305. CASTILLO (P), Historia y magia natural, Madrid, 1692, in-4to (MYS).

306. ABENDANA (P), Cuzari, libro de grande sciencia y mucha doctrina, traducido por Abendana, Amsterdam, (Bib. Nat. A 2954) (PHIL and MYS).

307. CARDOSO (B), Las Excellencias de los Hebreos, y las Calonias de los Hebreos, in4to, Amsterdam, 1679 (PHIL).

308. Dr JOSE A. ALVAREZ DE PERALTA (P), Iconografia Simbolica de los Alfabetos Fenicio y hebraico, Madrid, Baillère, 1898 (PHIL).

CHAPTER THREE

CLASSIFICATION BY SUBJECT MATTER

1. – WORKS ON THE MISHNA

(Bibliothèque Nationale)

310. R. MOSES MAIMONIDES. and R. ORADIA BARTENOVAE, Mischnat, traditiones, Sabionetx, 1563, 2 vols., in-4to (A. 828).
R. JUDAE SANCTI. Venitiis, 1606, folio (A. 829).
See also Nos. 830 to 834. – All these works are in Hebrew.

311. GUILLIEMUS SURENHUSIUS, Mischna, sive totius hebrœorum juris, rituum antiquitatum ac legum oratium systema, cum Rabbinorum MAIMONIDIS ET BARTENOVAE commentariis integris; quibus accedunt variorum auctorum notæ ac versiones in eos quos ediderunt codices: omnia a Guilielmo Surenhusio latinitate donata, digesta et notis illustrata Hebraicè et latinè, Amstelodami, Girard et Jacobus Borstius, 1698, 6 vols., folio (A. 834).
See also Nos. 835-849.
Mishna (best commentaries).

312. MOISE MAIMONIDES ET OBADIA BARTEN-OVE' Bib. Nat. A. 673, fol., Naples, 1490-92, Latin text published by SURENHUSIUS, 6 vols., Amsterdam, 1698-1703 (A. 674).

313. MISHNA in Spanish, Venice, 1606.

314. – in German, by Rabe, Onolzbach, 1761.

315. – in Hebrew, Berlin, 1834.

2. – WORKS ON THE TARGUM

(Bibliothèque Nationale)

316. PAULUS FAGIUS and ONKELUS, Thargum, 1546, fol. (A. 824).

317. UZIEL, Targum, Basel, 1607, fol., (A. 825).

318. UZIEL or FRANCISCUS TAYLERUS, London, 1649, in-4to (A. 826).

319. R. JACOB, F. BUNAM, Basel, in-4to (A. 827).

320. See also Nos. A. 435, A. 786, A. 2-332.

WORKS ON THE MASSORAH

(Bibliothèque Nationale)

321. BUXTORF, Tiberias (A. 822, 823).

3. – WORKS ON THE TALMUD

(Bibliothèque Nationale)

322. 1.—Talmud of Jerusalem. R. JOCHANAN, Talmud Hierosolymitanum, divisum in quatuor ordines, Venetiis, Daniel Bomberg, fol. (A. 840); another edition, Cracow, Isaac, Aron, 1607-1609, folio; 2. Talmud of Babylon.

323. RAB. ASCHE, Talmud Babylonicum integrum, ex sapientum scriptis et responsis compositum a Rab. Asche, centum circiter annis post confectum Talmud Hierosolymitanum, additis, commentariis, R. Salomonis Jarchi et R. Mosis Maimonidis, Venitiis, Daniel Bomberger, 1520, 1521, 1522, 1523; 15 vols, fol. (A. 842).

See also Nos. A. 843-857.

324. For condensations of the 'Talmud': Nos. 857-879.

325. For commentaries on the 'Talmud': Nos. 879-914.

326. For treatises on the 'Talmud': Nos. 915-917.

The Bibliothèque Nationale lists in its old catalogue one hundred and twenty-four works on the 'Talmud', for the most part works of considerable size.

4. – WORKS ON THE QABALAH IN GENERAL

(Bibliothèque Nationale, Wolf.)

1. Introduction to the Qabalah.

327. R. JOSEPH CORNITOLIS, Schaace Hedek portæ perlicia (Hebrew), Ruca, 1461, in4to (A. 964).

328. R. JOSEPH GECATILIA, Gan egiz, hortus lucis, sive introductio in artem cabalisticam (Hebrew), Hanover, 1615, folio (A. 965).

2. General works on the Qabalah.

329. R. AKIBA, Sepher Yetzirah (Hebrew), Mantua, 1562, in-4to (A. 966).

330. RITTANGELIUS, Sepher Yetzirah (Hebrew), Amsterdam, 1642, in-4to (Hebrew and Latin) (A. 957).

33. R. SCHABTAI SCHEPHTEL HORWITZ, Schepha Tal (Hebrew), Hanover, 1612, fol. (A. 968).

332. KNOOR DE ROSENROTH, Kabbala denudata (A. 969) (Latin).

333. PISTORIUS, Artis cabalisticæ scriptores (Latin), Basel, 1587, folio (A. 97o).

334. See also the treatises in Hebrew, Nos. 970-978.

335. JOSEPH DE VOYSIN, Trans. from Hebrew into Latin.

R. ISRAEL FILII R. MOSIS, Disputatio cabalistica de anima, et opus rhythmicum R. ABRAHAM ABBEN EZRAE, De modis quibus Hebræi legem solent interpretari, adjectis commentariis ex Zohar, aliisque rabbinorum libris, cum iis quæ ex doctrina Platonis convenere, Paris, Tussanus de Bray, 1658, in-8vo (A. 978).

336. AGRIPPA (Hen. Cor.), Phil. Occulta, (Book III); De Vanitate Scientiarum (Ch. LXVIII).

337. ALBERTI (Frid.Christian), Works.

338. ALTINGIUS (Jacob), In Dissertat. de Cabbale Scripturaria.

339. ANDREAE (Samuel), In Examine generali Cabbalæ philosophicæ, Henri Mari, Hernborn, 1670, in-4to.

340. BARTOLOCCIUS (Julius), Rabbinica Bibliotheca (passim), 1694, 5 vols., Rome, 1675-93, 4 vols., fol.

341. BASHNYSEN (Hen. Jac. Van), Disputationes II de Cabbala vera et falsa, Hanover, 1710.

342. BASNAGE (Jacob), Historia Judaica, Book III, Ch. X et. seq.

343. BERGER (Paul), In Cabbalismo Judaïco Christiano, Vitemberg, 1707, in-4to.

344. BUSCHERUS (Frédéric-Christianus), In Mensibus

Pietisticis (mense IV).

345. BUDDEUS (Jo. Franc), In observationibus Halensibus salutis, vol. I, observat. 1 and 16 and in Introductio in philosoph. Hæbreorum.

346. DE BURGONOVO (Archangelus), Ordinis minorum, Pro defensione doctrinæ Cabbalæ, Basel, 1600, in-8vo (pp. 53 and 54).

347. EJUSDEM, Cabbalistarum selectiora obscurioraque dogmata illustrata, Venice, 1569, in-8vo; Basel, 1587, folio.

348. CARHYIORIUS (Joh. Benedictus), Introductio in Theologiam Judaicam, Ch. VI.

349. COLBERG (Ehregott. Daniel), In Christianismo Hermetica Platonica.

350. COLLANGEL (Gabriel), In Dissert. de Cabbala, cum ejusdem polygraphia Galliœ edita, Paris, 1561.

351. DICKINSON (Edmond), In physica vetere et vera, Ch. IV and XIX.

353. DISENBACH (Martinus), In Judœo convertendo, p. 94, et converso, p. 145 et sqq.

354. DURETUS (Claudius), In the history of the origin of languages, Ch. VII.

355. FLUDD (Robertus), In Philosophia mosaica, et alibi, passim.

356. GAFFARELLUS (Jac.), Abdita divinæ Cabbalæ mysteria contra Sophistarum Logomachiam defensa, Paris, 1623, 4 teste Leone Allatio de Apibut Urbanis, Ejusdem tractatum de Cabbala, et in eum Mersenni notes M. S. S. in Biblioth. Peirescii memora, Colomesius in Galia Orientali, p. 154. Promisit et Cribrum Cabbalisisticum.

357. GALATINUS (Pet.), Book I, De Arcanis Cath. Veritat., Ch. VI.

358. GARZIA (Pet.), Vide supra Archangelus Burgonosensi.

359. GASTALDUS (Thom), In libris de Angelica potestate passim de Cabbala Judaica egit, eamque confutavit, teste Kirchero in Edipo Egyptiaco, vol. II, Part I, qui passim ad eum provocat.

360. GERSON (Christian), In Compendio Talmudis, Part I, Ch. XXXI.

361. GLASSIUS (Salomon), In Philologia Sacra, Book II, Part I, p. 302.

362. HACKSPANIUS (Theodoricus), In Brevi Expositione

Cabbalæ Judaicæ, Miscellaneis ejus Sacris subjuncta, p. 282 et sqq. qui speciatim, p. 341 et sqq. fuse de usu Cabbalæ in Theologgio differit.

363. HEBENSTREITIUS (Jo. Bat.), In dessertat. de Cabbala Log. Arithmo-Geometro-Mantica spargi nuper coepta, Ulm, 1619, in-4to.

364. HENNINGIUS (Jo.) in Cabbalologia sive Brevi Institutione de Cabbala cum veterum Rabbinorum Judaica, tum Poetarum Paragrammatica, Leipzig, 1683, in-8vo.

365. HOORNBECKIUS (Jo.), In libris VIII pro convincendis et convertendis Judœis, Book I, Ch. II, p. 89 et sqq.

366. HOTTINGERUS (Jo. Hen.), In Thesauro Philolog, Book I, Ch. II, Sect. V.

367. HOTTINGERUS (Jo. Henres.), Nepos, In notis ad discursum Gemaricum de Incestu Creatione et opere Currus, p. 41 et sqq.

368. KIRCHERUS (Alhanas), In Aedipo Aegyptiaco, vol. II, p. 1.

369. KNORR (Christianus), A. ROSENROTH, in Cabbala denudata, vol. I, Solisbac, 1677 and 1678; vol II, Frankfurt, 1684, in-4to. Vide Buddei Introduct., p. 281 et sqq.

370. LANGIUS (Joach.), In Medicina Medicina Mentis, p. 151, et sqq.

371. LANGIUS (Jo. Mich.), In Dissert. de Charactere primævo Bibliorum Hebr. et in Comment. de Genealogiis Judaicis.

372. LENSDENIUS (Jo.), In Philolog. Hebr. Dissert. XXVI.

373. LOESCHAR (Valent. Ernestus), In prænotionibus Theologicis, p. 288, et sqq.

374. LOBKOVITZ (Jo. Caramuella), Cabbalae Theologicæ Excidium, qua stante in tota S. Scriptura ne unum quidem verbum esset de Deo, Vide Imbonati Biblioth. Lat. Heb. p. 96.

374. EJUSDEM, Specimen Cabbalæ Grammaticæ, Brussels, 1642, in-12mo.

376. MIRANDULANUS (See Picus)

377. MORRESTELLIS (Pet.), Academia Artis Cabbalist, Paris, 1621, in-8vo, edita prorsus huc non pertinet, quippe quæ tantum de Arte Lulliana exponit.

378. MORUS (Henr.), In scriptis variis, de quibus

diligenter exponit. Rev. Jo. Franc. Buddeus in Introduct. in Philos. Hebraerum.

379. MULLERUS (Jo.), In Judaismo Prolegom. VI.

380. NEANDER (Michael), In calce Erotematum L. Hebr., P. 514 et sqq.

381. PASTRITIUS (Jo.), Cujus tractatum M. S. de Cabbala ejusque divisione et auctoritate laudat Imbonatus in Biblioth. Hebraeo, Latina, p. 126.

382. PICUS (Jo.) Mirandulanus, LXXII, Conclusiones Cabbalisticae et alia in Operibus ejus legenda. Conclusiones illae integrœ exstant in Rev. Budder Introduct., p. 230 et sqq. Conf. Archangelus Burgonov.

383. PISTORIUS (Jo.), Nidanus, in tomo I, Scriptorum Artis kabbalist., Basel, 1587, folio, quo continentur Pauli Ricii, Book IV, de cœlesti Agricultura, et opuscula nonnulla ejus alia: R. Josephi Castiliensis Porta lucis, Leonis Ebrai de amore Dei dialogi tres: Jo. Reuchlini Book III de Arte kabbalistica; item Book III de verbo mirifico: Archangeli Burgonoviensis Interpretationes in selectiora obscurioraque Cabbalistarum dogmata; et Abrahami liber Jezira. Lege de hac collectione Buddeum in Introduct. ad Histor. Philos. Hebr., p. 221. Rich Samaneni in Bibliotheca Selecta, vol. I, p. 322, et sqq., et Pet. Bælium in Dictionario edit. recentiss., vol. III, p. 2315 et sqq.

384. REIMMANNUS (Jac. Frider.), In Conata introduct. in Historiam Theolog. Judaicae, Book I, Ch. XV.

385. REUCHLINUS (Jo.), In libris III de Arte Cabbalist. Hagenoae, 1517, in-4to, Basel, 1550, et cum Galatino, Frankfurt, 1672, folio, item in Pistoris Scriptoribus Cabbalist., Basel, 1587.

386. RICCIUS (Paulus), In libris IV de cœlesti Agricultura et alia; vide part. I, No. 1817, Conf. Pistorius.

387. RITTANGELIUS (Jo. Steph.), In notis ad lib. Jezira, et libro de 'Veritate Religionis Christianae'.

388. ROSENROTH (See Christianus Knorr).

389. SCHERZER (J. Adamus), In Trifolio Orientali, p. 109 et sqq.

389b. SCHICKARDUS (Guilielmus), In Bechinath Happeruschim, Diss. IV.

390. SCHOTTUS (Casp.), In Technica Curiosa, Book XII, de Mirabilibus Cabbalae.

391. SCHUDT (Jo. Jac.), In Memorabilibus Judaicis,

part. II, Book VI, Chap. XXXI, p. 188 et sqq.

392. SENNERTUS (Andr.), Dissert. peculiari de Cabbala, Vitembe, 1655, in-4to, quae recusa est in Heptade II. Exercitatt. Pilolog. num. III.

393. SPERBERUS (Julius), Isagoge in veram triunius Dei et naturae cognitionem, concinnata an. 1608, nonc vero primum publici juris facta, in qua multa quoque praeclara de materia lapidis Philosophici ejusque mirabilissimo continentur, Hamburg, 1674. Hunc puto esse tractatum, in quo probasse sibi videtur, artem kabbalisticam omnium artium esse nobilissimam. Vide praefationem ejus ad Preces Cabbalisticas.

393b. EJUSDEM, Kabbalisticae Precationes, Latine, Amsterdam, 1675, in-8vo, et German eodem anno Amstelod. et Francofurti. Conf. Godefredi Arnoldi Hist. Haeresiologic., part. III, p. 16 et sqq.

394. VOISINIUS (Jos.), In notis ad procem, in Raym. Martini Pugionem Fidei, et ad. R. Israël, fil. Mosis. Disputat, Cabbalist.

395. WACHTER (Jo. Georg.), In Spinosismo Judaismi, Amsterdam, 1799, in-8vo, et Elucidario Cabbalistico, Rostoch., 1706, in-8vo.

396. WALTHER (Jo.), in Officina Biblica, p. 523 sqq.

397. WALTONUS (Brianus), In Prolegom. VII ad Biblia Poliglotta, Para. 30, 38.

398. ZIEROLDUS (Joh. Wilhelmus), In Introduct. ad Histor. Ecclesiast. Chap. III. Ex Judaeis, qui historice de Cabbala praeceperunt, potiores sunt Elias Levita in Tisbi Voce, R. Moses Corduero in R. Nephthali in praefat. et Menasse ben Israël in Conciliatione super Exodum, quaest CXXV, p. 249, et sqq. edit. Hispanicae.

5. – WORKS ON THE SEPHIROTH

(Wolf)

399. AEVOLUS (Caésar) (The Neopolitan), in the book of 'Ten Sephiroth', Venice, 1589, in-4to.

400. AQUINAS (Philippe), L'Interprétation de l'arbre kabbalistique, avec la figure de cet arbre, Paris, 1625, in-8vo, French. (Bib. Nat. A. 7.730), followed by 'Codices

manuscripti cab.' Gaffarel.

401. BASNAGE (Jacob), Histoire juive, Book II, Ch. XIV.

402. BUDDEUS (J. F.), Introduction à l'Histoire de la Philosophie hébraïque, p. 277 et sqq., 356 et sqq., last edition.

403. BURNEUS (Thomas), Archéologie philosophique, Book I, Ch. VII.

404. Carpzovius (J. Bened.), Introduction à la théologie juive (Int., p. 82), and Dissertatio de Vacca Rusa. part II, p. 56 et sqq., 1706, p. 161 et sqq., 170-177.

405. GUNDLINGIUS (Nicolas Hieron.), Historie de la philosophie morale, Part I, Ch. VII, p. 95.

406. HEUMANNUS (Christophe-Auguste), Acta philosophica, vol. II, No. 2.

407. HINKELMANNUS (Abraham), Detectio fundamenti Boehmiani, p. 20 et sqq.

408. KIRCHERUS (Athanas), Oedipus Aegyptiacus, vol. II, part I, p. 214 et sqq., 290 et sqq.

409. LOSIUS (Jean-Juste), Bega dissertationum Gressae, 1706, in-4to.

410. MEYEURUS (Johan), Dissert. theologica de mysterio SS. Trinitatis ex foliis V. T. libris demonstrato, Harderonii, 1712, in-4to.

411. MORUS (Henricus), In operibus philosophiae, p. 429 et sqq.

412. OLEARIUS (Gottfrid), In observationibus sacris super Matth., VI, p. 221 et sqq.

413. PFEIFER (August), In Critica sacra, p. 214 et sqq.

414. RITTANGELIUS (Jean-Stephanus), In notis ad lib. Iezirah et in lib. de Veritate religionis christianae.

415. DE ROSENROTH (Christianus Knorr), In Cabbala denudata, passim.

416. STENDNERUS, De mysterio Dei triunius, p. 294 et sqq.

417. VITRINGA (Campegnis), Liber I observat. sacrarum, Chap. X et XI.

418. VOISINIUS (Joseph), In Notis ad praemium Pugnunis fidei, p. 71 et sqq.

419. WACHTERUS (Jean-Georges), In Elucidario cabbalistico, Chap. III.

6. – WORKS ON THE SEPHER YETZIRAH

(Bibliothèque Nationale)

422. Sepher Yetzirah (in Hebrew), Mantua, 1562, in-4to (A. 996).

423. Artis cabalisticæ scriptores ex biblioth. Pistorii, 1587, folio (A. 970).

424. Abrahami patriarchæ liber Jesirah ex hebraee versus et commentariis illustratus a Guillemo Postello, 1552 (A. .Reserve, 6590).

425. Cuzari, libro de grande ciencia y mucha doctrina, traducido por Abendana, Amsterdam, 5423 (A. 1100).

426. Liber Jesirah qui Abrahamo patriarchæ adscribitur, una cum commetario Rabbi Abraham, Amsterdam, 1662 (A. 967).

427. MAYER LAMBERT, Commentaire sur le Sefer Jesira, Paris, 1891, in-8vo.

7. – WORKS ON THE PRACTICAL QABALAH

(Bibliothèque Nationale)

428. SCHEMAMPHORAS, Mss. 14-785, 14-786, 14-187.

429. SOLOMON'S SEAL, Mss. 25-314.

430. THE KEY OF SOLOMON, Mss. 25.244, 25.245.

APPENDIX

PERIODICALS

devoted in general to a study of the Qabalah

In French

'L'Initiation', director: Papus, monthly review of 100 pp., published regularly since 15 October 1888, Paris, 5 rue de Savoie.

'Rosa Alchemica', 43, Quai des Grands Augustins, Paris.

'Bulletin de la Société d'Etudes Psychiques à Nancy', 25 Faubourg Saint-Jean, Nancy.

'Bulletin du Centre d'Etudes Psychiques de Marseille', 41 rue de Rome, Marseille.

'La Résurrection', Saint-Raphaël (Var).

In English

'Light', 110, St. Martins Lane, London W.C.2.

'Star of the Magi', 617 La Salle Avenue, Chicago (U.S.A.).

'Psychic and Occult Views and Reviews', 239 Superior Street, Toledo, Ohio (U.S.A.).

'The Progressive Thinker', Chicago, Ill. (U.S.A.).

In German

'Psysische Studiën', Liedenstrasse 4, Leipzig.

'Die Uebersinnliche Welt', Ebersivalderstr. 16, Berlin.

In Spanish

'Revista International de Ciencias hiperfisicas', plaza de Santa Domingo, Madrid.

In Dutch

'Het Toekomstig Leven', Utrecht, Holland.

ALPHABETICAL TABLE
OF
AUTHORS MENTIONED IN THE BIBLIOGRAPHY

(The numbers refer to the classification numbers which precede each work.)

ALPHABETICAL TABLE
OF
WORKS MENTIONED IN THE BIBLIOGRAPHY

(The numbers refer to the classification numbers which precede each work.)

BIBLIOGRAPHY

Of works on the Qabalah
by Dr Marc Haven

PREFACE

The bibliography which we now present to students and scholars necessitates a short introductory note. Anyone wishing to undertake a fruitful study of the Qabalah should first learn the Hebrew language, acquaint himself with the customs, mores and religion of the Jewish people, know its history and that of the various religious sects which have come and gone among this people of theologians, priests and philosophers. So many books have been written on these subjects that it would be materially impossible to list them here; moreover, such studies can well be considered preliminary in scope. It seems to us then that a bibliography on the Qabalah need not include such works, and thus we have purposely omitted all publications concerning linguistics (grammars, dictionaries), history, ethnography, law, exoteric Jewish religion (rituals and commentaries thereon) and even the entire flood of Talmudic literature with its occasional gleams of enlightened teaching. We give only those works which may initiate the reader into the very theories of the Qabalah itself.

The listed works have not been classed according to date or language or subject. Our aim has been simply to indicate titles to those interested in extending their knowledge in the field, and thus we have established our lists according to the commonest method, that is, alphabetically by author.

For each book we have given only one edition, the first to appear. Should certain bibliophiles desire more complete information (*edit. princeps*) or even estimates of the commercial value of such and such a work, we remain at their disposition to furnish, insofar as possible, these complementary details.

The bibliographic notes from which we have extracted these pages are complete enough to allow us to do this in the majority of cases. For the works which we have ourselves requested from the Bibliothèque Nationale in Paris, we are able to furnish reference numbers; and we beg those who will have occasion to work in the Nationale to do the same, keeping a record of the numbers of the books on the Qabalah which they may obtain. Such a record will of course be most useful for those who come after them.

A final word on the manuscripts: the numerous Hebraic manuscripts, books or scrolls, the rare Qabalistic manuscripts, unique copies of which dot libraries, both public and private, such as the marvellous collection of our colleague Stanislas de Guaita, have not been indicated since our bibliography is aimed at students for whom such manuscripts are unfortunately destined to remain unavailable.

Dr M.H.

BIBLIOGRAPHY

Archangelus de Burgonovo. – Apologia pro defensione Cabalae. – Bosson, Al. Benaceius, 1564, in-16mo.
— Dechiaratione sopra il nome di Giesu secundo gli hebrei cabalisti. – Ferrara, Rossi, 1557, in-8vo.
— Cabalistarum selectiora Dogmata. – Venet, 1569, in-8vo.
Agrippa H.C. – Die Incertitudine et Vanitate scientiarum. – Antwerp, 1530, in-4to (French trans. by Jean Durand, Geneva, 1582, in-8vo).
— De Occulta Philosophia. – Libri tres, Lugd., Bernigos, 2 vols. in-8vo (French and English trans.).
— De la Noblesse et Précellence du sexe féminin. – French trans. by Gueudeville, Leiden, 1726, in-12mo.
J.-H. Alsted. – Physica harmonica. – Herbonae, Nassor., 1616, in-12mo.
Azariel. – Commentary on the doctrine of Sephiroth. – Varsch. 1798.
— Commentary on the Song of Songs. – Attona, 1763.
Andreas S. – Examen generale Caballae Henrici Mori. – Herbonn, 1670, 1 vol.
Aevolus Caesar. – De decem Sephirotis. – Venise, 1589, in-4to.
Abraham Akibah. – Sepher Ietzirah. – Mantua, 1552, 1 vol. in-4to.
Ph. d'Aquin. – Interprétation de l'arbre de la Cabale. – Paris, 1625, in-8vo.
— Explanatio verborum primi psalmi.
Isaac Abrabanel. – Rosch Emana. – Constant., 1505, in-4to.
— Mirhcbet Mamischne. – Sabionella, 1551, in-fol.
— Pirusch na torah. – Venise, 1579, in-fol.
— Zerah Pesach. – Constant., 1505, in-4to.
— Pirusch al nebüm. – S.L., 1641 et 1646, in-fol.
Asulaï Ch. – Schem Hagadolim. – Vienna, 1852.
Alcazar (R.P.L.) – Vestigatio arcani sensus Apocalypsis. – Ludg. 1618, in-fol.

Ahron de Karitene. – Comment. cabalistique de Simon Ostropoli. – Amsterdam, 1765, in-4to.

Ange Pechmeja. – L'Œuf de Kneph. – Bucharest, 1804, in-8vo.

Amelineau. – Essai sur le Gnosticisme égyptien. – 1887, in-4to.

Abraham Aben Daoud. – Sepher hakabalah. – Amsterdam, 1697, in-12mo.

Akiba Beer. – Maase haschem. – Amsterdam, in-4to.

Ahron ben Elia. – Kether Thora. – Goslow, 1867, 5 vol, in-8vo.

Jacob Abendana. – Leket Schoch. – Amsterdam, 1685, in-fol.

Ad. Bertet. – Apocalypse du bienheureux Jean dévoilée. – P. 1861, in-8vo.

Buxtorf, J. – Dissertationes philologuo-theologicae. – Basil, 1662, in-4to.

— Synagoga judaïca. – Basel, 1603.

— Exercitationes ad historiam arcae Fœderis. – Basil, 1659, in-4to.

Buddens. – Introductio ad historiam philosophiae Ebraeorum. – Halle, 1702.

Bee, P. – Geschichte aller Sekten der Juden und der Cabbalah. – Brunn, 1822, in-8vo.

Bachimius. – Pansophia enchiretica. – Norib, 1682, in-16mo.

Berger. – Cabbalismus judaico-christianus. – Witemb., 1707, in-4to.

Bashuysen. – Disputationes II de Cabbala. – Hanov. 1710.

Bechoü ben Asher. – Sepher Semlhan arba. – Venise, 1546, in-fol.

S.-J. Baird. – The Elohim revealed in the creation. – Philad., 1860, in-8vo.

Bungus. – Numerorum mysteria. – Berg., 1585, in-4to.

Beroaldus. – Symbola Pythagore. – Bonon, 1502, in-4to.

Jord. Bruni. – Opera omnia. – Fiorentino, Napoli, 1879 et sqq.

Campanella. – De Sensu rerum et magia. – 1620, in-4to.

— De Monarchia Messiae. – Aesü, 1633.

— Prodomus philosophiae instaurandae. – Frankfurt 1617, in-4to.

— Atheismus triomphatus. – Rome, 1631, in-4to.

Cudworth. – The true intellectual System of the Universe. – London, 1678, in-fol.

G. de Collanges. – Clavicule sur les 5 livres de Polygraphie. – in-4to, 1561.

Jo. Craig. – Theologiæ mysticæ principia mathematica. – London 1699, in-4to.

Ciaconnius. – De Vi trium verborum: Mane, Thecel, Phares. – Medial. 1814, in-8vo.

Moïse de Cordoue. – Or Neherav. – Venezia, 1554, in-4to.

Chaüun N. Ch. – Dibre Nechemja. – Berlin, 1713, in-4to.

Chiquivilla J. – Schaare Tsedek. – Koretz, 1785, in-4to.

Drach (Chevalier). – De l'harmonie de l'Eglise et de la Synagogue. – Paris, 1844, 2 vol. in-8vo.

— Lettre d'un rabbin converti aux Israélites ses frères – P. 1825, in-8vo.

— La Cabale des Hébreux. – Rome, 1846, in-12mo.

— Le livre Yaschar. – Paris, 1858.

— L'Inscription hébraïque de la sainte croix. – Rome, 1831, in-8vo.

Didvmi. – De Pronuntiationé divini nominis quatuor litterarum. – Parmæ, 1799, in-4to.

A. Dillmann. – Das Buch Henoch. – Leipzig, 1853.

Eisenmenger. Entdecktes Judenthum. – S. 1. 1700, in-4to.

Elias (Pandochæus). – Cf. O. Postel.

Eleutherii Aug. – De Arbore mali et boni. – Mathusii, 1561, in-8vo.

Eleasar ben Jehnda. – Sepher Rasiel. – Amsterdam, 1701, in-4to.

Emden Jacob. – Migdal Os. – Warsaw, 1886.

Freystadt. – Philosophia cabalistica. – Regim., 1832, in-8vo.

Marsile Ficin. – Opera Bas. H. Petri, 1561, in-fol.

R. Fludd. – (De Fluctibus.) (All his works.) In particular:

— Tractatus theologico-philosophicus. – Oppenh., 1607, in-16mo.

— Summum Bonum. – Frankfurt, 1629, in-fol.

— Philosophia moysaïca. – Gondæ, 1638, in-fol.

Franck. – Etudes orientales. – Paris, 1861, in-8vo.

— La Kabbale. – Paris, 1843, in-8vo.

Foucher de Careil. – Leibnitz et la Kabbale. – Paris, 1861, in-8vo.

Rabbi Gedaliah. – Schol seheleth haquabalah. – Amsterdam, in-16mo.

Rabbi Jose Gekatiliah. – Schaare aoura. – (Trans. in the coll. of Pistorius.)

— Ganoth Egoz. – Hanau, 1615, in-fol.

— Schaare Tsedek. – 1461, in-4to.

Rabbi Oriel Goronensis. – Sepher Sodoth.

De Goulianof. – Essai sur les hiéroglyphes d'Horapollon et quelques mots sur la Cabale. – Paris, 1827, in-8vo.

Gaffarel J. – Abdita divinæ cabalæ mysteria. – Chez Jérôme Blageart. – Paris, 1625, in-4to, 77 pp.

— Curiosités inouïes sur la sculpture talismanique. – S. 1, 1650, in-12mo.

— Codicum kabbalisticorum manuscriptorum. – Chez Jérôme Blageart. Paris, 1602, 50 pp.

Galatinus. – De arcanis catholicæ veritatis contra Judeos (with the De Cabala of Reuchlin) – Frankfurt, 1612, fol.

L. Grassot. – La Philosophie céleste. – Bordeaux, an IV, in-16mo.

Georgius Venetus. – De Harmania mundi. – Venet, B. de Vitalibus, 1525, in-fol.

Ginsburg. – The Kabbalah.

Gastaldus. – De Angelica Potestate.

Geiger Abr. – Etudes biographiques sur quelques rabbins kabbalistes. – Breslau, 1856 à 1864.

Rabbi Gersonides (Levi ben Gerson). – Milchemot haschem. – Rio di Trento, 1561, in-fol.

Grœtz. – Gnosticismus und Judenthum. – Berlin, 1846. – Frank und die Frankisten. – Breslau, 1868.

Gaffarel J. – Tom Adonoi. – De fine mundi de R. Elcha ben Daoud. – Paris, 1629, in-16mo de 39 + 24 pp.

— Mariales Gemitus. – Paris, 1638, in-4to.

— Nihil, fere nihil, minus nihilo. – Venet., 1634, in-8vo.

— Les Tristes Pensées de la fille de Sion. – Paris, 1624, in-12mo.

Gerondi Jona ha Hassid. – Schaare Teschubah. – Fano, Soncino (circa 1505), in-4to.

Meïr ibn Gabbaï. – Tolaat Jacob. – Cracovie, 1616, in 4to.

— Awodat Nakodesch. – Cracovie, 1578, in-fol.

Gerson ben Salomo. – Schaare haschamaïn. – Venise, 1547, in-4to.

Ghazzathi Nath. – Chemdath Hajamim. – 4 vol. in-4to, Venise, 1763.

Stanislas de Guaïta. – Au seuil du Mystère. – in-8vo. Paris, Carré, 1890,

— Le Temple de Satan. – In-8vo, Chamuel, 1891.

— La Clef de la magie noire. – In-8vo, Chamuel, 1897.

Habermann, J. – Magia und Weissheit der seehsten Buch Mosis. – S. 1., 1460, in-16mo.

Hackespan. – Exercitatio de Cabala judaica. – Altdorf, 1660.

F.M. Van Helmont. – Seder Olam. – 1693, s.1., in-16mo, 108 pp.

—Alphabeti hebraïci delineatio. – Salzb., 1667. in-12mo.

Hebenstreitius J.-B. – De Cabala. – Ulm, 1619, in-4to.

Henningius. – Caballologia. – Lipsi, 1683, in-8vo.

Hottingerus. – Discursus gemaricus de Incestu creationis et opere currus. – 1600, in-4to.

Sam. Hirsch. – Religions-philosophie d. Juden. – Leipzig 1842.

Abr. Herrera. – Schaare haschamaïm. – Beth. Elohim. – In-4to, Amsterdam, 1665.

H. Hoschke. – Jalkut Reubein. – in-fol., Amsterdam, 1780.

Horowitz S. – Megillath Sedarim. – Prague, 1793, in-8vo.

H. Joël. – Religions-philosophie des Sohar. – Leipzig, 1849.

Jellnick. – Beitrage zur Geschichte der Kabbalah. – Leipzig, 1852.

— Moses ben Schemtob de Léon. – Leipzig, 1851.

— Moses ben Norchman. – Leipzig 1853.

R. Isaac Luriah. – Etz Chaïm. – 1572, in-4to.

Jamblichus. – De Mysteriis. – Oxon, 1678, in-fol.

— De Vita pythagorica. – Leipzig, 1815, in-8vo.

Jacob ben Ascher. – Hoschen hamischpath, 1559, in-fol.

Joseph de Tvani. – Tsaphenoth phaneah. – Venise, 1648, in-fol.

Isaac Israëli. – Iesod Olam. – Berl., 1848, in-4to.

Iedaja ben Abraham. – Bechinat Olam. – Soncino, 1484, in-8vo.

Ichudah ha Levi. – Kuzari. – Hebrew trans. by Juda ben Tibbon – Fano-Soncino, 1506, in-4to.

— Numerous trans. in German, Latin, French, Spanish.

Isaac bar Elia. – Meah Schaarim. – Venise, Soncino, 1539, in-4to.

De Ianduno. – Questiones de physico auditu Helie Hebrei Cretensis. – Venet, 1501, 1 vol. in-fol.

R. Issachar Baer. – Commentaire au Schir haschirim (in Sepher mequor Hochmah). – Prague, 1610. – Trans in the Bibliothèque rosicrucienne, Paris, 1897.

Jaquelot. – Dissertation sur le Messie. – La Haye, 1699, in-

8vo.

Joseph ben Chalefta. – Seder Olam rabba vezuta. – Basel, 1578, in-4to.

R. Iachjia ibn Gedaliah. – Schelscheleth hakabbalah. – Amsterdam, 1697, in-4to.

Israël Iafé. Aor Israël. – Frif., 1702, in-fol.

Iungendres. – Specimen ... theologiæ mythicæ Judeorum. 1728, in-4to.

Alber Jhouney. – Le royaume de Dieu. – Gr. in-8vo. – Paris, comptoir d'édition.

H. Khunrah. – Amphiteatrum sapientiæ veræ. – Hanau, 1609, in-fol.

— De igne magorum. – 1783. in-16mo, 109 pp.

— Wahraftiger Bericht von philosophischen Athanor. – Leipzig, 1783, 58 pp.

Kurtz. – Das mosaïsche opfer. – Mitau, 1842, in-8vo.

Kircher. – Works. – In particular:

— Oedipus aegyptiacus. 3 vol. in-fol. Rome, 1652-54.

— Arithmologia seu de abditis numerorum mysteriis. – Rome, 1665, in-4to.

Knorr de Rosenroth. – Kaballa denudata. – 3 vol., Slazburg and Frankfurt, in-4to, 1677 et 1684.

Is Karo. – Commentarium in Pentateuchum. – Riva di Trento, 1558, in-4to, 188 pp.

Kleuker. – On the Nature and Origin of Incarnation among the Cabalists. – Riga, 1786 (in German).

Moïse Kimchi. – Maalach Schebilé Hadaath. – Venise, Bornberg, 1546, in-8vo.

A. Kohut. – Ueber die judische Angelologie und Demonologie. – Leipzig, 1866.

Lévi ben Gerson. – Milchamoth haschem. – Rive de Trente, 1560, in-fol., 75 pp.

— Commentaire sur Job. – Ferrare, 1477, in-4to. 119 pp.

Isodore Loëb. – Article Cabale in Grande Encyclopédie.

— Le taxo de l'Assomption de Moïse. – Paris. 1879, in-8vo.

Raymundi Lulli. – Arbor scientiæ. – In-4to, 1636.

— De Auditu kabalistico. – Venet. Paul de Vitalibu, 1518, in-12mo.

Lacour. – Aelohim ou les Dieux de Moïse. – Bordeaux, 1839, 2 vol. in-8vo.

Léon l'Hébreu (Aharbanel). – Dialoghi de amore. – Rome, 1535, in-4to. – French translation by Sieur du Parc. – Paris,

1556, in-16mo.

Lopackine. – Quelques traits de l'église intérieure. – Moscou, 1801, in-8vo.

Lodoïk (Comte de Divonne). – La Voie de la science divine. – Paris, 1805, in-8vo.

Lacuria. – Harmonies de l'être exprimées par les nombres. – Paris, 1853, 2 vol. in-8vo.

Lenain. – La Science cabalistique. – 1 vol. in-8vo, Amiens, 1823.

Eliphas Lévi. – *Works*.

Lobkowitz. – Specimen Caballæ grammatica. Brussels, 1642, in-16mo.

Le Feure. – Le Secret et mystère des Juifs jusques à présent caché. – Paris, in-8vo, 1562.

Phil a Limborch. – De Veritate religionis christiana amica collatio cum erudito Judeo. – Gondæ, 1627, in-4to.

Liharzik Fr. – Das Quadrat, in der Natur, 57 Tafeln der Tetragramme. – 1 vol. in-4to, Vienna, 1865.

Leon. – Rabbinische Legenden. – Vienna, 1821.

Leusden. – Questiones hebraicæ. – Basil, 1739, in-4to.

Lornei Michel Angelo. – La sacra scrittura illustrata, – Roma, 2 vol., in-4to, 1827.

D. Luria. – Kadmoth sepher hazoar. – Warsaw, 1884.

M. Ch. Luzzatto. – Chokar ve Mikubal. – Leipzig, in-16mo, 1840.

— 138 Regeln über die Kabbala. – Krakau, 1880.

Landauer. – Jehovah und Elohim. – Stuttgart, 1866.

Latif. Is. – Zurat ha Olam. Vienna, 1860.

— Kebuzat Chachamin. – (Dictionary of words difficult of interpretation found in the Zohar), Vienna, 1860.

Levinsohn. – Schorsche Lebanon. – (The supplement pertains to the Zohar.), Vilna, 1841.

Is. Loeb. – La chaîne de la tradition dans le Pirke Aboth. – Paris, 1889. – La vie des métaphores dans la Bible. – Paris, 1891. *Works* in particular.

R. Moses ben Maïmon. – More Nevouchim. – Latin trans. by Buxtorf. – Basel, 1629, in-4to – French trans. Munich, 3 vols.

Porta Mosis. – E. Pockok. – Oxoniæ, 1655, in-4to.

R. Moses de Cordoue. – Pardes Rimonim, et Thamar Deborah. – Mantoue, 1623, in-fol.

R. Moses ben Nachman. – Pirusch al hathorah. – Pesaro

Soncico, 1513, in-4to (Avel le Zeror hamor).

— Ozar Nechmad. Pressburg, 1837, in-4to.

— Wiknach Ramban. – (Edit, Steinschneider.) Berlin. 1860.

H. Mordatham. – Aureum speculum redivivum. – In-fol., 1785.

Henri Morus. – Psychozoïa. – In-8vo, 1640-47 (Cf. opera varia in Knou de Rosenroth.)

— A conjectural essay. – London, 1654, in-8vo.

Molitor. – Philosophie de la tradition. – French trans., Paris, 1834, in-8vo.

Siméon de Muis. – In psalmum XIX, trium rabbinorum commentarii. – Paris. Lébert, 1620, in-8vo.

Malfatti de Montengio. – La Mathèse. – Paris, 1839, in-8vo.

S. Munk. – Mélanges de philosophie juive et arabe, 1859, in-8vo.

Montecuccoli. – De Cabala. – Mutinae, 1612, in-4to.

Meïr ben Gabaï. – Meoroth Ehohim. – Venise, Juan Grifo, 1567, in-fol.

Menasseh ben Israël. – Mekoè Israël. – Amsterdam, 1697, in-32mo.

— Mishaïoth. – Amsterdam, 1633, pet. in-8vo.

— De Creatione problemata XXX. – De Resurrectione mortuorum. – Amsterdam, 1635 et 1636, in-16mo.

— Nischmath Chaijm. – Amsterdam, 1552, in-4to.

A. Margaritha. – Der ganz Judische glaub ... Leipzig, 1531, in-4to.

Misurachi. – Della Venuta del Messia. – Modana, Cassiani, 1826, 1 vol. in-4to.

J.-Fr. Meyer. – Edition, commentary and glossary of the Sepher Yetzirah (in German). – Leipzig, 1830, in-4to.

Michel Spacherus St. – Cabala speculum artis naturæ in alchymia Augustæ. – Schmidt, 1667, in-4to.

— Voarchadumia. – Venetiis, April 1530, in-4to.

J.O. Müller. – Des Juden Philo Buch von der Weltschopfung. – Berlin, Reimer, 1841, 1 vol. in-8vo.

Mises Fab. – Kabbala und Chassidismus. – Breslau, 1866.

Molcho Sal. – Sepher Hamphoar. – Amsterdam, 1709, in-4to.

Mordechoü ben Loe. – Eschel Abraham. – Fürth, 1701, in-fol.

R. N'Chuniah. – Sepher Habahir. – Amsterdam, 1651, in-4to.

— Soa haschem. – Amsterdam.

— Letter on the mysteries. Latin trans. by Paul Heredia.

Nieremberg (J.E.). – Curiosa y occulta philosophia. –

Madrid, 1643, in-4to.

Otto T.C. – Vali Razia. – Stettin, 1613, in-4to.

Le P. Olivier. – Alphabet de Cadmus. – Paris, 1755, gr. in 4to.

Pistorius. – Artis cabalisticæ ... Scriptorum tomus unus. – Basil., 1587, in-fol. chez Henricus Petrus, 26 ff., 979 pp.

Pfeiffer. – Antiquitates ebraicae. – Leipzig, 1685, in-12mo.

— Critica sacra. – Leipzig, 1688, in-16mo.

Picus Mirandula, J. Fr. – Works, and in particular:

— Cabalistarum selectiora dogmata ... – Venise, 1569, in-4to.

— Conclusiones 900. – S. L. 1532, in-8vo.

Guill. Postel. – Works, and in particular:

— Clavis absconditorum ... – Basel, 1547, in 4-to.

— De rationibus Spiritus Sancti, 11. II. – Paris, 1543, in-8vo.

– Liber de nativitate mediatoris ultima. – (About 1547, without place of origin.), in-4to.

— Liber Jesirah seu de formatione. – Paris, 1552, in-16mo.

Papus, – Works, and in particular:

— Le Tarot. – Paris, 1 vol. in-4to, 1893, Carré.

Patricius. – Magia philosophica. – 1 vol. in-16mo, 1640?

Philo Judæus. – Opera. Greek edition, Turnebus, 1552, fol, (numerous translations).

Reuchlin. – De Arte cabalistica 11. III. – Hagen, 1517, in-fol.

— De Verbo mirifico II. III. – Cologne, 1632, in-12mo. (*To be found in the collection of Pistorius.*)

P. Riccius. – Isagoge in-Cabalistarum eruditionem 1515, in-4to.

— Philosophica, prophetica ac talmudica disputatio. – 1514, in-fol.

— Compendium ... apostolicae veritatis ... – Papiæ, 1507, in-4to.

— Sol fœderis contra Judœos. – Papiæ, 1507, in-4to.

P. Riccuis. – De cœlesti Agricultura, 11. III. – Augustæ, Staymer, 1541, in-fol.

— De mosaïcis Edictis.

— De tertrino doctrinarum ordine. – 1510, in-4to. (*These three works are to be found only in the collection of Pistorius.*)

Riederer. – Die Bedenkliche und geheimnin—reiche Zahl Drey in Theologicis, Historicis und Politicis. – Frankfurt, 1732.

Roccha (Ant della). – Libro della pace e armonia. – Venetia, 1536.

Relandi. – Analecta rabbinica. – Ultraj., in-8vo, 1702.

— Antiquitates sacrae. – Traj. Bat., 1708, in-8vo.

Reggio J.-I. – Bechinath hakabbala. – Breslau, 1856.

— Torat Eloïm. – Vienna, 1818.

R. Schabtaî Scheptel. – Schepha-Tal. – Hanau, 1612, 1 vol., in-fol.

R. Simeon ben Jochaï. – The Zohar (attributed), containing: Midrach Hanelam; – Maïmer tha Chasi; Idra Rabba et Idra Suta; – Siphra Dzinoutha; – Sithreï Thorah; – l'Mukah; – P'Kudah.

Salomon ben Melek. – Michlof. Tofi. – Amsterdam, 1685, in-fol.

Salwigt. – Opus magokabalisticum. – Frankfurt, 1719.

R.-P. Esprit Sabathier. – Ombre idéale de la sagesse universelle. – In-16mo, 1679 (A re-edition in the Bibliothèque Rosicrucienne. Paris, 1897.)

Steebus J-Chr. – Coelum sephiroticum. – Mogunt, 1679, in-fol.

Jul. Sperberus. – Isagoge in veram Dei naturaeque cognitionem. – Hamburg, 1674.

— Kabbalisticae precationes. – Amsterdam, 1675, in-8vo.

J.-C. Schrammius. – Introductio ad dialecticam Kabbalorum. – 1703.

W. Sidelius. – De templo Salomonis mystico – Moguntiae, 1548, in-12mo.

Smith. – Article Caballah, in Dict. of Christian Biography.

Scherzer. – Trifolium orientale. – Leipzig, 1663, in-4to.

Schott. – Technica curiosa. – 1 vol. in-4to, Herbip., 1659.

Sennertus. – Dissertatio de Caballa. – Vitemb., 1655, in-4to.

Schickardus. – Mischpath Hamelek. – In-4to Tüb., 1628.

— Bechinath hapiruschim. – In-4to.

R. Samuel ben Abraham. – Keli hemda. – Venise, 1549-96, in-fol.

Strozae. – De dogmatibus Chaldaeorum. – Rome, 1617, in-4to.

Sonnenburg. – Arithmonomia naturalis. – Dresden, 1838.

Schultetus. – Imago tetrametallos Danielitica. – Witteb., 1670, in-4to.

Saadia Gaon. – Comm. on the Sepher Yetzirah. – Warsaw, 1873 (French trans. by M. Lambert, Paris, 1893.)

R. Salomon ibn Gebirol. – Mibchar hapeninim. – Soncino, 1484, in-4to.

R. Salomon b. Abraham b. Adred. – Arasba Teschuvoth. –

S.A., in-4to (Rome).

R. Samuelis. – Epistola de adventu Missiae. – Nurimb., 1498, in-4to.

R. Salomon Pariel. – Or Aïnim. – Soncino, 1516-1518, in-8vo.

Sommer. – Specimen theologiae Soharicae. – Gotha, in-4to, 1734.

Sohar. – 3 vol. in-4to. – Lublin, 1883. – Amsterdam, 1805 (ben Jochaï) cf. Siméon.

Steudner J. – Jüdische ABC Schul von Geheimniss des dreien Gottes. Spruch Rabi Botril über d. Buch Jesirah. – Augspurg, 1665.

Trithemius, J. – Works, and in particular: De Septem secundeis. – Cologne, 1567, in-12mo. – French trans. in the Rosicrucian collection, Paris, 1897.

— Quaestiones VIII ad Maximilianum. – Oppenhenn, 1515, in-4to.

Tholuck. – De Ortu Cabalae. – Hamburg, 1837, in-8vo.

— Peufismus seu Theosophia Persarum. – Berlin, 1821, in-12mo.

— Die speculative Trinitätslehre des spateren Orients. – Berlin, 8-vo, 1826.

Thubjana Abr. – Eschel Abraham. – Livourne, in-fol., 1683.

Vanim J.-C. – Amphitheatrum aeternae providentiae. – Ludg., 1615, in-8vo.

— De admirandis naturae ... Arcanis. – Lutet, 1616, in-8vo.

Vincent P.-E. – Rapport des notions anthropologiques basar, rouách, nephesch, sebh, dans l'ancien testament. – Paris, 1884.

Joseph Voisin. – Disputatio cabalistica. – Paris, 1658, in-8vo.

Veneti Fr.-Gr. – De Harmonia mundi totius cantica tria. – Venet., 1525, in-fol.

R. David-Vidal. – Kether Thorah, – Constantin. Soncino, 1536, in-4to.

Vital Ch. – Hagilgulim. – Wilna, 1886, in-8vo.

— Hagoralot. – Edit. J. Sapir, Jerusalem, 1863.

Virgulti (L.-Ph.). – La vera ideo del Messia. – Rome, 1730, in-8vo.

Valverdii (Barch.) – In Salomonis Alphabetum mysticæ et spiritualis expositiones. – Rome, 1589, in-4to.

Wagenseil. – Tela ignea Satanæ. – Altdorf, 1681, in-4to.

Wachter G. – Concordia rationis et fidei. – Amsterdam, 1692, in-8vo.

— Le Spinozisme dans le Judaïsme. – Amsterdam, 1699, in-8vo.

Elnudarium cabalisticum. – Rostoch, 1706, in-8vo.

Witsii. – Aegyptiaca — – Amsterdam, 1683, in-4to.

O. Weil. – Lois et mystères de l'amour. – Paris, 1880, in-16mo.

Zeller. – Vacca rufa. – Amsterdam, in-18mo.

Anonyme. – Somnia Salomonis regis filii David. – Venise, chez J.-B. Sessa, 1501, in-4to.

Dr MARC HAVEN

THE QABALAH OF THE HEBREWS

By the Chevalier DRACH

LETTER
FROM R.P. PERRONE TO THE AUTHOR

SIG. CAVALIERE

E stato per me di vera soddisfazione il leggere i preziosi fogli che a Lei piacque comunicarmi. Non solo in essi vi ho trovato una piena confutazione dell' impugnatore delle sane dottrine sotto il velo della recondita *Cabbala*, non ben conosciuta dal volgo de' lettori, ma inoltre una feconda e non comune erudizione in pruova della verità. Gliene facci, Sig. Cavaliere, le mie più sincere congratulazioni, e mi auguro il piacere di poter altra volta godere di un simile favore. Mi dico con sincere stima,

di V. S.
Collegio Romano, 30 Gen. 1864.

Umo devmo affmo
G. PERRONE d. C. d. G.

TRANSLATION

MONSIEUR THE CHEVALIER,

It was with true satisfaction that I read the precious pages which you so kindly sent to me. In them I found not only a complete refutation of that author who attacks the solid doctrines veiled within the Qabalah and so little-known to the common reader, but also a fertile and uncommon erudition in support of the truth. I give you, Monsieur the Chevalier, my sincerest compliments with the hope of one day enjoying again a similar favour. I remain, with sincere esteem,

of Your Lordship,

Roman College, 30 January 1864.

the humble, devoted and affectionate,

G. PERRONE of the C. of J.

TO HIS MOST REVEREND EXCELLENCY

MONSEIGNEUR PIERRE LACROIX

APOSTOLIC PROTONOTARY

SECRET CHAMBERLAIN OF OUR MOST HOLY
FATHER PIUX IX

NATIONAL CLERK OF FRANCE FOR THE HOLY SEE

CHEVALIER OF THE LEGION D'HONNEUR

MEMBER OF SEVERAL LEARNED ACADEMIES AND
SOCIETIES

HOMAGE

TO THE SACERDOTAL AND CIVIL VIRTUES

TO KNOWLEDGE VARIED AND HUMBLE

GIVEN BY

His most grateful servant

THE AUTHOR

WHAT THE HEBREWS TEACH CONCERNING THEIR QABALAH AND ITS ANCIENTNESS, PRINCIPAL DOCTORS OF THIS ESOTERIC SCIENCE, THE QABALAH, WHICH WAS FIRST TRANSMITTED ORALLY; THEN LATER SET DOWN IN WRITING. BOOKS SURVIVING FROM THIS WRITING. UNBELIEVERS HAVE SOUGHT TO DISTORT THE MEANING.

1. – THE WRITTEN LAW AND THE TWO ORAL LAWS, ONE LEGAL, THE OTHER MYSTICAL OR QABALISTIC.

The term *Qabalah*, which in Hebrew signifies *received tradition*, קבלה from the verb קבל, indicates by its very name that the science is considered by rabbis to be a traditional teaching. According to these teachers, it consists of traditions dating back to the most ancient times; for the core of the system, to Moses, and even to Adam. They say that the law-giver of the Jewish people received from God not only the written law, but also an oral one, that is, the former's interpretation, both *legal* or Talmudic and *mystical* or Qabalistic. Indeed, the Hebrews have never been permitted to interpret the word of God otherwise than in accordance with the tradition taught by the ancients or as a last resort in dubious cases, according to the decision of the supreme pontiff of a given epoch. See Deuteronomy XVIII:8 *et seq.*

These two parts of the oral law are thus composed only of traditions and logical deductions resulting therefrom. Of course there have slipped in, so to speak, a number of apocryphal and misrepresented traditions introduced by

Pharisees who falsified the meaning of the holy law; Our Lord condemned these in the harshest terms. But I must recall the rule I have given in several of my works: any tradition which bears the seal of true religion which, in the estimable words of Saint Augustine, goes back to the cradle of the human race,[1] is indubitably authentic. Certainly it is not a simple invention of the rabbis, this Divinity which consists of *three supreme splendours*,[2] distinct and yet inseparably united in a single essence of absolute oneness. Those who maintain that the Redeemer of Israel is to be at the same time truly God and truly man;[3] those who teach that the Messiah offers to *take upon himself* the expiation of all the sins of mankind;[4] those who

---

[1] Res ipsa quæ nunc christiana religio nuncupatur; erat et apud antiquos, nec defuit ab initio generis humani quousque ipse Christus veneret in carne. Unde vera religio, quæ jam erat, cat appellari christiana. Retract. I. XIII. 3.

[2] *Sephira*, ספירה, is translated by *numeration* or by *splendour*. The extracts I give further on show that the latter meaning is truest.

In my Harmony I cite certain authorities who affirm that this great mystery of the Trinity is to remain a secret known only to a few privileged beings, ליחידי סגולה, until the coming of the Messiah.

[3] See my Harmony, vol. I, pp. 70-107; vol. II, pp. 387-485.

[4] Zohar, Part II, columns 370,380: 'The Messiah appears and cries: "Let all sufferings, all spiritual unhealthiness of Israël come upon me!" And then all these things do come upon him. And if He had not ransomed Israël by taking them upon himself, no man would be capable of bearing the punishment which Israël deserves for the transgression of the holy law. These are the words of the prophet (Isaiah LIII:4): *Surely he has borne our sicknesses and carried our pains.*'

This is yet another proof against the rabbis that this chapter is relative to the Messiah.

The Midrash Yalkuth on the 60th chapter of Isaiah transcribes a long passage from the ancient book *Peciqta-Rabba*, recounting the confrontation between the Messiah and God the Father. *With joyous heart* the Messiah accepts the expiation of the sins of *all the children of Adam*, past, present and to come, despite the terrible picture God presents him of this agonizing atonement. This is not the Messiah awaited by the Jews. Theirs is to reassemble their scattered peoples, give them back Jerusalem and restore the temple, having subjugated the remaining nations of the earth. I say 'remaining' for the majority of them will be destroyed. Nowadays there are many Jews who no longer believe in the coming of the Son of David and who, should this come about even so, would not be prepared to follow him to Palestine. Finding myself in the magnificent country retreat of a wealthy man of Palestinian origin, I said to my host, 'If the Messiah came, you would leave this beautiful property with regret.' He replied, 'When he comes, we will ask him to take all the *goyim* (Christians) to the Holy Land and to leave us be here in France where we are perfectly content.'

teach us that the *Shiloh*, שילה , promised by the patriarch Jacob, is really the Messiah;[1] all these are consistently refuted by the modern Synagogue. No present-day rabbi would give the Zohar the following interpretation, in conformity with that of the Gospels, Matt. XXI:4, 5: *The poor man[2] seated on an ass*, foreseen by the prophet Zachariah (IX:9) is the Messiah, son of David.[3]

2. – PRINCIPAL DOCTORS OF THE QABALAH. THE ZOHAR.

The most distinguished teacher of the Qabalah, attracting the greatest number of eminent disciples, was the celebrated Simeon ben Yohai, a rabbi at the beginning of the second century A.D. The dialect he employed is definitely that of the Jews of the time, Syrio-Jerusalemite, into which numerous Greek and Latin terms had already found their way. As he himself affirmed, he taught the tradition and doctrine of masters far older than he, attributing a great amount to the prophet Elijah and to Moses, whom the Zohar calls *the faithful shepherd*, רעיא מהימנא , and to the angel Metatron. His disciples and their followers later put these lessons into writing, forming a single body of literature which was given the name of *Zohar*, זהר , that is, *light*. This composition apparently lasted several centuries, at least it continued for a long period of time to receive new additions, since in it mention is made of the part of the Talmud, the Mishna and the Gemarah, which are

---

[1] Zohar, Part I, Col. 504: 'The name *shiloh*, as it is here written, שילה, Genesis XLIX:10, indicates that this supreme and holy name of Divinity exists within Him. Such is the mystery here proclaimed.'

Rabbi Aolomon Yarhi interprets this name as *Messiah*, in accordance with the three Chaldean paraphrases of Onkelos, of Jonathan-ben-Uziel and of Jerusalem.

Sanhedrim treatment of the Talmud, Fol. 98 (back): '*Shiloh* is the name of the Messiah for it is so called in the prophecy of Jacob.'

[2] The Hebrew and vulgate versions of Zachariah bear the word *pauper* and not *mansuetus*. Saint Justin quoting this verse, no doubt from memory, combines the two meanings.

[3] The Zohar, Part I, Col. 505: Part II, Col. 171, and the *Talmud* (Sanhedrim), Fol. 98, quote this verse from Zachariah as designating the Messiah.

significantly posterior[1] and there is even a reference to the false prophet Mohammed,[2] Jewish historians assure us that only a small part of this volume has come down to us. Rabbi Ghedalia, in his chronical entitled שלשלת הקבלה, *chain of tradition,* fol. mihi 23 recto, Solkwo edition, writes: 'By oral tradition I have learned that this composition is so voluminous that if the totality of it were to be discovered, it would constitute the entire load of a camel.'

3. – TRACTS AND BOOKS COMPLEMENTARY TO THE ZOHAR.

The text of the Zohar, such as we possess it, includes several tracts which were successively inserted at various times.

---

[1] The author of the *Kabbala denudata,* Knorr Baron de Rosenroth, says in Vol. II, p.5 of the preface: 'Quod nec *gemara,* nec ullius libri talmudici, ullibi faciat (that is, the Zohar) mentionem.' This is an obvious error. The Zohar mentions the *Talmud* and its several divisions in more than one place. See, among others, Part I, Col. 347; Part II, Col. 357; Part III, Col. 45, 49, 290, 540, 541. Knorr himself gives in his first volume the Latin version of a book by Rabbi Joseph Ghicatilia, containing a passage from the Zohar in which mention is made of three tracts of the *Talmud,* entitled *Baba-gamma, Baba-metzia, Baba-batra.* See *Kabbala denudata,* Vol. I, Part I, p.184.

Further (p.7), Knorr writes: 'Adde quod etiam contra Christum in *toto libro* (that is, the Zohar) ne minimum quidem effutiatur, prout in recentioribus Judæorum scriptis plerumque fieri solet.' Another error. In the Zohar, Part III, Col. 546, *Jesus* is clearly named and spoken of in the most blasphemous manner. I quoted this passage from an Amsterdam edition in my Harmony, Vol. II, p.27 of the *Notice sur la cabbale des Hébreux.*

In some editions, especially those submitted to Christian censorship, this passage is left blank or marked with an asterisk, indicating that a number of words have been omitted.

Mr Franck, who appears to have studied the Zohar only in the very dubious edition of Rosenroth, repeats this error. On pages 106 and 107 of his *Kabbala* he says: '*not one time* is there mention (in the Zohar) of Christianity or its founder.'

As the work of the German Baron, *Kabbala denudata,* is the obvious source for all those who cannot read the original text of the rabbis, I have seen fit to point out its failings. 1. In the two volumes, the Hebrew characters where given are often strangely disfigured by numerous typographical errors. 2. The Latin translation of these texts is frequently inexact. 3. References to the Zohar are generally poorly annotated. 4. Not rarely one finds the quoted texts interrupted by what appear to be the beginnings of new sentences, but which are in fact only continuations of what precedes.

[2] Zohar, Part III, Col. 546.

Among these one finds the ספר הבהיר , *the illustrious book*. It dates from before the birth of R. Simeon-ben-Yohai, since its author was R. Nehunia-ben-Haqqaneh, who was alive thirty or forty years before the Incarnation of the Word. To complement the Qabalistic tome, there have been separately edited: 1. the תקוני הזהר , *complements of the Zohar*; 2. the זהר חדש, *the new Zohar*; 3. the Zohar of the Song of Songs, of Ruth, of Lamentations. Among Qabalistic books we must take care to mention the ספר יצירה , *the book of creation*, and several other ancient books, a part of which have been lost or remain hidden in unknown libraries. The Qabalistic commentary on the Pentateuch, ילקוט ראובני, gives extracts from many of these now unavailable sources. Included also in the number of principal Qabalistic works in the ספר רזיאל , *the book Raziel*; but this is rather a treatise on theurgy.

4. – RULE FOR QUOTING FROM THE ZOHAR.

Before proceeding, I think it fitting to give space to the formulation of a rule governing quotation from the Zohar. This book is divided in all editions into three more or less equal parts. The first on Genesis; the second on Exodus, the third on Leviticus and the two remaining books of the Pentateuch. It is further divided in some editions into *the greater Zohar*, זהר הגדול. , and *the lesser Zohar*, זהר הקטון.. The edition of Cremona, a folio edition, serves as a model for the pagination of the greater Zohar. The lesser Zohar's model is the edition of Mantua, in-4to. The former contains numbered pages and two columns per page; the latter gives only page numbers as there is no columnar division. The three Amsterdam reprintings in-8vo are page-numbered as in the Mantua editions. Thus the references to columns, so useful in research, relates only to the greater Zohar. The edition of Sultzbach bears· in its margins indications of the page and column numbers of the greater and lesser Zohar.

TRUE IDEA OF THE QABALAH. ITS USE IN THE SYNAGOGUE.

I am going to set forth what the Jewish Qabalah really is and I readily submit my theories and proofs to the appraisal of any man of good faith and sound judgement. It will be seen that according to the fundamental doctrine of the Qabalah, the universe is a creation *ex nihilo* of the infinite power of God.

Indeed, any science should have a practical aim. What, then, is the aim of the Qabalah? The principal document of the Qabalah, the Zohar, Part II, Col. 362, and all Qabalists, answer that this aim is the teaching of how to direct one's intentions in praying to God; which *splendour* or *attribute* of God should be addressed in such and such a state of need;[1] which angels should be invoked in order to obtain their intercession in certain circumstances; by what means one guards against the ill-will of wicked spirits which fill the air. It was precisely to indicate exactly these intentions, prayers and formulas that the rabbi Isaiah Hurwitz, a voluminous Qabalistic commentary giving the common prayers of the synagogue, a work entitled, שער השמים , *the gate of heaven*. From this aim, consequences can naturally be derived. The Qabalah teaches of a personal God to whom prayers should be addressed, whereas Pantheists make God out of themselves. They say, along with a crowned philosopher of Egypt: *Meus est fluvius meus, et ego feci memetipsum* (Ezek. XXIX:3).

I have seen rabbis who, hearing for the first time the claim that the Qabalah contains the principles of atheism, remained stupefied. It often happens that suddenly faced with a strange and ridiculous proposal, we find ourselves speechless. A crowd of answers tumbles into our mind, each jostling for first place, so to speak, and we do not know where to begin. These rabbis were able only to exclaim: But it is not possible! This is nonsense, madness. How so?! The devout Qabalists of these many centuries denying the existence of God?! כופרים בעיקר !

For doctors of the modern synagogue the diffusion of Qabalistic science represents an entirely different danger. Publishers of books on the Qabalah are not infrequently the object of rabbinical curses. Rabbi Yehuda Arih, known by the name of *Leon of Modena* writing in one of his works entitled חרי נהם , *the roaring lion*: 'I doubt that God will ever pardon those responsible for the printing of such books.' Indeed, a number of Israelites, distinguished as to learning and social position, have been led by the reading of Qabalistic works to

---

[1] Thus, according to the object of our prayers, we Christians address them particularly to one of the revered Persons of the Most Holy Trinity.

embrace the Catholic faith. I mentioned several of them in my *Harmony*, vol. 2, pp. 32-35. A disciple of this self-same Rabbi Arieh, *Samuel ben Nahmias*, member of a rich Venetian family, received baptism in his native city on 22 November 1649, under the name of Julius Morosini. He is the author of a voluminous and scholarly work in Italian, *The Path of Faith as Shown to the Hebrews*, Rome, Imprimerie de la Propagande, 1683, 2 vols., in-4to.

1. – QABALISTIC DOCTRINE OF EMANATION. THE TEN SEPHIROTH OR SPLENDOURS. THE THREE SUPREME SPLENDOURS.

Advocates of pantheism have occasionally called the Qabalah to their aid, since it so frequently speaks of *emanation*. Bending the term to their own uses, they have duped a great number of people, unable to verify the facts for themselves. Yet it is precisely this doctrine of emanation which gives the Qabalah its eminently Christian character, which no one of good faith can refuse to recognize. The demonstration of this quality is simple.

The Qabalah differentiates *all that is* into four worlds, each subordinate to the next. 1. The world of *Atziluth* (emanation). 2. The world of *Briah* (creation). 3. The world of *Yetzirah* (formation). 4. The world of *Assiah* (matter). The last three, stemming as the name implies from the world of creation, are creations *ex nihilo* of divine power, not at all emanations from the Essence of God. The texts which I will single out later on are quite emphatic in this regard.

Thus emanation ceases with the first world, the only *uncreated* one, remaining concentrated there. It is important to acquaint ourselves with the Qabalah's description of this first world. The world of *Atziluth* contains ten *sephiroth* (ספירות), that is, *splendours*. The first is the *supreme crown* (כתרעליון), also called, the *Infinite* (אין סוף). The second splendour emanates therefrom and is called *Wisdom* (חכמה). It is *Primitive Adam* (אדם קדמין), thus denominated so as to be distinguished from the *first man*. Let us note in passing that Saint Paul calls this incarnate splendour *novissimus Adam*, I Cor. XV:45. From this then, with the concourse of the supreme splendour whose concurrence is obligatory, emanates the third splendour,

Intelligence (בינה).

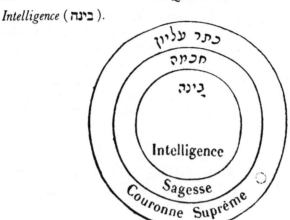

Such, teach the Qabalists, are the three Higher, or better, *Supreme* (עילאין) Splendours, the only ones called *Intellectual Splendours* (ספירות שכליות). Although distinct from one another, they are only a *single crown* (אחת עטרה); they are *one, the absolute one, unum absolutum* (יחיד המיוחד). This is why they are represented by these three concentric circles and why God Himself, *holy, holy, holy* (קדש קדש קדש) is represented by three *yod's* placed triangularly in a circle.

See my *Harmony*, Vol. I, p.309.

One must be quite blind not to perceive, or quite obdurate not to admit that these three splendours are the most holy and indivisible Trinity of Persons in the Divine Essence, *the one of absolute oneness*. The Qabalah proclaims this truth in terms identical with those of Catholic theology,[1] as will be seen from quotations given in a later place. But here I would like to cite a rather curious text. It is not the work of a Jewish Qabalistic but of Cicero, in his *De natura Deorum*, Book I, Para. 21 (No.28

---

[1] In my writings I have several times had the occasion to remark that when the synagogue and the Church come into agreement, it is always in the Catholic sense. Here we see the *Filioque* argument against the Photian schism.

in the Leipzig edition): 'Parmenides pictured something having the figure of a *crown*. He gives the name *stephane* (Gr., 'crown') to an unbroken circle, brilliant with light, and enclosing the *sky*; this is his name for God.'[1] Does he not then see the three supreme splendours forming a single *crown*? And let us mark it well, the first splendour encloses the whole within its continuous and endless circle. Cicero, understanding nothing of the sublime lesson of the philosopher of Elea, a lesson no doubt repeated from tradition, adds with the conceit characteristic of many a thinker: 'It is unimaginable that a circle could represent Divinity, or that such a figure could have any meaning.'[2] And yet Cicero must certainly have been aware that the Egyptians and other ancient peoples known for their wisdom represented by means of a serpent *in a circle*, tail in its mouth, the supreme God, eternal and infinite; in Qabalistic terms, אין סוף , *absque fine*.

The seven remaining splendours, each emanating from those preceding, are:

The fourth, *Grandeur* (גדולה), also called, *Benignity* (חסר).

The fifth, *Power* (גבורה), also called, *Severity, Rigorousness judgment* (מידת ודין).

The sixth, *Beauty* (תפארת).

The seventh, *Victory* or *Eternity* (נצח).

The eighth, *Glory* (הוד).

The ninth, the *Foundation* or *Basis* (יסוד).

The tenth, the *Kingdom* (מלכות).

These seven splendours make up a class apart under the generic denomination of *Knowledge* (דעת). *Knowledge*, says R. Joseph Ghicatilla, in his treatise שערי תורה (the gates of light), is the manner of being common to the divine representations coming after (the Splendour *Intelligence*), but no forming itself a separate *splendour*.

---

[1] *Stephanen* appellat continentem ardore lucis orbem, qui cingit *cœlum*, quem appellat Deum.

[2] In quo (that is, orbe) neque figuram divinam neque sensum quis-que suspicari potest.

2. – THE SEVEN SPLENDOURS AS DENOMINA-TIONALLY UNDERSTOOD, OR THE DIVINE ATTRIBUTES.

It is obvious to any clear-thinking mind that if the first three *Splendours*, ספירות , are God in three persons in the order of succession taught by the Catholic faith, then the seven following Splendours are, as is openly affirmed by the Qabalists, the *attributes* of God,[1] or more exactly, God in his *attributes*. Indeed, these include all the divine perfections. These Splendours are also *emanations*, for the divine attributes are inseparable from the Divinity, constituting a *perfect unity* among themselves and within God.

That the ten Splendours, in Hebrew, *Sephiroth*, are only the totality of the Supreme Being is proven by the divine name attributed to each of them:

The first is called אהיה , *I am who I am*.

The second, יה (shortened form of the name Jehovah).

The third, יהוה , pointed with the vowels of the divine name *Elohim*, אלהים .

---

[1] The divine attributes are distinguished as to *relative* and *absolute*. The former are the relations of the Divine Persons among themselves through the immanent action of generation and procession. The qualification *relative* does not, however, characterize sufficiently well the *non-absolute* attributes. Catholic theologians here include what they call the *properties* (proprietates), the *relations* (relationes), and the *notions* (notiones): to wit, innascibility, paternity, filiation, active spiration (spiratio) and passive spiration. There are thus four *properties*, innascibility, paternity, filiation and procession. The last three are personal proprieties (personales). Adding to these active spiration, we obtain the *relations*, numbering four.

It would be superfluous here to show how these formalities (formalitates) and even the very terms used by Christian theology are to be found in the Qabalah and various rabbinical works. The extracts quoted later will furnish some indication *first splendour*, the *Infinite* סוף חין (absque fine) with the sense of *leading to no origin whatsoever*, the *causa procatarchica* qualified as the *cause of all causes* עילה כל העילותetc.

The denomination *absolute attributes* is given to all the perfections which are the characteristics of the Divinity. These theologians distinguish as to *positive, negative* (in appearance), *quiescent* or *immanent, operative* or *transitive, primitive, derived, metaphysical, moral, communicable, incommunicable, proper, metaphorical*, etc.

The last seven *splendours* embody all these absolute attributes; all are to be found there, just as in the three supreme splendours one can clearly recognize the *relative attributes*, or better stated, the *five notions*.

The fourth, אלהּ , and according to others, אל , God.

The fifth, אלהים , God.

The sixth, יהיה, Jehovah.

The seventh, יהוה צבאות, Jehovah of the Powers.

The eighth, אלהים צבאות, God of the Powers.

The ninth, אל חי, living God.

The tenth, אדני, Adonai.

I stated that the divine attributes are *inherent* in God; this is taught by philosophy and Christian theology. Here are the words of the chief of present-day theologians, R.P. Peronné: 'Admitti nequit ulla realis distinctio inter Deum ejusque attributa, sive absoluta sive relativa, neque inter attributa absoluta ipsa. Si enim ejusmodi daretur distinctio, admitti in Deo deberet realis compositio atqui haec compositio in Deum cadere non potest, qui est omnino simplex; excludi igitur a Deo debet omnis realis distinctio, sive inter Divinitatem eiusque attributa absoluta ac relativa, sive inter attributa absoluta ipsa.' Prælect. theol., De Dei simplicitate, Prop. IV.

And to combat the criticism that the philosophy of a religious leader is necessarily prejudiced by theological thinking, let me quote a philosopher who can in no way be suspected of much zeal for Christian ideas. 'Hoc primum tene,' says Bayle, 'nihil esse in Deo quod non sit Deus atque adeo attributa divina non esse qualitates seu perfectiones ab Essentia divina distinctas, nisi secundum nostrum concipiendi modum.' Systema totius philosophiae. Metaphysicae specialis, chap. III, art. 3.

The Evangelist needs only a word to express this truth, to wit, that the attributes of God are essentially in God. *Deus charitas est.* I John IV:16.

3. – THE SEVEN SPIRITS OF THE APOCALYPSE, I:4.

The beloved disciple, fortunate enough to rest his head on the sacred heart of Jesus, recumbens in sinu Jesu, drew from this divine source a knowledge of the most profound and awesome mysteries. I will not hesitate to affirm that I see the ten *splendours* clearly referred to in the celebrated verse of his Apocalypse, I:4. Gratia vobis et pax ab eo qui est et qui erat et

qui venturus est, et a *septem Spiritus qui in conspectu throni ejus
sunt*. I hardly need repeat that these three tenses of the verb *to
be*, for *venturus est* is equivalent in Hebrew to *erit*, are, if I may so
express myself, the coin of the Divine Name Jehovah,   ,
whose constituent elements admirably denote the mystery of
the Most Holy Trinity. Learned commentators have already
demonstrated that the holy Apostle employs these three tenses
of the fundamental verb to designate the three reverend
Persons of God the One; and I myself have given a long
development in my *Harmony* to this signification of the
Tetragram. And so first we have the three *supreme Splendours*.
But what I wish above all to establish here is that the *septem
Spiritus* of this verse actually refers to the last seven splendours,
that is, God in his absolute attributes.

The opinion of those who take these seven spirits to be
angels seems inadmissible. For only God, to the exclusion of
any creature, even the most elevated of the celestial hierarchy,
has the right and the power to bestow that state of spiritual
grace called *gratia et pax*, a translation of the Hebrew
These two biblical terms clearly express the blessed union of
the soul with God, grace, the precious receptacle which is,
alas!, so fragile in the hands of weak mankind.

 ˙The fifth chapter distinguishes the *seven spirits* from the
angels in such a way as to leave no room for doubt. See verses 6
and 7. Nowhere in the Apocalypse does one find the angels
being called *spirits*. This salutation, *gratia et pax*, is the one
which Saint Paul repeats at the beginning of nearly all of his
epistles,[1] that treasure-trove of Christian theology. Now, the
great Apostle attributes this celestial gift, and rightly so, to
God alone: Gratia et pax a *Deo patre nostro et Domino nostro Jesus
Christo*. We are forced to conclude that in our verse from the
Apocalypse, Saint John is wishing the seven churches of Asia
grace and peace of soul in the name of all that is in God, his
hypostases and his attributes.

The preposition *et* before *a septem Spiritus* in no way
distinguishes these spirits from what precedes. Grotius, with
his commendably accurate eye, has remarked that as is so
common with the Hebrews and Greeks, this is an instance of
expressing the same thing in two different ways. He explains
in his commentary that the *seven spirits* are Divine Providence

---

[1] The only exception is the Epistle to the Hebrews.

manifesting itself in various fashions, referred to later, V:6, as the *eyes of God*: 'Et *oculos* septem, qui sunt *septem spiritus Dei*, missi in omnem terram,' says Saint John. Grotius adds: 'Et sic erit ... ; optatur enim pax *a Deo et septem Spiritibus*, id est, a Deo per hos septem Spiritibus, id est, a Deo per hos septem modos operante.' The Apostle of the Work (In principio erat Verbum) declares at the same time in his Apocalypse that the Word is God, and that consequently the seven spirits are inherent in him as they are in his father. He expresses himself thus in the fifth letter he writes at the instigation of Our Lord Jesus Christ: 'Hæc dicit qui habet septem spiritus Dei.'

A learned Jesuit, Father Alcazar, author of a vast commentary on the Apocalypse,[1] saw perfectly well that these seven spirits are nothing else, even in a literal sense, than the absolute divine attributes. This is Cornelius Lapidus's summary of the former's exposition: 'Alcazar per hosce septem spiritus accepit septem Dei virtues, sive *attributa* in quibus consistit integra Providentiæ perfectio. Porro hæc dotes sunt *in Deo*, suntque reipsa *ipse Deus*: unde *ab iss* pacem et gratiam suis precatur Johannes. Hæc ergo virtutes in Deo sunt immensæ, nec ullum habent finem, nec limitem; ideoque vocantur *spiritus* cum angelos Johannes in Apocalypsi *angelos* vocet, non *spiritus*.'

4. – THE SEVEN RADIANT LIGHTS OF THE APOCALYPSE IV:5. THE SEVEN EYES OF JEHOVA IN ZACHARIAH IV:10.

That these seven spirits are precisely the last seven *splendours* of the Qabalists is shown incontestably in Revelation IV:5. There it is positively stated that the seven spirits are *radiant lights* beaming forth from centres shining before the celestial throne. Et de throno procedebant fulgura et voces et tonitrua, et septem lampades ardentes, ante thronum, qui sunt septem spiritus Dei. This entire verse deals with nothing else but the subject we have been treating.

In Zachariah IV:10, these *lights, attributes, modes* of the Providence of God are called the *seven eyes of Jehovah, who walks*

[1] Very nearly all of Bossuet's exposition on the book of the Apocalypse is drawn from this commentary.

abroad over all the earth. Septem isti oculi sunt Domini (in Hebrew, *Jehovah*, of the triune God), qui discurrunt in universam terram. The Apostle Saint John in his turn declares these *eyes* to be the *spirits* of God. Et oculos septem (scil. Agni tamquam occisi), qui sunt *septem spiritus* Dei, missi in omnem terram. Qabalists do not fail to point out that in accordance with the text quoted from Zachariah, the seven splendours were symbolized by the seven lights of the temple's golden candlestick, and that these seven lights also represented the seven planets, by means of whose influence the rabbis believed Divine Providence manifested itself here below (עולם התחתון). Finally the ultimate confirmation of the sense of these seven spirits for Saint John is to be found in chapter V of his Apocalypse, where having attributed them to the Lamb, repeating the *Deus erat Verbum* of his Gospel, he gives an exact enumeration (verse 12) of the seven splendours: 1. Virtus 2. Divinitas 3. Sapientia 4. Fortitudo 5. Honor 6. Gloria 7. Benedictio.

It can be seen from the preceding pages that a great number of authoritative commentators have recognized in these seven spirits the divine attributes. Eichhorn, who distinguished himself in the eighteenth century by his great works on the Bible, took the final step and in his *Introduction to the New Testament*, vol. I, p.347, does not hesitate to admit that the seven spirits of the Apocalypse belong to the *sephirotic* (*sephiroth, splendours*) system of the Qabalah. 'Cabbalistisch sind,' says he, 'die sieben Geister Gottes.'

Such then is the Atziluthic world of the Qabalists, the only *uncreated* world, that is, God with his relative attributes (God as three persons) and his absolute attributes (his perfections, as God the One). Consequently, these first ten sephiroth are an indivisible whole. 'Mystery of mysteries of the Ancient of Days,' says the Zohar, 'which has not been given even to the angels on high.' (Zohar, Part III, Col. 243). This is the *Deum nemo vidit unquam* of Saint John, Ch. I, verse 18. Not even the angels, say the Church Fathers; for it is a question here of what theologians call *the comprehensive vision.*

5. – THE QABALISTIC TREE AND NOLITO TANGERE

Most commonly the ten Sephiroth are represented by the following figure, known as the *Qabalistic tree*.

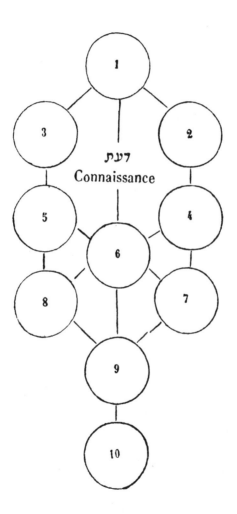

The various worlds, the hierarchies of angels, good as well as evil, the latter called *cortices,* קליפות, are all divided into the provinces of ten *Sephiroth*. Likewise, each *Sephira* in turn has its ten sephiroth. The result is a limitless number of Qabalistic trees. This is what is called the *orchard*, פּורדם . Qabalists teach that he who is bold enough to derive erroneous doctrines from the system *destroys the growing plants*, קוצץ בכטיעות; and that to wish to contemplate these sublime mysteries is *to go into the orchard* לפרדם כר.כם.

The Ilhaghiga talmud, reverse of fol. 14, names four individuals who dared *go into the orchard*. The first was stricken with sudden death; the second, with insanity; the third *destroyed the growing plants* and, despite his great advances in the holy doctrine, became impious and died impenitent; the fourth withdrew in time and no misfortune befell him.

I believe this is the place for these words from the admirable book, The Imitation: 'Si non intelligis, nec capis, quae infra te sunt, quomodo comprehendes quae supra te sunt?'

Qabalistic rabbis of the Middle Ages did not always back away from these examples of punishment. Sometimes they stirred up questions as strange as they were dangerous. They ask, for example: Since God fills all space, where did that cause of causes, the Supreme Crown, bring about the emanation of any other Sephira? It is as troublesome a question as asking what space the ubiquitous immensity of the Father could accord to the engendered Word. The answer they give is that the *Infinite* brought upon itself a sort of contraction, צמצום ; withdrew into itself, without however depriving space of its light. Certainly this is *going into the orchard* at its most audacious, and airing such questions brings one very close to *destroying the growing plants*. Moreover these Qabalists possessed too much of the *rabbi* to grasp that the Divine Essence in the world of Atziluth contains both the existence of the *cause of causes* and the generation or procession of *causes*, causatorum, as co-eternal phenomena, with neither beginning nor end, *nihil prius aut posterius*.

'Gloria sanctissimae et individuae Trinitati, Patri et Filio et Spiritui Sancto; sicut erat in principio et nunc et semper, et in saecula saeculorum. Amen.'

6. – EXTRACTS FROM QABALISTIC BOOKS

Note to the Reader.

I have drawn these excerpts only from books of incontestable authority. I might have increased the number sufficiently to make an enormous volume, but those to which I have limited myself are adequate to substantiate my position. The texts of Qabalists of the Middle Ages sometimes contain obscurities which I have not always succeeded in clarifying in my translation, despite a constant desire for scrupulous exactitude. Thus in several places I have allowed myself to add one or two words which I feel do much to render the exact meaning of the passage in question. Occasionally these same rabbis express themselves in a manner which will no doubt seem offensive to Catholic theologians. It must be remembered that although the content belongs to verbal tradition, the style is that of the rabbis who set it down in writing.

The first volume of my *Harmony* contains a great number of texts relative to our subject. As this work is, by the grace of God, rather widely circulated, I find it sufficient merely to cite it as a reference.

I. Zohar, Part III, Col. 307: 'There are *two* to which *one* is united, and these make *three*; and being *three*, they are only *one*. These *two* are the two *Jehovah's* of the verse, *Listen, oh, Israël*, etc. (Deut. VI:4). *Elohenu* (our God) joins with them. And this is the mark of the seal of God: TRUTH. And being joined together they are *one* in *matchless unity*.'

This is the *unissimus* of Saint Bernard.

II. Zohar, Part II, Col. 236, on the quoted text from Deuteronomy: '*Jehovah, Elohenu, Jehovah* (is) *one*. With a single unity, a single will, indivisible.'

III. Zohar, Part II, Col. 286, on the same text: 'The first *Jehovah* is the supreme point, the principle of all things. *Elohenu* is the mystery of the coming of the Messiah. The second *Jehovah* unites with what stand to the left in a single whole.'

IV. Zohar, Part III, Col. 116: 'Come, consider the mystery of this name *Jehovah*. There are three *degrees*, and each of these degrees is distinct from the others, and yet it is all a single whole, inseparable degrees joined together in unity.'

The Qabalah often uses the words *degrees* for the *hypostases* of our theology. The expression is to be found equally among the Church Fathers. Tertullian for example writes: 'Tres autem, non statu sed *gradu*; quia unus Deus, ex quo et *gradus* isti, et formae et species, in nomine Patris et Filii et Spiritus Sancti.' Adv. Praxeam, Chap. II.

V. Zohar, Part III, Col. 131: 'The hidden *paths*, the impentrable *lights*, the ten *words*, all issue from the lower point which is beneath *aleph*, . The *Sephiroth* emanate from the free will of God. The *Sephiroth* are not creatures, *absit!*, but *concepts*, *radiations* of the *Infinite*, and as such, they are eternal as the Infinite is eternal.'

It is almost superfluous to mention that *paths, lights, words*, here and elsewhere in the Qabalah, are the same as the

Sephiroth. The letter *aleph* is the particular symbol of the *Infinite.* The Zohar repeats this frequently.

VI. Zohar, Part III, Col. 302: 'To the Most Holy, praised be he!, belong three worlds where he remains hidden. The first is the supreme world (Atziluth), the most mysterious, which càn be neither seen nor known, except by him who remains hidden there. The second is that which touches the supreme world (Briah). The third is the one below these others, and so set apart at a certain distance. And this is the world of the angels of on high (Yetzirah).'

A little further on, speaking of the fourth world (Assiah), the Zohar says: 'Come, and consider that if man had not sinned, he would not have needed to taste death when leaving this world for the higher ones; but since he did sin, he must undergo death before he can rise to these other worlds. The spirit withdraws from the body which remains in this lower world; and then the spirit is *purified* in proportion to its guilt. Once this is accomplished, it attains terrestrial paradise. There it takes on another, luminous, form, but one which, as to shape and outline, is entirely similar to the previous one.'[1]

Something resembling *purgatory* is spoken of. In Part III, Col. 557, the Zohar discusses the *eternity* of suffering to which those who die impenitent are subject. 'Those,' it says, 'who descend to *the place of horror will not praise God* (Ps. CXV:2); for those who descend to this *place of horror* must remain forever in hell, בגיהנם ישתארין. Literally, *in gehenna permanebunt.*

---

[1] The constituent elements of the body are dispersed after its dissolution and re-enter the domain of inorganic matter. It follows that at the Resurrection the molecules of a given body may have passed through thousands of others, manifesting themselves successively on earth. How then, asks the rationalistic philosopher, can these numerous organisms re-form from material particles which have been so thoroughly scattered? We see that the ancient synagogue anticipated this objection. It affirms that souls take on bodies which are similar as to *shape and outline* in which they lived this life, but otherwise constituted. This view seems in no way contradictory to the Catholic faith. Indeed, Divine Truth teaches us that resurrected man will no longer be subject, as in this life, to material needs and gross appetites, *sed erunt sicut angeli Dei.* Matt. XXII:30.

An illustrious orator, the Most Reverend Father Félix of the Society of Jesus developed, in Notre-Dame de Paris, with his customary eloquence, this answer to the unbeliever's objection to the resurrection of the dead.

According to Druid theology, the soul, immaterial and immortal, wanders after death among the upper circles (*upper worlds* of the Zohar), surrounded by the stars.

VII. Complements to the Zohar. 'The revered and secret artisan who is being-non-being, אין , contains within himself the Three (higher) Sephiroth. The א (from this name) is the *Crown*; the ', *Wisdom*; the ן, *Intelligence*.'

The Qabalist, Rabbi Schabbathi, develops these words as follows: 'From the explanations we have given previously, one can form an idea of the mystery taught by the masters of the Qabalah, to wit, that the three first Sephiroth are considered to be a single entity. Now one might ask: Why do they say *are considered to be* and not simply *are* a single entity? Answer: Because these three, the Crown, Wisdom and Intelligence, are three *brains* and although they are manifest as single and unique, their wish is to not be confused since each of these brains is distinct from the two others. What is in the last seven Sephiroth is found in these three brains, and what is in the three brains is found in the ultimate unity, and what is in the ultimate unity is found in the infinite; thus there is no difference among the Sephiroth.'

VIII. Here the rabbi, after the example of the Zohar, Part I, Col. 27, Part III, Col. 376 and *alibi pluries*, compares the mystery of the Sephiroth to the integral parts of a tree, which in its totality is only a single and individual being. He continues thus: 'So it is with our present subject. The crown, the ultimate mystery, is the hidden root; the three brains are the trunk; they are united with their root. The other seven Sephiroth, the branches, are joined to the trunk which is the three brains; and all together are united with the root. This is why all of them together, the root and the three brains and the seven Sephiroth, are called an *absolute unity, a unique unity* אחדות אחד.' It is for this reason that the Doctors of the Qabalah have symbolized the ten Sephiroth by a tree, for they are like one as we have explained and as we will explain again. And if someone were to separate the Sephiroth from one another, *quod absit*!, and divide them, *quod absit*!, these same Doctors have said that this man would *destroy the growing plants*; for he would be as one who cut our tree to pieces or uprooted it from the source of all its vital sap.'

IX. Supplements to the Zohar, Fol. 17 recto, Livorno ed., with the commentary that accompanies the same text in the book Yetzirah.

The discourse attributed to the prophet is given in capital letters; the rest belongs to the commentary.

Discourse of the prophet Elijah. IT WAS YOU, OH, MASTER OF THE WORLD, WHO BROUGHT FORTH THE TEN PERFECTIONS. That is, the *Infinite*, praised be his name, caused the ten *Perfections*, which are the Sephiroth, to emanate from his own Essence, thus producing instruments of perfection for the perfection of evolving worlds. For it is through them that he creates, forms and makes all that he creates. The world *briah* (creation) forms the world *yetzirah* (formation) and makes the world *assiah* (matter). And he means that these ten Sephiroth are in the *Infinite*, praised be his name, like an instrument in the hand of an artisan, to be used for the perfection of God's works.

AND WE CALL THEM SEPHIROTH. That is, these *Perfections*, which he, praised be his name, has brought forth from his own Essence, are called *Sephiroth*. Elijah, of blessed memory, intends to make us understand that we must not make the error, absit! et absit!, of thinking and saying that the ten perfections are separate from him, absit!, as the tool is separate from the artisan. When an artisan goes to work, he takes up the tool, and when he has finished, he puts it down, leaving it in a place where it will be ready when he needs it again; for the tool is not inseparably joined to the artisan's hand by means of a continuous union, an eternal union. Thus you might fall into the error of thinking the same of the Sephiroth, likening them to tools which can be set down at will, and saying that they are something apart from the Infinite, praised be his name, absit! et absit!. This is why Elijah, of blessed memory, warns us that such is not the case. These ten Perfections which we call *Sephiroth*, a Hebrew word meaning *lights which shine*, shine with the very Essence of the Infinite, as fire is inherent in a burning coal. This fire is in the coal and could not exist without it. So it is for the Sephiroth; they are the sacred flames, lights which cause the occult hearth to glow, holy treasures of the Essence of the Infinite, praised be his name. They are all attached, bound, united to the Infinite, praised be his name, by a ceaseless and eternal union, connection, bond. And also they are united among themselves, inseparable for all eternity. Elijah calls them *Sephiroth*, which means *lights, splendours*. The root ספר of this noun signifies *to brighten, to shine with a brilliant light*, as is shown in the sacred texts, Exodus XXIV:10 and Job IV:7. This is Elijah's meaning in these words: USING THEIR LIGHT TO BRIGHTEN THE HIDDEN WORLDS WHICH DO NOT APPEAR AND THE WORLDS WHICH DO APPEAR. The sense is: using the Sephiroth to light the hidden and occult worlds which are:

1. The worlds of *Briah* (2nd world), referred to as *the throne of his glory*, numbering ten thrones, ten Briatic worlds. Their essential qualities and modes of existence are beyond our

comprehension, as I will show in the section treating the mystery of the four worlds, *Atziluth, Briah, Yetzirah* and *Assiah.*

2. The worlds of *Yetzirah* (3rd world), which form ten worlds of angels. These are likewise occult worlds, hidden from the material eye.

Now these two worlds, *Briah* and *Yetzirah,* are called *worlds which do not appear.* These in turn serve to light and create, not only through their intermediary, but out of their very substance, the visible worlds, perceptible to the senses and comprehensible for the intelligence of the material beings which inhabit the worlds of *Assiah* (4th world). Assiah also contains ten worlds, ten spheres, which are ten heavens. And our Doctors teach that these ten heavens are a five hundred years' walk from one to the next,[1] and each is a separate world, enveloping all the works of the six days of creation, that is, the spheres and all they contain, even to their very centre, the stars, planets, *cortices,* powers of impurity, and the demon of wicked thoughts.[2] These then are the *visible worlds.*

But let us return to the worlds of Elijah. AND THROUGH THEM (the Sephiroth) YOU HIDE AWAY FROM THE CHILDREN OF MEN. This means that the Infinite, praised by his name, having accomplished all actions through the agency of his Sephiroth, praised be their names, hiding himself, so to speak, in each action which is manifested only by the Sephiroth, praised be their names, and not by himself, *he conceals himself behind them,* like a man who hides from view by covering his entire person with a garment, so that only the garment is visible. God can only be known in his acts, and these are accomplished by his Sephiroth which are his garments.

Next he says: YOU UNITE THEM AND JOIN THEM TOGETHER. This means that although only the Sephiroth are manifest by their action on all worlds, their action is not independent of the Infinite. One must neither think nor say that the Sephiroth act alone and that the Infinite remains apart from what they do. This would be blasphemy; for they can only act by virtue of his all-powerful influence, which joins them together in perfect, absolute unity. They are a part of him as fire is a part of the ember. Thus he is the source and impulse of all their activity.

---

[1] The *Talmud,* tract Hhaghiga, reverse of Fol. 12, gives the Hebrew names of these ten heavens. The distance from one to the next is taken from the book Yetzirah which gives only *five hundred.* But the *Talmud,* same tract, Fol. 13 recto, adds *years.*

[2] We have already seen that by *cortices* the Qabalists designate fallen angels, wicked angels. According to the rabbis, it is the demon of evil inspiration, וכר הרע, that incites men to disregard and transgress the law of God.

AND SINCE YOU ARE THE CENTRE AND CORE, WHOEVER WOULD SEPARATE THESE TEN SEPHIROTH ONE FROM ANOTHER WOULD BE AS GUILTY AS IF HE WERE TO TEAR YOU ASUNDER, OH, MASTER OF THE WORLD. The Infinite is the centre of the flames with which the Sephiroth shine, for they shine only with the great, limitless light, and he clothes himself with the power of the lights which issue from him, in order to accomplish all his actions by them. Thus whoever would separate one from another by saying: the power of light that is in such and such a Sephira is not in such and such another Sephira, which has a power of different light, this man, in dividing the Sephiroth, would commit the enormous sin of cutting, dividing, splitting the unique Essence of the Infinite, praised be his name. For he is the most single of unities and the Sephiroth are emanations of this single unity. For him who would dare commit this grievous sin there is only the pit, perdition, death and the fires of hell's deepest abyss.

X. The Qabalistic system of the book Yetzirah, which the rabbis attribute to the patriarch Abraham, is entirely based on the dogma of the divine Trinity. It distinguishes in God *three Splendours*, Sephiroth, which merge in the *supreme Splendour*, constituting together but a single essence, to wit:

1. The *Infinite*, otherwise called *the supreme crown*.
2. *Wisdom*.
3. *Prudence*.

Qabalistic books also call these three supreme Splendours *the three paths, the three degrees, the three branches* (of the Qabalistic tree), *the three columns.*

(The text of the book Yetzirah is given in capitals.)

THE FIRST PATH IS CALLED THE IMPENET- RABLE INTELLIGENCE, SUPREME CROWN. IT IS THE PRIMORDIAL, INTELLECTUAL LIGHT, THE FIRST GLORY, INCOMPREHENSIBLE FOR ALL CREATED MEN.

Commentary of R. Abraham-ben-David, commonly called *Raabad*:

'The mystery of this *Path* is indicated by the letter aleph, א, א, ל, פ also form the word פלא , which signifies *The Admirable*. This denomination suits the first Path, for it is written: *And he shall be called ADMIRABLE, counsellor, the strong God.* Isaiah IX:6.'

This passage is remarkable. He recognizes that the ninth

chapter of Isaiah is relative to the Messiah, and that the Messiah is actually God, God made man. Parvulus enim natus est nobis, et filiis datus est nobis; et vocabitur nomen ejus *admirabilis.*

THE SECOND PATH IS THE ILLUMINATING INTELLIGENCE. IT IS THE CROWN OF CREATION, THE SPLENDOUR OF UNITY. IT IS RAISED ABOVE ALL THINGS. MASTERS OF THE TRADITION CALL IT THE SECOND GLORY.

Another rabbi, *Rabbi Saul,* speaking about this second path, expresses himself in analogous terms. Novissime diebus istis locutus est nobis in Filio, per quem fecit et saecula; qui cum sit *splendor gloriæ,* et figura substantiæ eius, sedet ad dexteram majestatis in excelsis. Rom. I:1, et. seq.

THE THIRD PATH IS CALLED THE HOLY INTELLIGENCE. IT IS THE FOUNDATION OF PRIMORDIAL WISDOM CALLED UNSHAKABLE FAITH. AMEN *is the root of the* QUALITY OF THIS FAITH. THIS PATH IS THE MOTHER[1] OF FAITH, FOR FAITH EMANATES FROM VIRTUE, THAT IS, FROM THE POWER WHICH IS WITHIN VIRTUE.

Our Holy Mother Church teaches that faith is one of the *fruits* of the *third path* of God, the Holy-Spirit.

Previously we saw that the term *degree* does not belong exclusively to the Qabalistic rabbis. The Qabalistic term *path* is an extremely ancient one. It is entirely Christian in CHARACTER, AND I bow reverently before my Divine Redeemer when he makes himself known as *The Path, The Way.* Saint Thomas asks him: Domine, quomodo possumus *viam* scire? And he answers: Ego sum *Via.* Six centuries earlier, Isaiah, the evangelical prophet, predicting in Chapter XXXV the coming of the Messiah, announces that there will then appear on earth the *holy path.* Et erit ibi semita et via, et *via sancta* vocabitur.

XI. Moses Nahmanides, commentary on the first verse of the book of Genesis: The doctrine of our teachers is that the word *bereschith,* בראשית , (signifying *in the beginning*) indicates that the universe was created through the agency of the ten Sephiroth. And this word designates particularly the Sephira

---

[1] The text gives *father,* as the Hebrew term, נתיב, which signifies *way* or *path* is a masculine noun.

called *Wisdom* (the second Person of the Supreme Trinity). This is the foundation of the entire subject of our text, for it is written: *Jehovah founded the world through wisdom.* Prov. III:19. Thus the word *bereschith* designates Wisdom. This is actually the second in the order of the Sephiroth, but the first to manifest itself.[1] Indeed, it is the beginning of beginnings. This is why the targum of Jonathan and Jerusalemite translate into Chaldean: Through WISDOM Jehovah created: בחוכמא ברא יי.[2]

XII. Commentary by the same Moses Nahhmanides on the beginning of Genesis, developed by the Qabalist, R. Isaiah Hurwitz, in his book *Shelah*, reverse of Fol. 271:

> The Most Holy, praised be his name, created all creatures, drawing them from absolute nothingness. And in the holy tongue we have no term but ברא (creavit) to express *to bring forth being from nothingness.* And there is nothing under or above the sun whose existence has not had a beginning. From the most absolute nothingness God drew a subtle, intangible, productive power capable of receiving palpable form. This is the primitive element which the Greeks called *hiule.* After *hiule* he created nothing more; but from this element he formed and fashioned all things, giving each a form appropriate to its intended function. And know that the heavens, with all they contain, are of this matter; and the earth also, and all things of the earth. The Most Holy, praised be his name, created the one and the other out of nothing. And they were created separately; then all things which accompany them were made. And this matter *hiule* is called in Hebrew *tohu,* תהו, and the form which this matter has been given is called *bohu,* בהו. This is what our doctors mean when they say in the book Yetzirah: *He formed TOHU and made an essence of that which was not.* Thus the text is literally clear. *In the beginning God created the heavens.* He drew their matter out of nothingness. *And the earth.* He drew its matter out of nothingness. And in this creation were created all the creatures of the heavens and of the earth.

XIII. R. Menahem de Recanati: 'The first three Sephiroth are called שכליות , *mentals, notions,* and not רצת , *knowledge,*

---

[1] These last words are to be found in the famous book *Pardes* by the Qabalist Moses of Cordoba. Also Saint John says that the *second* Sephira manifested itself to man and made known the *first* Sephira, which has never shown itself. Deum nemo vidit unquam. Unigenitus Filius, qui est in sinu Patris, ipse enarravit. John I:18.

[2] In printed Bibles only the Jerusalemite gives the version found by Nahhmanides in the targum.

attributes (as for the remaining seven).

XIV. R. Meir, son of Todros of Toledo: 'The three supreme Sephiroh are: *the supreme Crown, Wisdom* and *Intelligence*, and these are the *intellectual Sephiroth, the notions*; and the seven others are those which the Sepher Yetzirah names, ספור, *attributive Splendours*.

XV. R. Abraham Irira[2] in his book שער השמים, *the gate of heaven*: 'God in his ten Sephiroth does not communicate his nature to the three worlds of *Briah, Yetzirah* and *Assiah* ... The Sephiroth emanate from the primal *Infinite*, but in such a way as to be in nowise separate one from another. The Sephiroth are nothing more than *determinate divinity*. The worlds of Briah, Yetzirah and Assiah are creations ex nihilo. Such is not the case for the Sephiroth. They did not come out of nothing, but emanate eternally from the substance of the *primal Infinite*; and this, their immediate cause, undergoes no diminution, as a light communicating its brilliance to another light loses none of its strength. The Sephiroth are of the same nature as the primal Infinite, with this one difference, that the Infinite exists of itself, *est a seipso, causa sine causa*, and that the Sephiroth emanate from him, or in a word, are *caused* by the fundamental cause. From the most absolute unity of the Infinite *the celestial world* was born, העולם העליון, called in Qabalah, *primitive man, primordial Adam*, אדם קדמון, a Divine being which must not be confused, quod absit!, with *the first man, the first terrestrial Adam*, אדם הראשון . The primordial Adam is *one* and *many*, for all things are of him and in him, מניה וביה.

XVI. In the same book, Dissertation III, Ch. IX, Irira more amply develops this theme, discussing in detail the nature of the angels of the various hierarchies, a subject with which we cannot here concern ourselves.

The reader has just heard the voices of the greatest masters of the Hebrew Qabalah. I could easily have increased the number of my quotations. Now let us judge if unbelieving philosophers are justified in invoking the Qabalah in favour of pantheism.

---

[1] This is how the rabbis pronounce this name, אירירא, but the actual name of this celebrated Qabalist is *Herrera*. He was Spanish, from the city of Herrera.